# Family Law and
the Poor

*Contributions in American History*

SERIES EDITOR: *Stanley I. Kutler,* UNIVERSITY OF WISCONSIN

# FAMILY LAW AND THE POOR
## Essays by
## Jacobus tenBroek

## JOEL F. HANDLER
### Editor

Contributions in American History
Number 16

Greenwood Publishing Corporation
Westport, Connecticut

Copyright © 1964, 1965, 1971 by the Board
of Trustees of Leland Stanford Junior University

Library of Congress Catalog Card Number: 70-140918
SBN: 8371-5817-6

Greenwood Publishing Corporation
51 Riverside Avenue, Westport, Connecticut 06880

Printed in the United States of America

# Contents

# Editor's Note

This work originally appeared as a three-part article in the *Stanford Law Review* in 1964 and 1965 (vol. 16, pp. 257–317; vol. 16, pp. 900–981; vol. 17, pp. 612–682).

A few minor changes have been made for this collection. The original title of the article—"California's Dual System of Family Law: Its Origins, Development, and Present Status"—has been changed to the present one to reflect more accurately the general applicability of the work, even though the primary contemporary data were drawn from one state. Furthermore, the original three parts have been divided into six chapters, and a brief conclusion at the end of Part Two (pp. 978–981) has been omitted.

The original pagination appears in brackets at the bottom of the page so that existing references to the original essay can be found easily.

I wish to thank the editors of the *Stanford Law Review* for their cooperation and especially William Kroener for assisting me in preparing this volume.

# Jacobus tenBroek
# 1911–1968

Jacobus tenBroek was born in Alberta, Canada, in 1911. When he was a small boy, his family moved to California so that ten-Broek, blinded in an accident, could attend the State School for the Blind in Berkeley. He was graduated from the University of California at Berkeley in 1934 with highest honors in history and went on to earn two postgraduate degrees from the University of California at Berkeley Law School—an Ll.B in 1938 and a J.S.D. in 1940. As a student, tenBroek was on the staff of the *California Law Review* and was a member of the Order of the Coif. After earning an S.J.D. from Harvard Law School, where he was a Brandeis Research Fellow, tenBroek joined the faculty of Chicago Law School. He returned to California in 1942 and began a teaching career at the University of California at Berkeley which lasted for a quarter-century. There he made outstanding contributions in his leadership of the speech and political science departments and the Academic Senate.

In 1934, with Dr. Newel Perry, his teacher at the State School for the Blind, and others, tenBroek founded the California Council for the Blind. Six years later, with Perry's encouragement, the young professor founded the National Federation for the Blind. His goal was to remove the blind from their traditional isolation and to stimulate their associations with each other in order to organize for self-advancement. He stressed a philosophy of normality, equality, and productivity and put it into practice by personally conducting many campaigns and activities for the welfare of the blind. These ranged from the removal of public and private employment discrimination to the improvement of educational and welfare provisions and administration.

In May 1950 tenBroek was appointed by the governor of California, Earl Warren, to fill an unexpired term on the State Social Welfare Board. He was subsequently reappointed to three additional four-year terms.

tenBroek had long envisioned a world federation of the blind of all nations, and he was elected president of the International Federation of the Blind at its organizational meetings in 1964.

In his rigorous work as administrator, organizer, spokesman, and formulator of legislative proposals for all these organizations, tenBroek's scholarly work on welfare theory was translated into practical achievements on behalf of his fellow blind and all the culturally and socially deprived. He earned wide recognition from social work organizations, public and private welfare officials, and the press and radio as a dynamic leader in the field of social welfare. He was praised for fighting a heroic battle for all the disadvantaged groups who could not effectively speak for themselves.

During his career, tenBroek published more than fifty articles and monographs and authored or coauthored four books. His works on family law, public assistance, and the law of the poor consistently predate the attention given to these subjects by the majority of his colleagues; and they laid the intellectual foundations for the current development of welfare law.

In his book, *The Antislavery Origins of the Fourteenth Amendment* (published in 1951 and recently republished under the title *Equal Under Law*), tenBroek rediscovered forgotten origins of the Thirteenth and Fourteenth amendments to the Constitution of the United States. This book foreshadowed the widespread use and interpretation of those amendments by the Supreme Court, which have occurred since then. Another book, *Prejudice, War and the Constitution* (1954), a study of the Japanese-American detention in World War II, received a Woodrow Wilson Award in 1955 for its significance for democratic practice. His five articles on *Extrinsic Aids in Constitutional Construction,* written in the late 1930's, are only now beginning to be acknowledged as innovative work on the interpretation of basic documents of government. A good example of tenBroek's scholarship put into action can be seen in his monograph, *The Right to Live in the World: The Disabled in the Law of Torts,* in which he presents an analysis of the origins and present status of the relevant doctrines in the law of torts and proposes a theory of readaptation to meet modern demands for the integration of the disabled into the mainstream of society. Indeed, this is the main theme and objective that runs throughout tenBroek's scholarly works and practical pursuits: the search for ways to take care of those in need —not to foster dependence and therefore a loss of freedom, but to find ways to promote the achievement of a productive role in society.

# Editor's Introduction

More than twenty years ago, Jacobus tenBroek published his famous constitutional argument on behalf of the poor. The arguments that he raised then and subsequently validated through extensive documentation—namely, that the law discriminates against the poor on the basis of their poverty and, as such, violates the equal protection clause of the Fourteenth Amendment of the United States Constitution—finally appeared, in 1970, to be on the threshold of acceptance. His purpose as a legal scholar (and this was only one of the many roles he assumed on behalf of the poor) was to attack the wall created by law that separated the poor from the nonpoor; his goal was to integrate the poor with the rest of society.

tenBroek, in an article coauthored with Joseph Tussman entitled "The Equal Protection of the Laws,"[1] is credited with coining the phrase "substantive equal protection."[2] At the time that the article was published (1949), the equal protection clause was rarely argued or accepted by the courts. In Justice Holmes's words, it was "the last resort of constitutional arguments."[3] The authors' purpose was to show the usefulness of the clause in defense of the poor.

All laws cannot apply to all people equally; legislation must impose special burdens or grant special benefits to particular groups, classes, or individuals. Courts traditionally held that the

---

1. 37 CALIF. L. REV. 341 (1949).
2. Karst & Horowitz, *Reitman v. Mulkey: A Telophase of Substantive Equal Protection*, in THE SUPREME COURT REVIEW 39 (Kurland ed. 1967).
3. Buck v. Bell, 274 U.S. 200, 208 (1927).

demands of the equal protection clause can be reconciled with the legislative right to classify only if the basis of the classification is "reasonable." "The Constitution," the authors said, "does not require that things different in fact be treated in law as though they were the same. But it does require, in its concern for equality, that those who are similarly situated be similarly treated."[4] A classification is reasonable (and therefore not violative of the equal protection clause) if it includes all persons who are similarly situated with respect to the purposes of the law.

When statutes are challenged on equal protection grounds, courts generally defer to the legislative judgment. Particularly with regard to business and economic legislation, the Supreme Court has presumed validity as long as there was some reasonable relationship to a statutory purpose. Validity has been presumed even where the reason for the statute was not clear. tenBroek and Tussman urged additional equal protection standards. They argued that for some human traits, no legislative classification should be permitted. "The assertion of human equality," they said, "is closely associated with the denial that differences in color or creed, birth or status, are significant or relevant to the way in which men should be treated. . . . Laws which classify men by color or creed or blood accordingly, are repugnant to the demand for equality, and therefore, such traits should not be made the basis for the classification of individuals in laws."[5] They suggested, by way of example and with remarkable prescience, that segregation laws be declared invalid on the basis of "the forbidden classification doctrine." As a fallback position—in the event that the forbidden classification doctrine seemed too extreme—tenBroek and Tussman urged that when certain classifying traits were involved, presumptions of constitutionality be reversed, and the Court should scrutinize the legislation most carefully in terms of reasonable relationship to statutory purpose to see whether the legislation was discriminatory toward certain groups. They urged the Court to insist on the legislature's purity of motive.

At the time "The Equal Protection of the Laws" was published, the only "authority" that tenBroek and Tussman had was the classic dictum of Justice Jackson, concurring in *Edwards v.*

---

4. Tussman and tenBroek, *op. cit.*, at 344.
5. *Ibid.*, at 353.

*California:* "The mere state of being without funds is a neutral fact—constitutionally an irrelevance, like race, creed, or color."[6] Five years after the publication of their article, the Supreme Court decided *Brown v. Board of Education.* That case and its progeny have put race, if not in the forbidden classification category, at least very close to it.[7] Then, the Court began to use the equal protection clause to invalidate state statutes which had the effect of denying indigents rights in criminal procedure that others enjoyed. In *Griffin v. Illinois,* the Court held that Illinois must provide transcripts to indigent appellants since transcripts, which were available for a fee, were necessary for appeals. Mr. Justice Black said, "In criminal trials a State can no more discriminate on account of poverty than on account of religion, race, or color."[8]

This was the state of the law—Justice Jackson's dictum, the *Brown* decision, and a few criminal procedure cases—when ten-Broek published his work in the *Stanford Law Review* in 1964 and 1965 on the dual system of family law. tenBroek showed, through a massive presentation of evidence, that, for most matters of concerns to the family, there are in fact two systems of family law—one for the poor and one for the rest of society. He traced the origin of separate systems from Elizabethan England to its reception in America and its full flowering in the 1960's. His principal examples in the nineteenth century are New York and California and, in the twentieth, California. But these states are only case study examples; this is in fact a study of the development of the dual system of family law in America.

Most of the family law of the poor derives from the welfare system. The dual system took hold at the point when the public took responsibility for the relief of the poor; its guiding principle has always been the protection of the public purse. The result has been to create, in tenBroek's terms, a wall of separation between the poor and the rest of society with regard to family law. The basis of the classification is poverty. tenBroek argued that poverty should be treated the same as race and, on the basis of the *Brown*

---

6. 314 U.S. 160, 184 (1941).
7. 347 U.S. 483 (1954). See *Developments in the Law: Equal Protection,* 82 HARVARD L. REV. 1065, 1088–90 (1969).
8. Griffin v. Illinois, 351 U.S. 12, 17 (1956); Gideon v. Wainwright, 372 U.S. 335 (1963) (state must provide trial counsel for indigents); Douglas v. California, 372 U.S. 353 (1963) (state must provide counsel for indigents when appeal is granted as of right).

decision, be declared a forbidden classification. He saw substantive equal protection as the constitutional weapon to be used to break down the wall of separation and integrate the poor with the rest of society.

tenBroek was an optimist. Although his work traced four hundred years of discrimination against the poor, he spoke of "a new spirit in constitutional law [that] has given positive signs of its future potential,"[9] and, for a time, events seemed to be fulfilling his expectations. After the publication of his work, the equal protection clause was used to strike down discriminatory legislation in a number of fields, including race, criminal procedure, voting, and illegitimacy. Rather than being the "last resort of constitutional argument," scholars were calling for the application of the clause in schools, law enforcement, and welfare.[10] The wall of separation began to break down.

The constitutional development of the equal protection clause, after tenBroek's work on the dual system, proceeded along two parallel lines. One development was the growing judicial hostility to classifications based on wealth, which was beginning to look like an "invidious classification." In addition to the criminal justice cases, the Supreme Court struck down classifications based on wealth in voting cases.[11] Although not applicable to family law, the approach of this line of decisions was directly in point with tenBroek's central argument—that when important or fundamental interests are involved, there can be no classifications based on wealth. The other line of development had been to strike down distinctions made *between* classes of welfare recipients; for example, lower federal courts have struck down residency requirements, maximum grants on aid, and men-in-the-house rules on the grounds that these rules arbitrarily discriminate between similarly situated welfare recipients.[12]

The 1969 Supreme Court term began auspiciously. The Court

---

9. 17 STAN. L. REV. 681.
10. See, *e.g.*, Karst & Horowitz, *supra; Developments in the Law, supra; compare* Michelman, *Forward: On Protecting the Poor Through the Fourteenth Amendment*, 83 HARVARD L. REV. 7 (1969). For an article critical of tenBroek's argument, see Lewis & Levy, *Family Law and Welfare Policies: The Case for "Dual Systems,"* in LAW OF THE POOR 424 (tenBroek ed. 1966).
11. Harper v. Virginia Board of Elections, 383 U.S. 663 (1966), 372 U.S. 353 (1963).
12. Shapiro v. Thompson, 394 U.S. 618 (1969) (residency requirements); Kaiser v. Montgomery, Civ. No. 49613 (N.D. Cal., Aug. 28, 1969) (maximum grants); King v. Smith, 277 F. Supp. 31 (M.D. Ala. 1967); aff'd, 292 U.S. 309 (1968).

held that termination of welfare assistance before an evidentiary hearing was a denial of due process. In that case, the Court acknowledged the importance of welfare. "The crucial factor," said the Court, "is that termination of aid pending resolution of a controversy over eligibility may deprive an *eligible* recipient of the very means by which to live while he waits. Since he lacks independent resources, his situation becomes immediately desperate."[13] Was not then the right to welfare in reality the right to live and therefore a fundamental right? Lower federal courts had been edging toward this position. In *Rothstein v. Wyman,* the court pointed out that unless the indigent and unemployed have at least the bare minimum for existence, they are incapable of exercising constitutional rights and liberties. The court continued:

> Legislation with respect to welfare assistance, therefore, like that dealing with public education, access to public parks or playgrounds, or use of the mails, deals with a critical aspect of the personal lives of our citizens, whether such assistance be labelled a "right," "privilege," or "benefit." . . . Its importance is magnified by the defenseless and disadvantaged state of the class of citizens to which it relates, who are usually less able than others to enforce their rights. . . . We believe that with the stakes so high in terms of human misery the equal protection standard to be applied should . . . more nearly approximate that applied to laws affecting fundamental constitutional rights. Poverty is a bitter enough brew. It should not be made even less palatable by the addition of unjustifiable inequalities or discriminations.[14]

Then, on April 6, 1970, a divided Court decided the case of *Dandridge v. Williams.*[15] At issue was Maryland's "maximum grant regulation." Maryland calculated the standard for need for families on welfare by the number of children in the family and their living conditions. The standard of need increased in proportion with each additional child, but there was a maximum amount that any family could receive regardless of the number of children. Parents of large families brought suit claiming that the Maryland system discriminated against them invidiously merely because of size. A needy child in a large family (i.e., over the maximum limit) receives nothing compared to a similarly situated needy child in a small family. The parents claimed the

---

13. Goldberg v. Kelly, 397 U.S. 254 (1970).
14. 303 F. Supp. 339, 346–47 (S.D.N.Y. 1969) (citations omitted).
15. 397 U.S. 471 (1970).

classification of families by size was too broad and unreasonable and thus violated the equal protection clause.

Speaking for a five-man majority, Mr. Justice Stewart's opinion displayed a remarkable lack of sensitivity to the plight of poor people. He pointed out that there are two standards that the Court can use in applying the equal protection clause. If the interests involved were protected by the First Amendment guarantee of free speech, the Court would apply a strict standard and see whether the state law overreached in its classification. On the other hand, if the matter involved "state regulation in the social and economic field, not affecting freedoms guaranteed by the Bill of Rights," then the classification was permissible as long as it had some reasonable basis. And where does welfare fit—with fundamental human rights or with the regulation of business or industry? Justice Stewart said that he recognized the "dramatically real factual difference" between welfare and business regulation. "The administration of public welfare assistance . . . involves the most basic economic needs of impoverished human beings." But this was still not enough. The classification of impoverished human beings was to be judged by the same standards as the regulation of gas companies and optical dispensers. Welfare did not involve a fundamental right, and the Court would not apply the strict standard of the equal protection clause.

The callousness of Justice Stewart toward the plight of the poor was displayed in another passage of his opinion. The families argued that one of the effects of the Maryland system was to force needy children out of their families. Not so, said the Justice, "for even if a parent should be inclined to increase his per capita family income by sending a child away, the federal law requires that the child, to be eligible for AFDC payments, must live with one of several enumerated relatives. The kinship tie may be attenuated but it cannot be destroyed." In other words, to avoid impoverishment, a mother must shop around for an eligible relative to take in her excess children.

The equal protection clause has been described as a moral standard which allows the Court, in establishing constitutional doctrine, to contribute to our thinking about social justice and ethical conduct.[16] Until *Dandridge,* this had been true.

---

16. FREUND, ON LAW AND JUSTICE 35 (1968).

tenBroek's work, as represented by this volume, must be studied to appreciate fully what the system of family law in the United States has done to the poor. The principal state interest in discriminating against the poor has been the overriding desire to save public money. In this respect, Maryland is no different from Elizabethan England. tenBroek showed how this desire has spawned a whole system of unjustifiable inequalities and discriminations. In order to live, the poor must accept the conditions of public assistance, which make their family relationships different from those of the rest of society. The *Dandridge* case is only one example of discrimination based on poverty.

It took the Court a half-century to learn that "separate but equal" could never be meaningful in matters of race, and, in the years following the *Brown* decision, we began to learn of the extent and pervasiveness of a whole system of racial discrimination. The same is true in the family law of the poor. tenBroek had great faith that constitutional law could be the weapon to attack this system. But if views such as Justice Stewart's are to prevail and dominate, then the equal protection clause has once more become "the last resort of constitutional arguments." If that is the case, we must seek other routes to achieve the goals of social justice embodied in the equal protection clause.

Family Law and
the Poor

# 1

# Introduction

California family law, particularly that dealing with the child, derives from four principal sources: the Elizabethan Poor Law,[1] the Aid to Families With Dependent Children Law (AFDC),[2] the California codes of 1872, and the common law. The main features of these four legal complexes are in many respects different, in some important respects contradictory, and in all respects in need of review and reform. Since the poor law and the AFDC Law provide public financial assistance to the destitute, they are basically similar although they vary in the groups covered, the conditions of eligibility for assistance, the amount and form of the grant, the provisions for relatives' responsibility, and the tax and governmental source of money. The codes and the common law are similarly closely related because the codes nullified or adopted common-law rules and because courts have intermeshed code interpretations and common-law decisions. Although in different times, subject matter areas, and degrees there has been, and still is, some intermingling of provisions and concepts among all four of these legal complexes, it is apparent that the major gap lies between the two public aid laws on one hand and the codes and common law on the other, rather than between the members of each of the pairs.

Thus we have two systems of family law in California: different in origin, different in history, different in substantive provisions, different in administration, different in orientation and outlook. One is public, the other private. One deals with expenditure and

---

1. 43 Eliz. 1, c. 2 (1601).
2. Cal. Welfare & Inst'ns Code §§ 1500–80.

conservation of public funds and is heavily political and measurably penal. The other deals with the distribution of family funds, focuses on the rights and responsibilities of family members, and is civil, nonpolitical, and less penal. One is for underprivileged and deprived families; the other for the more comfortable and fortunate. The first is embodied in the California poor law[3] and the AFDC Law, administered through state and local agencies and subject to continuous legislative attention. The other is embodied in the codes of 1872 which were founded on the Field Draft Codes in New York, incorporating some New York common-law rules and some poor law provisions as they existed in New York, and on some early California community property, divorce, and other statutory provisions—all judicially administered and developed with only occasional legislative change.

In the context of family law, no less than in school racial segregation, one might ask whether "separate" is not "inherently unequal," generating among aid recipients "a feeling of inferiority as to their status in the community that may affect their hearts and minds in ways unlikely ever to be undone."[4]

---

3. CAL. WELFARE & INST'NS CODE §§ 2500–611.
4. Brown v. Board of Educ., 347 U.S. 483, 494 (1954).

# 2

# The Poor Law
# and the Common Law
# in England

The famous statute of 43 Elizabeth, the Elizabethan Poor Law, was both a consolidation of earlier Tudor statutes and a consummation of English experience with care of the poor. A growth rather than a creation,[5] it contained almost nothing new but fixed the character of poor relief for three centuries not only in England but in America as well. Today its principal features linger in the welfare programs of all of our states.

Precisely, the Elizabethan Poor Law is Chapter 2 of 43 Elizabeth. Other welfare statutes were enacted in the forty-third year of Queen Elizabeth. Welfare statutes enacted earlier remained in effect thereafter. Welfare programs, customs, and practices, particularly in the towns, affected the character of the national program and were not displaced by it. All of these properly may be regarded as parts of the Elizabethan poor law system. That system embraced the following main provisions. Impotent poor were to receive direct relief from funds collected by taxation.[6] "[C]onvenient places of Habitačon" were to be erected for them on the wastes and commons within the parish.[7] Hospitals and almshouses such "as shalbe in the said Countie" were to be tax-supported in amounts determined by the justices of the peace in quarter sessions.[8] In general, begging was forbidden.[9] Employable poor were

---

5. Leonard, Early History of English Poor Relief (1900). This pioneer work is still a leading study.
6. See 43 Eliz. 1, c. 2, § I (1601); 39 Eliz. 1, c. 3, § I (1597); 14 Eliz. 1, c. 5, § XVI (1572). Statutes of the Realm Printed by Command of His Majesty King George III (1816) is the source of reference to English statutes throughout this Article.
7. 43 Eliz. 1, c. 2, § IV (1601); see 39 Eliz. 1, c. 3, § V (1597).
8. 43 Eliz. 1, c. 2, § XII (1601); 39 Eliz. 1, c. 3, § XIII (1597).
9. 7 Jac. 1, c. 4 (1609); 39 Eliz. 1, c. 4, §§ II, III (1597); 39 Eliz. 1, c. 3, § X (1597);

to be put to work in manufacturing projects organized by overseers of the poor.[10] The able-bodied refusing to work were to be sent to houses of correction.[11] Rogues, vagabonds, and vagrants were to be punished.[12] Poor children were to be put to work or apprenticed.[13] Relatives were made responsible for the maintenance of their destitute kinsmen.[14] Only those who had settlement in a community were entitled to its aid,[15] and what constituted settlement and the methods of its acquisition were carefully circumscribed. Paupers and potential paupers without settlement were to be excluded or expelled from the community. "[A] competent Sume of Money . . . owte of every County or Place Corporate" was to be fixed by the justices of the peace in quarter sessions for the support of the poor prisoners of the King's Bench and Marshallsea; a minimum of twenty shillings yearly was sent from each county for each prison.[16] Special provisions were made for destitute, sick, and maimed soldiers and mariners.[17]

Earlier provisions on charitable uses, encouraging establishment of private foundations, defining their purposes, and establishing machinery for checking diversion of their resources, were codified and expanded. "[B]y Deede inrolled in the High Court of Chancery" a benevolent person of means could create and endow in perpetuity a charitable corporation, empowered to receive real and personal property and with an organizational structure and purposes prescribed by the founder. Commissions could be appointed by the Chancellor "to enquire . . . of all . . . such Guift . . . and of the Abuses and . . . Falsityes defrauding of the Truste Intente . . . ."[18] The preamble list of charitable purposes, given

---

14 Eliz. 1, c. 5 (1572); 27 Hen. 8, c. 25 (1535); 22 Hen. 8, c. 12 (1530); 11 Hen. 7, c. 2 (1495).

10. 43 Eliz. 1, c. 2, § I (1601); 39 Eliz. 1, c. 3, § I (1597); see 18 Eliz. 1, c. 3, § IV (1575–1576).

11. See 43 Eliz. 1, c. 2, § II (1601); 39 Eliz. 1, c. 3, § III (1597); 18 Eliz. 1, c. 3, § IV (1575–1576). See also 14 Eliz. 1, c. 5, § XXII (1572); 3 & 4 Edw. 6, c. 16, § VI (1549–1550); 1 Edw. 6, c. 3, § XI (1547); 27 Hen. 8, c. 25, §§ VI, X (1535–1536).

12. 7 Jac. 1, c. 4 (1609); 39 Eliz. 1, c. 4, §§ II, III (1597); 39 Eliz. 1, c. 3, § X (1597); 14 Eliz. 1, c. 5 (1572); 27 Hen. 8, c. 25 (1535); 22 Hen. 8, c. 12 (1530); 11 Hen. 7, c. 2 (1495).

13. 43 Eliz. 1, c. 2, §§ I, III (1601); 18 Eliz. 1, c. 3, § IV (1576); 27 Hen. 8, c. 25, § 6 (1535–1536).

14. 43 Eliz. 1, c. 2, § VI (1601); 39 Eliz. 1, c. 3, § VII (1597); 18 Eliz. 1, c. 3, § I (1576).

15. 13 & 14 Car. 2, c. 12 (1662); 14 Eliz. 1, c. 5, § XVI (1572); 27 Hen. 8, c. 25 (1535–1536); 11 Hen. 7, c. 2 (1495); CLARKE, SOCIAL ADMINISTRATION INCLUDING THE POOR LAWS 169 (1935).

16. 43 Eliz. 1, c. 2, § XII (1601); 39 Eliz. 1, c. 3, § XIII (1597).

17. 43 Eliz. 1, c. 3, §§ I, XV (1601); 39 Eliz. 1, c. 3, § XVI (1597).

18. 43 Eliz. 1, c. 4 (1601); 39 Eliz. I, c. 5–6 (1597). See also 14 Eliz. 1, c. 14 (1572).

great interpretive weight by courts in succeeding centuries, was almost completely secularized.

The application of the Elizabethan poor law system to our present society has been severely and properly criticized. Historically it may be viewed as all of the following, whatever the apparent contradictions: the outcome of the inadequacy and disruption of nongovernmental sources of charitable aid; an economic, social, and political necessity in the century of the Tudors; aimed more at civil disorder than at economic distress; oriented toward the fading agrarian age rather than the urban industrial poverty that was its principal instigating cause; overemphasized the personal causes of poverty and sought to solve them by excessive doses of criminal law; recognized the economic causes of poverty and sought to overcome them by providing work through government-made or sheltered employment; a great code of social legislation and a landmark of social progress.[19]

Four features of the Elizabethan poor law system are of special importance to us: its parliamentary development, its assumption of public responsibility for the poor, its relationship to the Statutes of Labourers,[20] and its bearing on the creation of a family law of the poor.

## Parliamentary Development of the Poor Law

Parliament played a leading role in the development of the English poor law system. The contrast is with the courts rather than the executive. The judicial role was of little importance. The relation of the poor law system to the economic life of the nation, to population movements, to civil disorders, and to tax levies and public expenditures committed it, as now, to the special care and continuous surveillance of the legislature from almost the beginning of the constitutional framework of government. The Statute of Labourers, intimately associated with the poor law system and the origin of important parts of it, was passed in 1350 when the legislative function of Parliament, and indeed Parliament itself

19. Standard modern works on the history of poor relief in England are: ASHLEY, AN INTRODUCTION TO ENGLISH ECONOMIC HISTORY AND THEORY (4th ed. 1925); DE SCHWEINITZ, ENGLAND'S ROAD TO SOCIAL SECURITY (1943); 4 HOLDSWORTH, HISTORY OF ENGLISH LAW (1924); JORDAN, THE CHARITIES OF RURAL ENGLAND 1480–1660 (1962); JORDAN, PHILANTHROPY IN ENGLAND 1480–1660 (1959); LEONARD, EARLY HISTORY OF ENGLISH POOR RELIEF (1900); TIERNEY, MEDIEVAL POOR LAW (1959); WEBB, ENGLISH LOCAL GOVERNMENT: ENGLISH POOR LAW HISTORY, PART I, THE OLD POOR LAW (1927), PART II, THE LAST HUNDRED YEARS (1929).

20. 25 Edw. 3, st. II (1350–1351), preceded by the Ordinance of Labourers, 23 Edw. 3, c. I–VIII (1349).

as a representative body, was in its infancy.[21] The next great period
of statutory development, both of the poor law system and of the
nation, was the transforming era of the Tudors. Among varied
Tudor statutes reorganizing government, fixing the relation of
church and state, and regulating the economy[22] were a new statute
of laborers[23] and the intermediate and final stages of the poor law
statutes.[24] Thus the family law of the poor, which evolved as an
integral part of the labor and poor law systems, was the creation
of Parliament and was then as today primarily statutory. The family law of the rest of the community was created by the common-
law courts. It was integrated into the main body of the nation's
statutory law only as it was a part of the feudal law of inheritance
and wardship. Here the role of the courts was primary and that
of Parliament secondary. This conforms to a general observation
made by Holdsworth with respect to the influence of statutes on
the overall development of the law: "It is on matters of public
law, or on matters which affect the economic life of the nation,
that the influence of the statutes has been the strongest. On matters of private law, such as the law of contract and tort, it has been
the weakest."[25] Land law was an exception because its feudaliza-
tion made it in effect the public law of the nation and because in
any event it must always be closely connected with commerce and
industry. "Apart from the land law, the Legislature has been content to leave the task of developing private law to the lawyers. It
has only intervened occasionally to amend and supplement."[26] Thus
in this manner the family law of the poor came to be dominantly
legislative, the family law of the rest of the community dominantly
judicial.

---

21. Other famous and enduring statutes enacted about the same time—the Statute of
Treasons, 25 Edw. 3, st. 5, c. 2 (1351–1352), and De Natis Ultra Mare, 25 Edw. 3, st. 1
(1351–1352)—dealt with such basic public questions as the relation of the individual to
the state and the nature of allegiance.

22. The Acts of Supremacy, 5 Eliz. 1, c. 1 (1562); 1 Eliz. 1, c. 1 (1558); 26 Hen. 8,
c. 1 (1534), and others carrying out the Reformation, 32 Hen. 8, c. 12 (1540); 23 Hen. 8,
c. 9 (1532); 23 Hen. 8, c. 1 (1531–1532); 22 Hen. 8, c. 14 (1531); 21 Hen. 8, c. 12 (1529);
21 Hen. 8, c. 5 (1529); statutes of treasons devoted largely to the same end, 13 Eliz. 1, c. 1
(1571); 1 Eliz. 1, c. 5 (1558); 1 & 2 Phil. & M., c. 10 (1555); 1 & 2 Phil. & M., c. 9,
(1555); 1 M., st. 1, c. 1 (1553); 5 & 6 Edw. 6, c. 11 (1552); 1 Edw. 6, c. 12 (1547); 33
Hen. 8, c. 23 (1541–1542); 26 Hen. 8, c. 13 (1534); the Statute of Uses, 27 Hen. 8, c. 10
(1535), and the Statute of Wills transforming the land law, 32 Hen. 8, c. 1 (1540); and
statutes regulating trade and industry, see, *e.g.*, 5 Eliz. 1, c. 7, 8, 12, 21, 22 (1562); 28
Hen. 8, c. 8, 14 (1536); 27 Hen. 8, c. 9, 21, 13, 14 (1535); 6 Hen. 8, c. 8, 9, 12 (1514);
5 Hen. 8, c. 2, 4 (1513); 4 Hen. 8, c. 6, 7 (1512).

23. 5 Eliz. 1, c. 4 (1562).

24. 39 Eliz. 1, c. 3 (1597); 18 Eliz. 1, c. 3 (1575); 14 Eliz. 1, c. 5 (1572); 5 Eliz. 1,
c. 3 (1562); 5 & 6 Edw. 6, c. 2 (1552); 27 Hen. 8, c. 25 (1535); 22 Hen. 8, c. 12 (1530).

25. HOLDSWORTH, SOME LESSONS FROM OUR LEGAL HISTORY 45 (1928).

26. *Id.* at 45–46.

## Poor Law Assumption of Public Responsibility

The central concept and great achievement of the Elizabethan poor law was the firm establishment of the principle of public responsibility to maintain the destitute. Through it, the final step was taken, permanently shifting a part of the burden to relieve economic distress from the ecclesiastical, private, and voluntary to the civil, public, and compulsory. The assumption of responsibility, moreover, was made by the nation and its application was nationwide. The obligation was to be discharged, however, by an assessment on the inhabitants and occupiers of property of the parish. Administration was to be entrusted to the principal local officials—the justices of the peace of the county aided by parish officials, overseers of the poor, and churchwardens, by town officers, "the Maiors, Bailifs, or other Head Officers of everie Towne and Place Corporate and Citie within this Realme, being . . . Justices of Peace," and by every alderman of the City of London within his ward.[27]

Professor W. K. Jordan, the latest of the historians extensively to study the subject, says that 43 Elizabeth, chapter 2, "was carefully and unambiguously drafted; a brilliantly conceived system of administration was established in which the remotest parish was linked with Westminster; and the whole realm was declared to be a single community of responsibility for the relief of poverty which threatened to overwhelm the private resources of any single locality."[28] Following the style of the age, 43 Elizabeth, chapter 2, is better characterized as rambling, imprecise, and inartistic. More importantly, it cannot be said to have "established" "a system of administration," especially one linking the remotest parish with Westminster. The most that can be said is that 43 Elizabeth, chapter 2, marked a stage in the development of such a system. Nor was it "conceived" by the act's authors, "brilliantly" or otherwise. It grew: in part it had already been established; in part it remained to be established; and the process was muddlingly evolutionary. Most importantly, "the whole realm" was not declared to be "a single community of responsibility for the relief of poverty." The

---

27. 43 Eliz. 1, c. 2, § VII (1601). Justices of the peace were appointed by the King's commission or became members of it by occupying principal positions in chartered towns. 2 BARRY, THE PRESENT PRACTICE OF A JUSTICE OF THE PEACE 558 (1790). For a study of the interplay of local and national forces in the appointment of justices of the peace and the administrative and judicial functions of these officers see BARNES, SOMERSET 1625–1640, ch. III (1961).

28. JORDAN, PHILANTHROPY IN ENGLAND 1480–1660, at 126 (1959).

statute did not make the nation a single welfare state. It did not create a nationally financed and nationally administered welfare system, make available a national subsidy to localities with inadequate resources to meet the local need, or provide a method of channeling resources from the wealthier localities to the poorer or those in greatest need. The nation did not even set the standards or amount of assistance or define need. It did not levy the tax, prescribe its condition, or order its relationships[29] to other taxes or expenditures. These were to be determined by local officials,[30] and the largest unit over which the burden might be spread was the county or the town, not the nation. "[I]f the saide Justices of the Peace doe perceive that the Inhabitance of any Parishe are not able to levie amonge themselves sufficient Sum*m*es of Money for the Purposes," then they "shall and may taxe rate and assesse" other parishes in the hundred for the sake of the poor parishes, "and if the saide Hundred shall not be thought to the saide Justices able and fitt to releive the . . . sever*all Parishes not able to pro*vide for themselves," then the justices "shall rate and assesse" any other parish "within the . . . County . . . as in their discrecion shall seeme fitt."[31] Any person who found himself aggrieved by any tax or other act of the churchwardens or overseers could appeal to the justices of the peace who were authorized at their general quarter sessions to dispose of the matter "as to them shalbe thoughte convenient,"[32] their order being conclusive and binding all parties. Public housing for the impotent poor erected on the wastes and commons within the parish was to be "at the gene*r*all Chardges of the Parishe or otherwise of the Hundred or Countie,"[33] and almshouses,[34] hospitals,[35] and houses of correction[36] were a county responsibility.

Accordingly, the resources of the locality continued to fix the limit of assistance, no matter how overwhelming might be the

---

29. 43 Eliz. 1, c. 2, § XI (1601), did fix the maximum and minimum of the tax. It was not to exceed "six-pence" nor fall below a "halfpenny." For cases on rating and taxing see 9 CHITTY, STATUTES 250 (1895).

30. The overseers of the parish poor, the churchwardens, and "fower three or two substanciall Housholders . . . noiated . . . under the Hande and Seale of two or more Justices of the Peace," were "to raise weekelie or otherwise by taxaXon . . . such competent . . . sümes of Money as they shall thincke fytt." 43 Eliz. 1, c. 2, § I (1601).

31. 43 Eliz. 1, c. 2, § II (1601). Italicized letters in quotations indicate letters added because of the unavailability of characters representing them in the original.

32. 43 Eliz. 1, c. 2, § V (1601).

33. 43 Eliz. 1, c. 2, § IV (1601).

34. 43 Eliz. 1, c. 2, § XII (1601).

35. *Ibid.*

36. 18 Eliz. 1, c. 3, §§ V, VI (1576).

threat of poverty. To the private resources of the locality now were added the public resources, not just as a matter of fact and common practice, at least in the big towns, but as a matter of national requirement. Forty-three Elizabeth, chapter 2, declared the nation to be many communities of responsibility for the relief of poverty —as many communities as there were counties, towns, and parishes. Thus the significant thing about 43 Elizabeth, chapter 2, was that by it "the whole realm" declared *local* public responsibility for the relief of poverty in the form of a mandatory directive which the localities were legally obligated to effectuate. Gradually administrative means were found by which the nation might make good the legal mandate.

Professor Jordan explains the emphasis on the locality, not in terms of the absence of national fiscal and administrative machinery to do the job directly and the availability of the existing units of local government, but in terms of the Tudor preoccupation with problems of vagrancy.[37] All who have investigated the subject insist vagabondage was common;[38] perhaps it reached the proportions of a "chronic plague."[39] Police methods were ineffective to meet the problem, particularly in agricultural communities but also in the towns. By "sealing off" poverty in the locality, by bringing vagabondage to rest in the parish where it could be controlled and dispersed, Jordan says, the Tudors concluded the dangers of social disorder connected with vagabondage could be ended.[40] Considering today's arguments for county administration and control of the poor law system—that relief is thus closer to the taxpayer who will keep expenditures down, that there is local knowledge of the conditions of poverty and the needs of the poor, that local politicians wish to retain the preserve for themselves,

---

37. JORDAN, PHILANTHROPY IN ENGLAND 1480–1660, at 78–83 (1959).

38. See 4 HOLDSWORTH, *op. cit. supra* note 19, at 394.

39. According to Jordan, the vagabonds "moved across the countryside in droves, swarming into funerals for doles, infesting cities, and living in many cases by alms supplemented by a beggary tinged with criminality." JORDAN, PHILANTHROPY IN ENGLAND 1480–1660, at 78 (1959). In the manner of modern critics of the Aid to Dependent Children program, he assigns characteristics to the vagrants: they "settled into a rootless and wandering life from which they came in time to have no desire to be redeemed"; "to a remarkable degree" they were "self-perpetuating," "a breed of men, their women and children" who "insulated themselves from a society of which they were no more than a festering part." *Id.* at 78–79; *cf.* LEONARD, *op. cit. supra* note 19, at 221: "A man who was unemployed and had no resources had either to beg or to steal. If he begged, he was whipped; if he stole, he went to one of the terrible prisons of the time. The bands of armed vagrants, who made themselves terrible by their numbers and defied the law, were therefore only a natural consequence of the social conditions of the period. Repressive measures were tried but did not succeed because force could not restrain a man from begging if that was his only means of escaping starvation."

40. JORDAN, *op. cit. supra* note 39, at 80.

that administration from afar is inefficient—Jordan's vagrancy thesis can easily be seen to be only part of the explanation.

Direct local administration and exclusive local financing became then and has remained part of the Elizabethan poor law system. One immediate and long-range consequence of this distribution of authority, administration, and cost was that great reliance was placed on settlement and removal provisions. These served to identify the community responsible for providing support in each case and to keep down relief expenditures. Only those who had been born in a community or had long lived there were eligible. Other poor persons were kept out or removed to the place of their settlement. The size of the taxing and paying unit thus was determinative. From the community's point of view it supported only its own. From the pauper's point of view, he was bound to the place of his misfortune, restricted in his free movement and his personal opportunity. From society's point of view, the economy was fragmented, rendering more difficult the solution of economic problems that were regional and national. All of this is true today.

### Poor Law Assumption of Public Responsibility and Private Charity—Statute of Charitable Trusts

The public responsibility assumed by the Elizabethan poor law was not intended to be exclusive. It was designed to build on and supplement existing charitable programs conducted by local government units or by private institutions and foundations. The Tudors had a great impact on traditional charitable activities and institutions. Begging, an established and reputable practice for many groups during the Middle Ages as well as a necessary one, was first severely regulated and then generally outlawed. Social, trade, craft, and religious guilds, all of which made the performance of a charitable function a regular part of their work, drastically declined in the sixteenth century as a result of economic forces and state regulation.[41] The confiscation of part of their property under Edward VI[42] in 1547, Stubbs concludes, "was one unquestionable cause of the growth of town pauperism."[43] The church had a jurisdiction over the poor somewhat akin to that over marriage, divorce, and testamentary disposition and intestate succes-

---

41. 5 Eliz. 1, c. 4 (1562); 22 Hen. 8, c. 4 (1530–1531); 19 Hen. 8, c. 7 (1503); Cheyney, An Introduction to the Industrial and Social History of England (1901).
42. 1 Edw. 6, c. 14, § VII (1547).
43. 3 Stubbs, Constitutional History of England 620 (5th ed. 1903).

sion of personal property.[44] It discharged its charitable duty toward them through the beneficed clergy in their parishes, through the mendicant friars, and through the almoners of the monasteries. Though church charity probably declined before 1536, expropriation of the monasteries then and in 1539[45] accelerated the process.[46] Henry VIII did not confine his activities to the expropriation of the monasteries. By the Statute of Superstitious Uses passed in 1531,[47] he and Parliament laid a restraint on the creation of trusts for most religious purposes.[48] That statute, the statutes abolishing the authority of the Pope in England,[49] the statutes suppressing the monasteries,[50] and the complex of doctrines and activities known as the Reformation diverted great wealth into private charitable foundations that would have flowed into religious channels. This alone would have made the functions, legality, and public supervision of these institutions, which accordingly became the principal remaining source of private charity,[51] more immediately

---

44. TIERNEY, MEDIEVAL POOR LAW 4–5 (1959).

45. 31 Hen. 8, c. 13 (1539); 27 Hen. 8, c. 28 (1535–1536).

46. Historians are in dispute about how sharply the expropriation reduced charitable activities. De Schweinitz thinks, "This action, like the Black Death in the 14th century, gave dramatic point to an already bad situation. A social resource, inadequate at its best, was now substantially diminished. What was more, one of the great symbols of charity had been removed, and there was consequently double occasion for public action." *Op. cit. supra* note 19, at 19.

47. 23 Hen. 8, c. 10 (1531–1532).

48. Assurances and trusts of lands to the use of parish churches, chapels, churchwardens, guilds, fraternities, commonalties, companies, or brotherhoods, or for obits forever or for three or four score years or for a continual service of a priest were thereafter declared to be void if made for a term exceeding twenty years. An exception was made in the case of cities and corporate towns where by ancient custom devises into mortmain had been permitted. The statute also was not to apply to lands which, under the wills of two former aldermen of the City of Norwich, were to be employed "for the discharge of Tolles and Customes within the . . . Citie and at the gates of the same, for the discharge of poore people within the same Citie, of taxes and tallages . . . for the clensing of the Stretes." These distributions had to be certified into the Court of Chancery. 23 Hen. 8, c. 10, § V (1531–1532). By 1 Edw. 6, c. 14 (1547), past dispositions made for certain superstitious uses were forfeited to the king.

49. 28 Hen. 8, c. 16 (1536); 24 Hen. 8, c. 12 (1532–1533).

50. 31 Hen. 8, c. 13 (1539); 27 Hen. 8, c. 28 (1535–1536).

51. Private charitable foundations had been less important than the church but more so than the guilds. The long history of private foundations was closely related in the Middle Ages to the accumulation of property by the church and the efforts of the king and the feudal barons to prevent it. The mortmain statutes provided for the forfeiture of land conveyed to religious bodies or to individuals for their use. 15 Rich. 2, c. 5 (1391); 18 Edw. 1, st. I, § 3 (1289–1290); 7 Edw. 1, st. I (1297); 9 Hen. 3, c. 44 (1225). Early in the fifteenth century the Chancellor began to issue subpoenas for the enforcement of uses, 3 SCOTT, TRUSTS § 348.2 (1939), and in 1414 Parliament passed a statute providing for the investigation and reform of charitable foundations of all sorts, testifying to their extent at the time and to the strength of the belief that they were misapplying their resources. The preamble described the objective to be "to sustain impotent men and women, lazars, men out of their wits and poor women with child, and to nourish, relieve and refresh other poor people." 2 Hen. 5, st. I, c. 1 (1414). More than 5,000 charitable trusts still subsisting in the first half of the nineteenth century had been created before 1601. SCOTT, TRUSTS § 348.2. De Schweinitz concluded that there were at least 460 charitable foundations in England at the time of the Reformation. *Op. cit. supra* note 19, at 15.

pressing national problems.[52] But the forces and vast political re-organization which gave rise to these problems were also setting other changes and programs in motion.[53]

Under the Tudors charitable foundations and the law of charitable trusts were developed in connection with the poor law. As the state assumed public responsibility for the poor, it built upon private charity and sought to encourage it. At best, such charity was an alternative to public expenditure; at least, it served as a method of reducing the cost. As the poor law system evolved, the Tudors sought to assure that charitable foundations devoted their resources without diversion or misapplication, that private and public charitable works were interrelated administratively, and that the establishment of private charitable foundations occurred, especially in the area covered by the public responsibility. While we cannot ignore pressures arising from the political changes of the times and the developing *parens patriae* and police functions of the state, it is probably not too much to say that the modern law of charitable trusts evolved as an integral part of the poor law system and did so primarily because of the assumption of public responsibility by that system, with the resulting necessity of finding means of keeping down public expenditures.

In 1551 after a temporary regression in poor law development, Edward VI revived the poor law statutes of Henry VIII.[54] At the same time he directed the bishops to inquire into the manner in which hospitals were applying their funds.[55] In 1572 Elizabeth undertook a poor law reformulation,[56] and the all-important step was taken of authorizing compulsory taxation for the relief of the destitute.[57] The impotent poor were to be registered in the parish of their settlement, and those not settled were to be removed. Some might be relieved in hospitals. Provision was made for the supervision of these and other charitable foundations by the bishops and the justices. But now the legislation went further: the preamble[58]

---

52. BRISTOWE, HUNT & BURDETT, TUDOR'S CHARITABLE TRUSTS, THE LAW OF CHARITIES AND MORTMAIN 2 (4th ed. 1906).
53. Charitable trusts were apparently never treated as falling within the Statute of Uses, 27 Hen. 8, c. 10 (1535–1536), which converted the equitable interests of a beneficiary in a use into a legal title with a right of immediate possession or within the Statute of Wills, 32 Hen. 8, c. 1 (1540), which made it possible to dispose of land by will to persons other than corporations. Some say that the statutes had the indirect effect of bringing questions of the validity of charitable uses within the cognizance of common-law courts. BRISTOWE, *op. cit. supra* note 51, at 2.
54. 5 & 6 Edw. 6, c. 2 (1551).
55. 5 & 6 Edw. 6, c. 2, § VI (1551).
56. 14 Eliz. 1, c. 5 (1572).
57. 14 Eliz. 1, c. 5, § XVI (1572).
58. "Diverse well disposed and charitable persons" had given "lands, tenements and

presupposed the previous legality of charitable trusts and proclaimed a policy of encouraging them. Those who created charitable trusts were told that their grants, gifts, and devises would be valid even though the recipient corporation was not accurately named in the instrument.[59] The machinery and programs of the poor law were further linked to the functions and encouragement of private charitable foundations in the revision of 1576. The able-bodied indigents were put to work on stocks of goods supplied by the overseers of the poor, and houses of correction were to be established and used as a work-enforcement mechanism. At the same time provision was made that "landes holden in free soccage" might be given for twenty years for the maintenance of houses of correction and stocks for the poor.[60] The last and greatest of the reviews of the poor law before 1601 was also the last and greatest review of the law of charitable trusts. The close interdependence of the two fields can be seen from the topics and order of the statute's sections as enacted in 1597. Chapter 1 dealt with the decay of towns and houses of husbandry; chapter 2 with tillage and enclosure; chapter 3 with the poor law proper, containing all the provisions which four years later constituted 43 Elizabeth, chapter 2; chapter 4 with the punishment of vagabonds and beggars; chapter 5 with the lawfulness and methods of establishing charitable trusts; chapter 6 with the public responsibility and administrative machinery for enforcing such trusts.[61] The new method of creating a charitable

---

hereditaments to the relief and sustentacion of the poor" in one hospital founded by Henry VIII and in the three founded by Edward VI as well as in other hospitals. The hope was expressed that "many more hereafter will likewise charitably give." 14 Eliz. 1, c. 14 (1572).

59. See note 51 *supra*.

60. 18 Eliz. 1, c. 3, § IX (1576).

61. Chapters 5 and 6, with slight variations, became chapter 4 of 43 Elizabeth and were made perpetual by 21 James I, chapter 1 (1624). The preamble of chapter 5 recalls that at the preceding session of Parliament it had been declared lawful for a person to give his lands, tenements, and hereditaments in fee simple "by Feoffament Will in writing or other Assurance" "as well to thuse of the Pore as for the Provision Sustentacon or Mayntenance of any Howse of Correccion, or abiding Howses or of any Stocks or Stoares." This "good law," however, was found not to have the effect intended because hospitals, houses of correction, and abiding places could not be erected or incorporated without obtaining special license from the Crown. This obstacle was now to be removed so that such establishments might be founded "with as great ease and little charge as may be" by simply enrolling a deed in Chancery. 39 Eliz. 1, c. 5 (1597); 2 COKE, INSTITUTES OF THE LAW OF ENGLAND 719 (1642).

Coke, who participated in the development and framing of the law, described its purpose as follows: "[T]he charges of incorporation and of the licence of Mortmaine in these days grow so great by one meanes or other, as it hath discouraged many men to undertake these pious and charitable workes, whereas in former times such workes of piety and charity for the poore did ever passe *in forma pauperis,* and so we hope to see it againe." 2 COKE, *op. cit. supra* at 722. The model of the statute, Coke tells us, was 13 Elizabeth, chapter 17 (1571), "for the erection and foundation of an Hospitall by Robert earle of Leicester . . . ." 2 *id.* at 725.

trust was simply to enroll a deed in the High Court of Chancery. The charitable objects mentioned are those of the poor law itself: to erect "hospitals, measons de dieu, abiding places, or houses of correction . . . as well for the finding, sustentation and reliefe of the maimed, poore, needy or impotent people, as to set the poore to work . . . ."[62] These purposes were expanded into the historically definitive list of twenty-one in chapter 4 of 43 Elizabeth. In addition to providing the simplified method of trust creation and identifying the permissible charitable purposes, the act endows the charitable trust with its legal attributes: a body corporate and politic having perpetual succession, it may sue and be sued and take land as well as personalty "without License or Writ of *Ad Quod Damnum*, the Statute of Mortmain or any other Statute or Law to the contrary notwithstanding."[63] The founder was left completely free to determine the form of the establishment, the method of its operation, its ordinances and statutes, its head, members, and the number and kind of poor to be served, and the discharge of the visitorial function.[64] Responsibility and authority to see that the charitable trusts were carried out according to the intentions of the founder was devolved upon the Chancellor. He was empowered to appoint commissions to inquire by jury into any breaches of trust or misapplication of resources.[65] He was authorized to make such orders and decrees "as the said good, godly and charitable uses may be truely observed in full, ample and most liberal sort, according to the true intent and meaning of the Founders or Donors thereof."[66]

## The Poor Law and the Statutes of Labourers

Any welfare system primarily operates upon and is for the benefit of the working classes of the nation and must be regarded, in modern times no less than in the Middle Ages, as an indispensable part of the overall system of labor legislation. Whatever might be said in welfare terms of the necessity to deal with the particular needs of individuals and families, the unemployed segment of the

---

62. 2 *id.* at 719.
63. 39 Eliz. 1, c. 5 (1597).
64. Coke says that the orders governing the establishment were to contain "two especiall things, viz. daily prayer to Almighty God: and that the Master and Brethren be not idle, but that they and every of them exercise such worke meet for them . . . ." 2 COKE, *op. cit. supra* note 61, at 725.
65. According to Coke the Chancellor could inquire into these nine things: abuses, breaches of trust, negligence, misimployments, not imploying, concealing, defrauding, misconverting, and misgovernment. 2 *id.* at 711.
66. 39 Eliz. 1, c. 6, § 1 (1597).

population stands in an economic and social relationship to the employed segment. How the state regulates that relationship, through what machinery and for what ends, and the extent to which it leaves regulation to the operation of unregulated forces are intricate problems of politics and general economics no less than of welfare. The social scientists' solutions to these problems are likely to reflect views about the relative roles of the personal and nonpersonal causes of poverty and the degree to which poverty is morally reprehensible, related to correctable traits of character, and subject to control by penal sanctions.

At its origins and during its sixteenth-century evolution, the poor law was an integral part of the overall system of labor controls, and its characteristics derive partially from that source. As the centuries slipped away, the general system first moderated and then dissipated. The poor law, however, neither died nor greatly changed. In this sense as it prevails today the poor law is an anachronism.

The pattern of labor controls had been established in the Ordinance and Statute of Labourers of 1349–1351,[67] designed to make available to the feudal lords an adequate supply of agricultural workers when the Black Death and other social and economic factors had created a critical labor shortage. Poor and idle persons were regarded, as de Schweinitz says, "not as a problem in destitution but as a seepage from the supply of labor."[68] The problem was seen as one of getting any unemployed manpower to work. Enforcement provisions were crudely direct, uncomplicated by any ideas about economic incentives or psychological persuasion. Under severe penal sanctions, men and women "able in body and within the age of three score years" were required to work for anybody who wanted them. They had to work, not at wages determined by individual or collective bargaining—since part of the problem had been that "many seeing the necessity of masters, and great scarcity of servants, will not serve unless they may receive excessive wages"—but at wages frozen at those "accustomed" in "the twentieth year of our reign of England, or five or six other common years next before." Prices were also fixed but somewhat more flexibly.[69] Laborers were not to quit their jobs and move

---

67. 25 Edw. 3, st. II (1350–1351), preceded by the Ordinance of Labourers, 23 Edw. 3, c. I–VIII (1349).

68. De Schweinitz, England's Road to Social Security 6 (1943).

69. Sellers of "all manner of victuals" were "bound to sell the same . . . for a reasonable price, having respect to the price that such victuals be sold at in the adjoining places,

about in search of other employment but to remain with their masters and in their towns. Finally begging was prohibited as was giving alms or "anything to such who may possibly labor or presume to favor them in their sloth so that thereby they may be compelled to labor for their necessary living."

The lash of necessity, the terrors of the jail house, and legally imposed geographical and occupational immobility were the devices used to drive men to work at wages pegged to earlier times and conditions. To the avowed economic motive for this repressive system was added an incidental allusion to prevention of immorality and crime: the able-bodied who lived by begging were thought, not only to refuse to labor, but to give themselves over "to idleness and vice, and sometimes to theft and other abominations." The Statutes of Labourers contain an unspoken distinction between the employable and the impotent, those not "able in Body" or not within "the age of three score years," "such who could [not] possibly labor" and who could not therefore be "compelled to labor for their necessary living." But no provision is made for the impotent; they are not even expressly exempted from the operation of the statute. We must look to the Statute of Labourers of the fourteenth century for some of the characteristics of the poor law system developed in the sixteenth century, though the economic circumstances of the age and, one would suppose, the applicability of the methods were quite different.

In the sixteenth century the increased efficiency of a rising class of yeoman farmers brought unemployment or only seasonal labor to marginal workers. Sheep raising, the base of the cloth manufacturing centers and of trade, shifted the use of land, causing some agricultural depopulation—though just how much is a topic of historical dispute. Early industrial and commercial revolution brought with it a rapid urban growth and a new class of urban industrial workers, the source of a new kind of poor and the victims of a new kind of poverty. Their employment depended on special skills; their living depended on trade and production subject to periods of slump and complete stagnation; and when unemployment came their destitution was absolute, unrelieved by the means of partial support available in agricultural communities. Most importantly the sixteenth century saw a sharp population rise, perhaps as much as forty percent, resulting in a substantial rural

so that the same sellers have moderate gains, and not excessive, reasonably to be required according to the distance of the place from whence the said victual be carried."

and urban labor surplus.[70] To these distinctive economic and social factors of the age must be added the stock causes of widespread poverty: storms, droughts, crop failures, and food shortages; inflation; severe and recurrent epidemics; unrest, disorders, and localized rebellions.

If many of the problems of the sixteenth century were new and different, remedies were old and familiar. With variation in detail, the overall pattern of rigid labor control embodied in the fourteenth century Statutes of Labourers[71] was reaffirmed and revitalized by a 1562 act "towching dyvers Orders for Artificers Laborers Servantes of Husbandrye and Apprentises."[72] The stated purpose was to "banishe Idleness advance Husbandrye and yeelde unto the hired person bothe in the tyme of scarsitee and in the tyme of plentye a convenient proporcon of Wages."[73] What "a convenient proporcon of Wages" was the statute left to the annual determination of the justices of the peace.[74] But the essential feature of the act for present purposes is that it sought to "banishe Idleness" and "advance Husbandrye" by compulsory labor. Persons between the ages of 12 and 60, not "retained" and without independent means of support, were compelled to serve in husbandry; artisans were ordered to work in their trades for anybody who wanted them; artificers and "persons as be meete to labour" were to be caused by local officials to serve "mowing reaping shearing getting or inning of Corne Grayne and Heye";[75] unmarried women between the ages of 12 and 40 were required to go to work; and youths under 21 were obligated to bind themselves as apprentices. Hours of labor—twelve hours a day in summer and from dawn to dusk in winter—were set by the statute itself. Thus, labor was apportioned among the various occupations and particularly

---

70. In his recent study of this subject, Jordan concludes that, during the first four decades of the seventeenth century, "something like eight percent of the population of any urban and industrial complex in England were quite chronically at or below the line of poverty as then most harshly defined, while in periods of trade depression or pestilence this proportion could rise . . . to as much as twenty per cent." JORDAN, *op. cit. supra* note 39, at 68.

71. This legislation had been reenacted at least thirteen times in the century following its original enactment. See CHEYNEY, AN INTRODUCTION TO THE INDUSTRIAL AND SOCIAL HISTORY OF ENGLAND 106–28 (1901).

72. 5 Eliz. 1, c. 4 (1562).

73. 5 Eliz. 1, c. 4, § I (1562).

74. Because of its minute regulation of apprenticeship and of the relations between masters and journeymen, this act, which remained in force in England for two hundred and fifty years, is sometimes denominated a "great industrial code," CHEYNEY, *op. cit. supra* note 71, at 156, and it certainly had the effect of preempting by national legislation a field of regulation formerly occupied by the craft guilds. It thus contributed, along with already operative economic forces, to the decline of those once powerful organizations.

75. 5 Eliz. 1, c. 4, § XV (1562–1563).

directed into agriculture to further the economic policy of the state in favor of that industry and to diminish the dangers of scarcity and famine which were epidemic in the century.

State efforts to control price and distribution of the food supply accompanied these labor controls which, in turn, were counterparts of the close regulation of all other parts of the economy. Export of grain and its movement within the country were closely managed by the Privy Council; producers were compelled to bring their supplies to market, as were those who held cargoes in ships in harbor; corn badgers and local dealers were strictly supervised.[76] The common-law crimes of forestalling, regrating, and engrossing were statutorily defined and strengthened;[77] combinations to raise the price of victuals were made crimes.[78]

The result of the centuries-old English labor legislation reformulated in the Elizabethan statute of 1562 was a system of complete paternalism: no free labor, let alone a free labor movement, existed. Substantially all persons without visible means of support were required to work. They had little choice of the type of work or of employer and no chance to bargain for wages; combining to do so was made a crime.[79] In general, the employer-employee relationship was that of master and servant, based on fixed wages and work hours and for a fixed term which neither party could terminate at will. Breach of the relationship without cause or termination without a quarter's notice resulted in a forty-shilling forfeiture when done by the master and in corporal punishment and coerced return to labor when done by the servant. A servant fleeing into another shire was to be arrested and returned; servants who finished their terms could not go elsewhere to work without a testimonial certificate that they were free to do so. The master might correct his underage servant in moderation;[80] the servant who assaulted the master, the mistress, or their agents was liable to imprisonment and other corporal punishment. Because the master

---

76. By 5 Eliz. 1, c. 12 (1562–1563), "Drover of Cattell Badger Lader Kidder Carrier Buyer or Transporter of Corne or Grayne Butter or Cheese" were required to procure a license from the justices of the peace. To be eligible for such a license, a person had to have dwelled in the shire for three years, be married, be at least thirty years of age, and be a householder "and not Howshold Servaunt nor Retainers to anny *person* or *persons*." The license was only good for one year. See 4 HOLDSWORTH, HISTORY OF ENGLISH LAW 373–87 (1924).

77. 5 Eliz. 1, c. 12, § II (1562); 5 & 6 Edw. 6, c. XIV (1551–1552); see 4 HOLDSWORTH, *op. cit. supra* note 76, at 375–79.

78. 7 Edw. 6, c. 5 (1552–1553) (regulation of wine prices); 2 & 3 Edw. 6, c. 15 (1548); 25 Hen. 8, c. 2 (1533–1534); 24 Hen. 8, c. 3 (1532–1533) (regulation of meat prices); 3 Hen. 8, c. 8 (1511–1512).

79. 2 & 3 Edw. 6, c. 15 (1548).

80. 4 BARRY, THE PRESENT PRACTICE OF A JUSTICE OF THE PEACE 46 (1790).

was damaged by the loss of the services to which he was entitled, he might justify an assault in defense of his servant, bring an action against a third person who injured the servant or enticed him away,[81] or assist his servant in law suits against third persons despite the general prohibition against maintenance.[82]

These rules applied with special force to apprentices who were denominated by Blackstone and generally regarded as a "species of servant."[83] The apprenticeship was established by an indenture, according to which the apprentice was to dwell and serve the master for a term of years. He was to obey all the lawful commands of the master, preserve the master's secrets and protect his interests, and remain with him unless given leave. "[A]t cards, dice, or any other unlawful games, he shall not play; taverns or alehouses he shall not frequent; fornication he shall not commit; matrimoney he shall not contract . . . ."[84] The master was obligated to instruct the apprentice in his "trade, science or occupation."[85] He was to supply him "meat, drink, washing, lodging and apparel, both linen and woollen, and all other necessaries fit and convenient."[86]

Holdsworth saw this complex of labor and industrial regulation as a "necessary consequence" of the commercial and industrial policy of the Tudors and the provisions of poor relief as "an essential part" of it.

> [F]ixed rules of law as to wages, and the other measures taken by the government to provide employment and cheap food, were necessary for the protection of the economically weak. The prohibition of a com-

---

81. 3 & 4 Edw. 6, c. 16, § XI (1549–1550); 4 Barry, *op. cit. supra* note 80, at 50–51; 4 Holdsworth, *op. cit. supra* note 76, at 383.

82. 1 Blackstone, Commentaries on the Laws of England 429 (Cooley ed. 1899).

83. 1 *id*. at 426.

84. 4 Barry, *op. cit. supra* note 80, at 368.

85. *Ibid*.

86. For the standard form of indenture see 4 *id*. at 367. By the Statutes of Labourers the classes of persons who might take apprentices were limited so as to favor some occupations and to discourage others. Householders with half a ploughland in tillage were entitled to take an apprentice between the ages of 10 and 18. City-dwelling householders over 24 exercising any art, mystery, or manual occupation there might apprentice the son of a freeman "not occupieng Husbrandrye nor being a labourer." 5 Eliz. 1, c. 4, § XIX (1562–1563). Youths were not to be bound to the "Misteries or Craftes of a Marchante . . . Mercer Draper Goldesmithe Ironmonger Imbroderer or Clothyer" unless they were the sons of the masters or their parents were freeholders of 40 shillings a year. 5 Eliz. 1, c. 4, § XX (1562–1563). Inferior tradesmen might take the sons of anybody as an apprentice. 5 Eliz. 1 c. 4, § XXIII (1562–1563). These trades included smith, wheelwright, ploughwright, millwright, carpenter, roughmason, plasterer, sawyer, lime-burner, brickmaker, bricklayer, tyler, slater, healyer, tyle-maker, woolen weaver weaving household cloth only, fuller, burner of ore and wood ashes, thatcher or shingler. For limitations on the number of apprentices in specific callings see 14 Car. 2, c. 5 (1662); 1 Jac. 1, c. 17 (1603–1604) (hats and felts). The master generally received a sum of money as consideration for the arrangement. In 1530 Parliament, seeking to prevent excessive charges of apprentices enter-

bination to raise wages, and the separate remedies provided to compel workmen to keep their contracts, were necessary in order to secure the peace of the State and the rights of the employer. . . . Those who obtained relief through the poor law did not occupy, as they occupy in modern times, a peculiar status of their own.[87]

But all of the elements of general labor control had existed in England from the middle of the fourteenth century when a different economic and political theory prevailed. Therefore although quite compatible with Tudor economic policies, they were a "necessary consequence" no more of them than of quite different principles. If wages were publicly fixed, then prices, especially on necessaries, had also to be fixed; forbidding combinations to raise wages and prices was in effect only another way of saying that wages and prices were fixed. Moreover, in a system of set wages and prices where wage and price differentials may not be used to apportion workers among the various industries and to compel men to work where assigned, the public authority may have to do so. Controlling any one of these elements in the economy entails controlling others. Contrary to Holdsworth's view, neither protection of the economically weak nor securing the rights of employers is a governing motive in this economic theory.

Holdsworth's conclusion leaves something to be desired also in relating the overall system to particular features of the poor law. If labor is compulsory, then vagabondage and begging might be prohibited as an enforcement measure. In 1349 that measure was conditioned by labor shortage and would seem dependent on it. If everybody must work in time of labor surplus and industry, commerce, and agriculture cannot be regulated to absorb the surplus, then the state must provide the work. But why must everybody work in these circumstances; why should the state supply the employment and coerce the labor, particularly if it was not to be on necessary public works?

The answers supplied in the sixteenth century are the same as those used today; they have little connection with the industrial and general labor policies of the Tudors.[88] The first answer

ing the guilds, set the entrance fee at a maximum of 2 shillings, 6 pence. 22 Hen. 8, c. 4 (1530).

87. 4 HOLDSWORTH, *op. cit. supra* note 76, at 404.

88. One possible answer is that the working class occupies a status, the function of which is to work. Holdsworth leans toward this theory in his attack upon the doctrine of equality. "The preservation of some of the medieval feeling in favor of a due subordination of class to class, and of a separation between different classes which had different duties to perform, has had happy results upon English society and the English state. A strict caste

is that the state, which was then assuming a public obligation for the support of the able-bodied unemployed as well as of the impotent, might by this method minimize its expenditures while at the same time accomplishing its objective. In the seventeenth century the principles of public responsibility and coerced labor developed together. The first great statute by which the state undertook to stimulate and organize private relief for the impotent directed local officials to insure that those with "lymmes stronge ynough to labour" be "kepte in contynual labour, whereby evry one of them may gette theyr owne [sustenance] and lyving with their owne handes."[89] The association of the two principles was continued in the statutes of 1547,[90] 1549–1550,[91] and 1572.[92] With the firm establishment of the principle of public taxation for the relief of the destitute in the last statute, the state undertook work relief in earnest. In 1576 work relief was taken out of the realm of a general order to local officials; under explicit statutory instruction local officials were to gather "a competent Store and Stocke of Woole Hempe Flaxe Iron or other Stuffe" and to deliver a portion to each poor and needy person "to bee wrought into Yarne or other Matter." The poor person was to be paid "accordinge to the deserte of the Worcke," and the officials were to sell the product.[93] Those able-bodied who refused to work or who spoiled the material supplied them were to be sent to the house of correction—one or two of which were ordered erected in each county—"there to be straightlye kepte, as well in Diet as in Worke, and also punisshed from tyme to tyme . . . ."[94]

The second answer concerns vagrancy and vagabondage and notions of their causes, effects, and cure. Idleness was thought to be a result of personal choice rather than economic conditions. Based on personal fault it was personally correctable if only the will were instilled. Accordingly the Tudors, like their predecessors, unleashed the furies of the criminal law against combined idleness and poverty. "Ruffelers, sturdy vagabonds, and valiant beggars" were to be seized, tied naked to the end of a cart and whipped

system is favorable to corruption and fatal to progress; but a system which persists in ignoring all differences between classes, and in attempting to realize the fantastic doctrine of the equality of all individuals of the state, is favorable to social discontent and consequent unrest, and fatal to individual effort." 4 *id*. at 406.

89. 27 Hen. 8, c. 25, § IV (1535).
90. 1 Edw. 6, c. 3 (1547).
91. 3 & 4 Edw. 6, c. 16 (1549–1550).
92. 14 Eliz. 1, c. 5 (1572).
93. 18 Eliz. 1, c. 3, § IV (1575–1576).
94. *Ibid*.

through the nearest market town until bloody, and then returned
to the places where they were born or last dwelt, each there to "put
hymselfe to laboure lyke as a trewe man oweth to do." That no
work was to be found in that place did not matter. If "loitering,
wandering, and idleness or vagabondage" continued, the punishment was repeated, successively augmented by having the upper
gristle of the right ear "clean cut away" and eventually by death.[95]
Other penalties added from time to time were slavery for two
years and then for life,[96] assignment to the galleys, and banishment
from the realm.[97] The explanation provided in one of the statutes
was that "ydleness" was

> the mother & rote of all vyces, whereby hathe insurged & spronge &
> dayly insurgeth & spryngeth contynual theftes murders and other hay-
> nous offences & great enormytes. . . . [I]n all places throughe out this
> Realme . . . Vacabundes & Beggers . . . dayly do increase in greate
> & excessyve nombres into great routs and companies . . . to the high
> displeasure of God the inquyetacon & damage of the Kyng's People &
> to the marvaylous disturbance of the Comon Weale of this Realme.[98]

These violent penalties failed. The alternative eventually
adopted was the institution whose name characterizes its function,
the house of correction. There the "sturdy rogue" could be starved,
worked, punished, and thereby reformed. By a resolution of the
judges and a statute of 1610, it was made explicit that not only
rogues and vagabonds but disorderly persons and merely idle persons were eligible for this treatment.[99] Moreover, they were to receive no allowance but such "as they shall deserve by their owne
labour and work."[100] Coke thought the proper working of the
poor law depended on the houses of correction. When justices of
the peace diligently performed their duty in this respect "there
was not a Rogue to be seen in any part of England, but when
Justices and other Officers became *tepidi*, or *trepidi*, Rogues, etc.
swarmed againe."[101]

> [F]ew or none are committed to the common Gaole amongst so many
> male-factors, but they come out worse then they went in. And few are
> committed to the House of Correction, or Working House, but they
> come out better.

---

95. 22 Hen. 8, c. 12, § III (1530).
96. 1 Edw. 6, c. 3 (1547).
97. 39 Eliz. 1, c. 4, § IV (1597).
98. 22 Hen. 8, c. 12 (1530).
99. See 7 Jac. 1, c. 4 (1609–1610); 2 COKE, *op. cit. supra* note 61, at 731.
100. 7 Jac. 1, c. 4, § IV (1609–1610).
101. 2 COKE, *op. cit. supra* note 61, at 729.

And where some are of opinion, that in particular Townes a discreet and expert workman may set the young and idle people as voluntaries on worke: Certainly, the youth on both sexes hath (in the time of this great negligence) gotten such a trade of picking theevery, stealing of wood, and the like, through idleness, as they will never be brought to worke, unlesse they be thereunto compelled (and the rather, for that some of the Parents and Masters have benefit by them) but compelled they may be, and this great worke happily effected, if by the order of the Justices of the Peace these statutes be put in due execution.[102]

However the poor law and the general pattern of labor controls might fit into the overall economy and economic theory of the times, the paternal, custodial, coercive, and punitive attitudes in the Elizabethan poor law were part of the same attitudes existing throughout the whole system of labor control. Special applications might have to be devised for those under the poor law, and additional or even different reasons might justify their use; but the principal ideas, institutions, and practices of the general system were almost automatically extended to the special. Those who were capable of work were compelled to engage in it whether for a private master or for the overseers of the poor in sheltered projects or in houses of correction. In the case of able-bodied poor, often described as vagrants and vagabonds but including the merely idle as well as the disorderly, additional reasons for compulsory labor were to minimize public expenditure through the partial or total self-support of the individual and to reform the miscreant idler. Laborers were not free to move about from place to place without authorizing certificates under threat of incurring the harsh penalties meted out to sturdy rogues. That the relief recipient should be similarly circumscribed was thus a part of a well-established general pattern, but the reasons were quite different: to identify the locality responsible for support and to curtail relief costs. Children of the laboring classes were required to be apprenticed, including children of families on poor relief. The special statutes requiring that poor children be put to work or apprenticed thus applied general policies to the particular group. Lightening the relief load was added to the three general objectives of the child labor system: To render the abilities of the children "in their several stations, of the greatest advantage to the commonwealth";[103] to provide children with training in "husbondrie or other craftes . . . by the

---

102. 2 *id*. at 734–35.
103. 1 BLACKSTONE, *op. cit. supra* note 82, at 451.

whiche, they may gette their livinges when they shall come to age";[104] to assure that children are "accustomed and brought up in Laboure and Worke, and then not lyke to growe to bee ydle Roges."[105] The objective of lightening the relief load intruded urgency and special administrative machinery into gathering poor law children from their families and distributing them to masters which did not exist as to the rest of the laboring class. Indeed, public authorities might assign such children to masters whether they were willing to receive them or not. But in general there was no distinction of principle between laboring class families on and off relief as to the work requirement of their children.

## The Family Law of the Poor

Under 43 Elizabeth, chapter 2, children were to be taken from parents thought by the churchwardens and overseers of the poor unable to keep and maintain them regardless of whether the parents were recipients of poor relief. Families were not to be kept together and aided. Mothers' aid was not a conception of 43 Elizabeth. Prescribing no standards, the statute explicitly placed the decision within the administrator's unconfined discretion, and it was held that the churchwardens and overseers need not aver even that the parents were unable to maintain the child.[106] The statute is silent about parental rights, nor does it intimate that any existed to be skirted, nullified, or safeguarded.[107]

---

104. 27 Hen. 8, c. 25, § VI (1535–1536).
105. 18 Eliz. 1, c. 3, § IV (1575–1576).
106. 1 BARRY, *op. cit. supra* note 80, at 88. Later a rule was introduced that a child under seven should not be separated from its mother for the purpose of being maintained by the parish. Regina v. Clarke, 7 Ell. & Bl. 186, 119 Eng. Rep. 1217 (Q.B. 1857).
107. The King v. Inhabitants of Hamstall Ridware, 3 T.R. 379, 381–82, 100 Eng. Rep. 631, 632–33 (K.B. 1789) see 1 BARRY, *op. cit. supra* note 80, at 81–82. *The King v. Inhabitants of Hamstall Ridware*, interpreting 43 Elizabeth, chapter 2, 178 years after its enactment, illustrates the great reliance on feelings, morals, and judicial notions of the principle of social welfare and the complete absence of any reference to parental rights. The question was whether the two justices who had to approve the apprenticeship made by the churchwardens and overseers might act separately or had to act concurrently. The judges held that, since the function was judicial and not merely ministerial, the justices had to act concurrently. "*Chief Judge Lord Kenyon.* [W]hen the nature of this case is considered, it appears to be one of the most serious subjects that fall within the decisions of the justices. For they are empowered by this Act of Parliament to take children out of the arms of their parents, and to bind them out as apprentices till they are 21 years of age. The law has made them the guardians for those children, who have no others to take care of them. And who ought to judge of the fitness of the persons, to whom the poor children are thus to be apprenticed? Not the overseers—they are frequently obscure people, and perhaps in managing the business of the parish are not always attentive to the feelings of the parents. But the Legislature intended that the magistrates should have a check and control over the parish officers in this instance; and in my mind they are called upon to examine with the most minute and anxious attention the situations of the masters, to whom the apprentices are to be bound, and to exercise their judgment solemnly and soberly before they allow or

Although setting the children to work was provided as an alternative to apprenticing, how this was to be done and whether by methods used for adults was not indicated. In any event, the statute principally emphasized apprenticing as the method to provide for the maintenance of children of the poor. The "competent sums" to be raised by taxation for purchasing stocks on which to put the able-bodied to work and for relieving the impotent were also to be used for apprenticing poor children. How the money was to be employed for this purpose is not specified, but presumably it was to supply the bargain price to the master. The churchwardens and overseers were to bind children to be apprentices "where they shall see convenient."[108] It was held that this phrase referred to the selection of the masters rather than of the children, and thus persons were not free to decline children assigned to them. As the selection of the children was entirely within the discretion of the local officials, so was the selection of the masters.[109] Lord Kenyon said, "The general object of the . . . [poor law statute] was to compel all of those who had any property in the parish, to contribute their due proportion towards the maintenance of the poor; and the receiving of apprentices is one mode of contributing to their general relief."[110] Unwilling masters had a right of appeal to the justices in quarter sessions. Masters selected were usually those "who by their possessions or manner of living have occasion to keep servants . . . ."[111] Merchants, gentlemen of fortune, and clergymen were equally eligible with others and might be compelled to take a child.[112] Persons not part of the community were exempted. Since assigning a child was only a mode of assessing the poor law tax, choice had to be made among inhabitants and occupants of parish property; only they were liable for the tax. Besides,

disallow the act of the parish officers; for which purpose it is necessary that they should confer together. *Ashhurst*, J. The act of the justices in this case is in its nature an act of judgment. They are the guardians of the morals of the people, and ought to take care that the apprentices are not placed with masters who may corrupt their morals. . . . *Grose*, J. This act is peculiarly of a judicial nature; for the magistrates are appointed the guardians of those who have no other. They should therefore exercise their judgment in this case with great deliberation."

108. 43 Eliz. 1, c. 2, § III (1601).

109. For evidence as to the reaction of parents and masters see BARNES, SOMERSET 1625–1640, at 184–85 (1961).

110. The King v. Clapp, 3 T.R. 107, 113, 100 Eng. Rep. 480, 483 (1789); see 1 BARRY, *op. cit. supra* note 80, at 85–86. A later statute, 8 & 9 Will. 3, c. 30, § V (1696–1697), quieted lingering doubts about this interpretation of the phrase and enforced by distress administrative orders against unwilling masters.

111. 1 BARRY, *op. cit. supra* note 80, at 88.

112. *Ibid.* (merchants); 1 BLACKSTONE, *op. cit. supra* note 80, at 426 (gentlemen of fortune and clergymen).

if outsiders could be compelled to accept children of the parish, each community could transfer its burdens to others.

The indenture used for apprenticing the pauper child was similar to that for other children though the standard of care by the master may have been somewhat lower. The churchwardens and the overseers of the poor were parties on the one side, the master on the other. The master agreed to instruct the child in his "craft, mystery or occupation" and to supply him with "sufficient meat, drink, apparel, washing, and lodging, and all other things needful or meet for an apprentice." However, there is less emphasis on serving the master and more on behaving toward him "honestly and obediently in all things . . . and honestly and orderly toward the rest of the family . . . ."[113]

Once the poor law plan assumed the obligation to care for poor children, characteristic tendencies implicit in that assumption manifested themselves. The state found ways to minimize the cost. Apprenticing is one such grand device; the full exploitation of private resources another.

Strangely, while the famous list of charitable uses in 43 Elizabeth, chapter 4, includes "Educacõn and prefermente of Orphans . . . Marriage or Poore Maides . . . Supportacõn, Ayde and Helpe of younge Tradesmen," apprenticing of poor children was conspicuously absent. The deficiency was corrected in 1609 by a statute[114] comprehensively regulating the handling of private charitable funds given for the placement of children and apprentices and integrating administration of the funds in the poor law system. The preamble states that great sums of money had already been and would in the future be freely given to cities, boroughs, towns, parishes, and individuals "to be contynually imployed in bynding out of Apprentizes of a great Number of the poorest sorts of Children unto needefull Trades and Occupacions . . . ." Nomination and placing of apprentices and employment of the funds were entrusted to the parson or vicar, together with the constable, collector, churchwardens, and overseers of the poor. The funds were to be used within three months of their receipt[115] and to remain in continual use. If there was more money than was required in the parish, "then such of the poorest Children of any of the Parishes

113. 4 Barry, *op. cit. supra* note 80, at 369.
114. 7 Jac. 1, c. 3, § I (1609–1610).
115. 7 Jac. 1, c. 3, § III (1609–1610).

next adjoyning shalbe bound Apprentices" therewith.[116] First choice was to be given "to the poorest sorte of Children [not over fifteen years of age] whose Parents are least able to releive them."[117] Masters and mistresses receiving an amount along with an apprentice were to be bonded in double the sum "upon condicion to repay" it at the end of the seven years or within three months thereafter or within one year after their deaths should that occur during the term, "soe as the said Moneys may be againe ymployed for placing such Apprentice [with] some other person of the same Trade . . . ."[118] At the behest of private complainants, the Chancellor was to enforce the trust of these privately given funds by appointing commissions of investigation empowered to recover misapplied funds from those who misapplied them or from "the able Inhabitants . . . as in the discrecion of the said Comissioners . . . shalbe thought fittest." Appeal could be taken from the commissioners to the Chancellor, who was authorized to issue any decree.[119]

To those who are unable to work the arguments of the controlled economy cannot apply. They have no role in the economic system, and that system does not call for their support and cannot justify it. This is especially true if one disregards rehabilitation, not a prevalent idea for the impotent in the time of the Tudors, and if one supposes that the unemployables are a fixed group of persons with absolute characteristics rather than a group the size and membership of which are fluid, marginal, and relative to economic conditions. The cost to the public of supporting this group could not be reduced through their earnings derived from labor. However, a device was hit upon which ever since has been used for that purpose—the legal liability of financially able relatives. This device was first legislatively enunciated in 1597[120] and then found a permanent place in the poor law in 43 Elizabeth.[121]

> [The parents, grandparents, and the children of] everie poore olde blind lame and impotente person, or other poore person not able to worke, beinge of a sufficient abilitie, shall at their owne Chardges releive and maintain everie suche poore person, in that manner and accordinge to that rate, as by the Justices of the Peace of that Countie where suche sufficient persons dwell, or the greater number of them, at their generall

---

116. *Ibid.*
117. 7 Jac. 1, c. 3, § IV (1609–1610).
118. 7 Jac. 1, c. 3, § II (1609–1610).
119. 7 Jac. 1, c. 3, § VI (1609–1610).
120. 39 Eliz. 1, c. 3, § VII (1597).
121. 43 Eliz. 1, c. 2, § VI (1601).

Quarter-Sessions shalbe assessed; upon paine that everie one of them shall forfeite twenty shillings for everie monthe which they shall faile therein.[122]

Not only were the relatives made legally liable specified, but the amount of their liability and the manner in which they relieved their poor kinsmen were committed to the discretion of the justices of the peace, and the penalty for failure to comply was set by the law at twenty shillings for each month of nonsupport.

In view of later pronouncements on the nature and source of relatives' support obligation, particularly that of the parents for the child, it is important to emphasize, not only that this principle was introduced into the law by the poor relief statutes, but also that in that context the parent's support obligation was not linked to property rights in the child, did not stand in any reciprocal relationship to the parent's right to the services and earnings of the child, and was in no way connected with rights to custody. Quite the contrary, legal liability of relatives was designed to indemnify the public and to minimize its costs in relieving the poor. Some rational basis had to be found for selecting the relatives to be held liable and, in view of the purpose of the provision, the circle of liable relatives had to be made as wide as possible. Natural duty, moral responsibility, and voluntary assumption of liability by the act of begetting point at least to the parent, and some of these are obviously inapplicable to other relatives. "It is a principle of law," said Blackstone, referring not to law in general but only to the poor law, "that there is an obligation on every man to provide for those descended from his loins."[123] Under the poor law the obligation ascended as well as descended in a direct line; not only the parents and the grandparents but the children were made liable. Direct consanguinity was the test.

Lightening the public burden for support of the poor equally motivated the creation of both parents' legal liability for their illegitimate children. Indeed, much of the improvement in the legal status of the bastard child and of its mother in the long course of Anglo-American legal history derived from this source. An Elizabethan statute of 1575, which survived for centuries and was widely adopted in America, spelled out the reasoning in excruciating detail.

---

122. 43 Eliz. 1, c. 2, § VI (1601).
123. 1 BLACKSTONE, *op. cit. supra* note 82, at 447–49, 454.

Concerning Bastards begotton and borne out of lawful Matrimonye (an Offence againste God's Lawe and Man's Lawe,) the said Bastards being now lefte to bee kepte at the Chardges of the Parishe where they bee borne, to the greate Burden of the same Parishe and in defrauding of the Reliefe of the impotente and aged true Poore of the same Parishe, and to the evell Example and Encouragement of lewde Lyfe: It ys ordeyned and enacted by the Aucthorytye aforesaid, That two Justices of the Peace, . . . [within which] Parishe suche Bastarde shalbee borne, (upon Examinacion of the Cause and Circomstance,) shall and maye by their Discretion take Order as well for the Punishement of the Mother and reputed Father of suche Bastarde Childe, as also for the better Releefe of everye suche Parishe in part or in all; and shall and maye lykewyse by lyke discretion, take order for the keepynge of everye such Bastarde Childe, by chardging [the] Mother or reputed Father with the Paymente of Monie Weekely or other Sustentacion for the Releefe of suche Childe, in suchewise as they shall thincke meete and convenient: And yf after the same Order . . . [the] Mother or reputed Father . . . shall not for their parte observe and perfourme the said Order . . . then everye suche partye so making Defaulte in not perfourminge of the said Order, to bee committed . . . to the Common Gayle . . . ."[124]

By a statute of 1609–1610,[125] justices of the peace were to commit lewd women with bastard children to the parish houses of correction for one year. Offending again, they were to be committed until they could provide "good suerties for . . . good behaviour . . . ."[126] Lewd women with bastard children not chargeable to the parish were not subject to the provisions of the act, again emphasizing the consequences of the public assumption of responsibility for the support of the poor.

To the general system imposing liability on financially able relatives and the special system dealing with the parents of illegitimate children was added a third provision[127] applicable to fathers and mothers with legitimate families. It was designed to reach with penal sanction those who had no financial ability but their capacity to labor. "Many wilfull people, fynding that they having Children, have some hope to have Reliefe from the Parish wherein they dwell, and being able to Labor, and therebie to releive themselves and their Familyes, doe neverthelesse rune awaie out of their Parishes and leave their Famylyes upon the Parish."[128] Such persons were to "endure the Paines" meted out to incorrigible rogues.

124. 18 Eliz. 1, c. 3, § I (1575–1576).
125. 7 Jac. 1, c. 4, § VII (1609–1610).
126. *Ibid.*
127. 7 Jac. 1, c. 4, § VIII (1609–1610).
128. *Ibid.*

In addition, a mother or father threatening to run away was to be sent to the house of correction unless he or she could provide sufficient surety for the discharge of the parish. In this manner were first legislatively censured the irresponsible parent seeking to escape family burdens by flight and also that most pathetic figure of the relief system, the parent who found that his children would be better cared for if he left them.

Thus the steps taken in sixteenth-century England, culminating in the statute of 43 Elizabeth by which the public undertook responsibility for the support of the poor, had as one of their consequences the establishment of the legal liability of various relatives for the support of their poor kinsmen. In the special case of bastard children, the liability extended only to the mother and putative father. In the case of other poor who were unable to maintain themselves by labor, the liability extended to other relatives—to grandparents and children—and did so regardless of the minority or majority of the poor persons. Legal sanctions were provided; at first the common gaol and later the house of correction for parents of illegitimate children; the house of correction for deserting parents of legitimate children; a fixed sum of money for other liable relatives. The sums to be contributed and the manner of maintenance by a relative were to depend on the relative's ability and were to be fixed by the justices of the peace.

The main thesis developed in these pages may be recapitulated somewhat as follows: The Elizabethan poor law system proved an historical repository and a fertile source of special legal provisions about the poor. These governed their subjection to public control, their condition of idleness or labor, their freedom of choice of living arrangements, their right to travel and settle where they pleased, their personal and civil rights, and their family relationships. Regulation of those family relationships included the denial or subordination of parental rights to custody, control, and determination of training or education, the imposition of a support obligation upon relatives, descending and ascending in a direct line and eventually laterally as well, implementation of public concern about the paternity of bastards and the liability of both parents for their support, and the establishment of the criminality of parental desertion.

The poor law was thus not only a law *about* the poor but a law *of* the poor. It dealt with a condition, and it governed a class. The special legal provisions were designed not to solve the causes and problems of destitution but to minimize the cost to the public of maintaining the destitute. They were accordingly concomitants of the central concept and the great achievement of the poor law— the assumption of public responsibility for the support of the poor —and of the necessity it entailed of keeping public expenditures down. Once the public agreed to pay the bill, it acquired a pressing concern about the size of the bill and an active interest in finding methods for reducing it. The impulse to invent and apply devices which did so was implicit in the poor law principle itself, and the devices invented and adapted for this purpose, originally and from time to time thereafter, were as characteristic of the poor law as the public acceptance of the basic responsibility. Other motivations sometimes contributed to the same ends—for example, economic concepts about the relationship of public support of the poor to the availability and standards of labor, ethical concepts about the need for the individual to work, and criminological concepts about the social results of idleness and vagrancy—but these forces were only contributory and in any event applied principally to the able-bodied or employable. The seminal source of the law of the poor, pervasive and enduring, adaptive of features drawn from other practices and institutions and inventive of new ones, applicable to the destitute of all conditions—the unemployable as well as the merely unemployed—was the need to curtail public expenditures and to conserve public funds once the public undertook the burden at all. As will be shown, its creative and adaptive force is still felt today.

The course of the common law was quite different both in the path it followed and in the substantive rules of family relationship it produced. Those rules were primarily the work of the courts. Missing are the legislative and public character of the concern. In the absence of the prod of the public financial interest, the doctrine of relatives' liability for support of the poor did not appeal to the judges. In feudal law the property relationship prevailed over the personal relationship or natural family ties.[129] Indeed, Radin and Plucknett agree that English family life was profoundly and

---

129. See generally PLUCKNETT, A CONCISE HISTORY OF THE COMMON LAW 545 (5th ed. 1956); POLLOCK & MAITLAND, HISTORY OF ENGLISH LAW BEFORE THE TIME OF EDWARD I, ch. 7 (1895); RADIN, ANGLO-AMERICAN LEGAL HISTORY, ch. 35 (1936).

adversely affected by such feudal rules as primogeniture, exclusion of the half-blood, and the disabilities of coverture.[130] Feudal law did not recognize the family as such or assign rights and duties to its members by virtue of membership. Property rights were the only privileges which the king's courts would enforce between father and son and between husband and wife.

Between father and son, the most important rules related to wardship of heirs. The feudal law singled out the heir for special treatment among all the children. The heir was the natural heir— that is, the child or kinsman—but he received his inheritance by virtue of feudal rules which the ancestor could not alter by his will.[131] Wardship, as a feudal incident, was the right to be a guardian of a minor heir or heiress. The father was entitled to that right; on his death it passed not to the mother but to the lord of the infant's land, leading Plucknett to say that "the orphaned infant was treated as an adjunct to his lands."[132] The same was true of the infant heir who was not orphaned; the guardian had custody of the estate and probably of the person of the ward. The guardian was obligated to provide for the maintenance and education of the ward out of the revenues of the estate. Beyond that, he was legally free to dispose of the revenues in his own interest.[133] Many great medieval statutes and other documents, including Magna Charta itself, sought to curtail the abuse so flourishingly potential under this system which treated guardianship and paternal power as merely profitable rights.

Since property is the key to the feudal relationship of guardian and ward, father and heir, the source of rules governing the parent-child relationship when the child is not an heir, when he is a younger brother or sister of the heir or any of the children of the propertyless classes, must be found elsewhere. Plucknett states that parental rights over these children "seem to be based on the singular fiction that they are 'servants' within the scope of the old labor

---

130. PLUCKNETT, *op. cit. supra* note 129, at 544–45; RADIN, *op. cit. supra* note 129, at 524.

131. As late as 1557 a statute against abducting children from their parents applied only to heiresses. 4 & 5 Phil. & M., c. 8 (1557–1558).

132. PLUCKNETT, *op. cit. supra* note 129, at 545.

133. 1 POLLOCK & MAITLAND, *op. cit. supra* note 129, at 303. Pollock and Maitland summarize the relevant law as follows: "The guardian's rights in the person, in the marriage, in the lands of the heir are regarded as property; they are saleable, assignable rights; large sums are paid for the wardships and marriages of wealthy heirs; indeed, so thoroughly proprietary and pecuniary are these rights that they can be disposed of by will; they pass like chattels to the guardian's executors."

law."[134] Radin, too, emphasizes that to some extent the status of the minor child is assimilated to that of the servant.[135] This is not to say that all of the rights between master and servant applied to the relationship between parent and child. The servant had rights in the relationship which could not be claimed by the child—rights to its continuance during the contracted term, to the payment of wages, and to maintenance during sickness and disability. Between father and child, there were no legally enforceable rights; the child was not entitled to the father's care, protection, or support. He remained in his father's household at the complete sufferance of the father, who could turn him out any moment without regard to the child's need or the father's ability.[136] For physical mistreatment the child had no right of action against his father, though here the criminal law might assist him.

On the other hand, while no legally enforceable rights existed between parent and child, the father had some right as against third parties and at this point it was the master-servant analogue that was relied upon. As in the case of master and servant, the father and child might maintain each other's lawsuits and might justify the defense of each other's persons.[137] The parent was liable for the torts of the child only if the child was acting as the father's servant in the discharge of some employment.[138] Action by a parent against a third person for abducting, enticing away, or harboring his child might be either in assumpsit or in tort. In assumpsit the theory was that the defendant had impliedly undertaken to pay for the services of the child; the action in tort was trespass on the case for the wrong and consequent loss of the child's services.[139] The father had a right of action against a wrongdoer who injured his child *per quod servitium amisit*, the same ground upon which the master had a right of action against the tort-feasor of his servant. The seduction of a daughter fell into this class; the daughter herself had no right of action, but the father could sue alleging loss of the

---

134. PLUCKNETT, *op. cit. supra* note 129, at 545.
135. RADIN, *op. cit. supra* note 129, at 503.
136. HALE, HISTORY OF THE COMMON LAW OF ENGLAND 32 (6th ed. 1820); PLUCK-NETT, *op. cit. supra* note 129, at 544; POLLOCK & MAITLAND, *op. cit. supra* note 129, at ch. 7, § 3; RADIN, *op. cit. supra* note 129, at ch. 35.
137. 1 BLACKSTONE, COMMENTARIES ON THE LAWS OF ENGLAND 450 (Cooley ed. 1899); 2 COKE, INSTITUTES OF THE LAW OF ENGLAND 564 (1642); 1 HAWKINS, PLEAS OF THE CROWN 458, 459 (Curwood ed. 1824). See generally HALE, *op. cit. supra* note 136, at Analysis p. 32.
138. See MADDEN, PERSONS AND DOMESTIC RELATIONS 399 (1931).
139. *Id*. at 437; *cf*. Evans v. Walton, L.R. 2 C.P. 615 (1867).

daughter's services. A century after feudal tenures were formally abolished and after general guardianship and chancery protection of children had been firmly established, the assimilation of the status of the minor child to that of the servant still shaped the course of the law. This is reflected in Blackstone's remark that the father "may indeed have the benefit of his children's labor while they live with him and are maintained by him; but this is no more than he is entitled to from his apprentices or servants."[140]

Blackstone, reviewing the law governing the relationship of parent and child in the last half of the eighteenth century, found little to report. His chapter on this topic is therefore devoted to general discussion, mostly of civil-law principles, and reference to moral obligations. The discussion in itself, however, is interesting because it, too, gives little solace to later opinions which emphasize parental rights to custody and to the child as property and assert that these are founded on the common law. His analysis of parental rights and duties has almost nothing to do with property rights and hardly mentions custody. Parental duties are three: Protection, maintenance, and education.[141] The first two are natural duties; the third derives from them. The duty of protection is so strongly enforced by nature that it required "rather a check than a spur" in the municipal laws.[142] The duty of maintenance is "an obligation . . . laid on them [the parents] not only by nature herself, but by their own proper act, in bringing them into the world . . . ."[143] "By begetting them, therefore, they have entered into a voluntary obligation to endeavor, as far as in them lies, that the life which they have bestowed shall be supported and preserved."[144] Blackstone credits Montesquieu with

> a .very just observation upon this head: that the establishment of a marriage in all civilized states is built on this natural obligation of the father to provide for his children; for that ascertains and makes known the person who is bound to fulfil this obligation; whereas, in the promis-

---

140. 1 BLACKSTONE, *op. cit. supra* note 137, at 453.

141. As regards education, the parent has conferred little benefit upon his child "by bringing him into the world . . . if he afterwards neglects his culture and education," letting him grow up like "a mere beast, to lead a life useless to others and shameful to himself." Blackstone acknowledges English laws were defective in enforcing the duty of education except in one particular: "The poor and labourious part of the community, when past the age of nurture, are taken out of the hands of their parents, by the statutes for apprenticing poor children; and are placed out by the public in such manner, as may render their abilities, in their several stations, of the greatest advantage to the commonwealth." 1 BLACKSTONE, *op. cit. supra* note 137, at 451.

142. *Id.* at 450.

143. *Id.* at 447.

144. *Ibid.*

cuous and illicit conjunctions, the father is unknown; the mother finds a thousand obstacles in her way, shame, remorse, the constraint of her sex, and the rigour of laws, that stifle her inclinations to perform this duty; and besides, she generally wants ability.[145]

Providence has seen to the fulfillment of the duty of support "more effectually than any laws, by implanting in the breast of every parent that . . . insuperable degree of affection which not even the deformity of person or mind, not even the wickedness, ingratitude, and rebellion of children, can totally suppress or extinguish."[146] Some help to Providence, however, has not been amiss in all "well regulated states." In England that help was supplied only by the Elizabethan Poor Law.

In England the common law did not seek to augment the poor law. Neither by judicial decision nor indeed by statute was any general liability created in parents to support their minor children, let alone their adult children or other relatives. The courts continued to find that parents were under a natural duty and a moral responsibility but not a legal obligation. The Elizabethan poor laws stood alone as the only legal provisions upon the topic. This was still true at the time of the establishment of state government in California and the beginning of Field's work on his Draft Codes in New York. In 1840, in a suit against the father for care and medical attendance supplied his minor son, the English judges held that "in point of law, a father who gives no authority, and enters into no contract, is no more liable for goods supplied to his son, than a brother, or an uncle, or a mere stranger would be."[147] If the son is left to starve, the exclusive remedy of the law is to apply to the parish poor law authorities who will "compel the father, if of ability, to pay for his son's support."[148]

---

145. *Ibid.*
146. *Ibid.*
147. Mortimore v. Wright, 6 M. & W. 482, 486, 151 Eng. Rep. 502, 504 (Ex. 1840).
148. Shelton v. Springett, 11 C.B. 452, 456, 138 Eng. Rep. 549, 550 (1851).

# 3

# The Poor Law,
# the Common Law, and the Field
# Draft Codes of New York

The English poor law system reached its full development by 1601, six years before the English settlement in Jamestown, nineteen years before the landing at Plymouth Rock, and sixty-three years before the English conquest of New York. Professor Riesenfeld has shown how step by step, settlement by settlement, and colony by colony it became deeply embedded in community life and legal order.[149] With variations in time and degree and by a more flexible pattern, the common law of England followed a roughly similar course. Since New York proved a principal channel by which family law ideas eventually were transmitted to the legal system of California, it is necessary to trace the poor-law and common-law reception in that state.

## The Poor Law

The reception of the Elizabethan poor laws in New York followed the usual pattern with some early variation resulting from settlement by the Dutch who "treated the care of the poor as a matter of charity and a function of the church."[150] In 1661 a rudimentary poor law system, similar to early Tudor legislation, was begun. The Director General and Council of New Netherland ordered that weekly collections be made for the poor in all villages and settlements, that the "lazy and vagabond . . . as much as possible be rebuked," and that the deacons of New Amsterdam give

---

149. See Riesenfeld, *The Formative Era of American Public Assistance Law*, 43 CALIF. L. REV. 175 (1955). See also Riesenfeld, *Law-Making and Legislative Precedent in American Legal History*, 33 MINN. L. REV. 103 (1949).

150. Riesenfeld, *The Formative Era of American Public Assistance Law*, 43 CALIF. L. REV. 175, 219 (1955). See generally BRANSCOMBE, THE COURTS AND THE POOR LAWS IN NEW YORK STATE 1784–1929 (U. CHI. SOC. SERV. MON. 1943), SCHNEIDER, THE HISTORY OF PUBLIC WELFARE IN NEW YORK STATE 1609–1866 (U. CHI. SOC. SERV. MON. 1938); SCHNEIDER & DEUTSCH, HISTORY OF PUBLIC WELFARE IN NEW YORK STATE 1867–1940 (U. CHI. SOC. SERV. MON. 1941).

aid to persons residing in the outlying villages only if they brought with them certificates "of their character and poverty."[151] By the Duke of York's Laws of 1665, compiled from the laws of the other colonies, levies and assessments were to be made in the parishes for the support of the poor.[152] In 1683 the system was expanded;[153] the duty of support was laid on every "Citty Towne and County."[154] Steps were taken to prevent and discourage vagabonds and other idle persons "to come into this province." Before being admitted as inhabitants, persons without a visible estate or a manual craft or occupation were required to give security against becoming paupers. Masters of vessels were to report a list of passengers "with their Qualityes & Condiçons" and to retransport undesirables out of the province.[155] Extensive settlement and removal provisions were enacted in 1721[156] and remained in effect until 1773 when they gave way to even more extensive provisions based on the English statute of 1662.[157] The statute of 1773 also contained responsible-relatives and absconding-parents provisions. A bastard law modeled on 18 Elizabeth, chapter 3, was enacted in 1774.[158] In 1784[159] and 1788 while adapting its laws to the new state government, New York repealed all of its colonial statutes dealing with the poor and reorganized, collated, amended, and reenacted them in a series of separate statutes dealing with bastards,[160] apprenticeship,[161] disorderly persons,[162] and "the better settlement and relief of the poor."[163] The general pattern was that of Elizabeth with a number

151. Laws & Ordinances of New Netherland 1638–1674, at 411 (O'Callaghan 1868).
152. See Colonial Laws of N.Y. 1665, at 24 (Duke's Laws).
153. See Colonial Laws of N.Y. 1683, ch. 9, at 131.
154. *Ibid.* That this provision did effect a secularization see Colonial Laws of N.Y. 1721, ch. 410, at 56.
155. For the machinery of the tax later provided for this law see Colonial Laws of N.Y. 1691, ch. 6, as amended, ch. 96 (1701), as amended, ch. 133 (1703). For the establishment of the system in New York City see *id.* 1695, ch. 47. For a special tax for New York City following "a calamitous distemper" see *id.* 1702, ch. 115.
156. Colonial Laws of N.Y. 1721, ch. 410, at 56.
157. Colonial Laws of N.Y. 1773, ch. 1600, at 513. *Compare ibid. with* 13 & 14 Car. 2, c. 12 (1662).
158. Colonial Laws of N.Y. 1774, ch. 1679, at 689. *Compare ibid. with* 18 Eliz. 1, c. 3 (1575–1576).
159. N.Y. Sess. Laws 1784, ch. 35.
160. N.Y. Sess. Laws 1788, ch. 14.
161. N.Y. Sess. Laws 1788, ch. 15.
162. N.Y. Sess. Laws 1788, ch. 31.
163. N.Y. Sess. Laws 1788, ch. 62. The New York Laws of 1788 also dealt with the relationship between freed Negroes and the town obligation to support paupers. Masters freeing slaves by manumission or by will were required, if the slaves were over fifty years of age or had not sufficient ability to provide for themselves, to enter into a bond in a sum not less than £200 to keep the freedmen from being town charges. Such slaves freed without this security remained free, but the master or his heirs, executors, and administrators were liable for their support. If the slave was under fifty or had ability to maintain himself, no security was required. But the master had first to procure a certificate from the overseers

of adaptations due to different economic and geographical circumstances.

Every city and town was required to maintain its own poor. Individuals and families then county responsibilities were to be continued as such.[164] Administration was entrusted to overseers of the poor and justices of the peace, in whose complete discretion rested the determination of the amount of and eligibility for aid. The amount of the poor relief budget was to be fixed by the freeholders and inhabitants of the town assembled at their annual meeting, and that sum was to be raised in the town by the county supervisors. The overseers were to keep a register of the poor on relief, showing the amount and period of the grant and the cause of the necessity. Poorhouses were to be established as "convenient dwelling" places for the "lodging and accommodation of the poor," where they were to be kept, maintained, and employed on assigned work, the income to be used for their support. Those refusing to go to the poorhouse when assigned were to be removed from the register and denied all relief.

Elaborate and rigorous provisions on settlement and removal were instituted: every effort was made to limit acquisition of legal settlement to persons likely to be self-supporting, to exclude those likely to be dependent, and to impose the burden of relief on the townsmen who aided the stranger in coming or remaining.[165] Those likely to become public charges were to be removed to the place of their legal settlement within the state or into the state from which they came. Settlement provisions for immigrants were far more liberal than those for wandering natives. Mariners who were without settlement either in New York or in any other of the United States and other able-bodied persons from foreign countries were allowed to gain settlement in the city or town where they first resided for one year.[166] Shipmasters were required to report on all of their passengers, to return those who became public charges, and to enter a heavy bond "conditioned that the person so imported shall not become a charge to . . . any . . . city or town in this state."[167] The 1824 form of this provision was held consti-

of the poor and two justices of the peace as to the Negro's age and ability. See N.Y. Sess. Laws 1788, ch. 40, Warren v. Brooks, 7 Cow. 218 (N.Y. 1827). See the exception in N.Y. Sess. Laws 1816, ch. 45.

164. In 1809 counties were made responsible for the support of paupers without settlement. N.Y. Sess. Laws 1809, ch. XC.

165. N.Y. Sess. Laws 1788, ch. 62.

166. *Ibid*.

167. *Ibid*.

tutional by the United States Supreme Court on the ground that paupers carried a moral pestilence akin to physical pestilence against which a state might erect a quarantine barrier.[168] An effort was made to employ the poor by freeing them from the immobility imposed by local relief and settlement provisions. Even though they could not give the requisite security against becoming paupers, poor persons were allowed "to abide . . . and follow any honest employment" in any town where they could find work if they presented a certificate from the overseers of the poor of their place of legal settlement acknowledging responsibility for them.[169]

The American counterpart of the English vagabondage statutes appeared in the New York compilation of 1788 under the title of "An act for apprehending and punishing disorderly persons."[170] The classes of disorderly persons comprehensively included those unlawfully returning to the city or town from which they had been removed, those who "not having wherewith to maintain themselves live idle without employment," idle persons not having visible means of livelihood, those who beg publicly in the town where they dwell or who wander abroad and beg, and jugglers, fortune-tellers, others in a "like crafty science," and common prostitutes. The disorderly were to be committed to the bridewell or house of correction until they could provide for themselves or until the justices of the peace could "place them out in some lawful calling as servants, apprentices, mariners or otherwise."[171]

Relatives' responsibility provisions of 43 Elizabeth, chapter 2, were adopted by New York with little change. To the parents, grandparents, and children, New York added the grandchildren. The twenty-shilling penalty for each monthly refusal to pay the amount fixed by the justices of the peace was made ten shillings per week to be sued for by the overseers of the poor. The relatives were to provide relief in the manner approved by the overseers and ordered by the court of general sessions.[172] The statute provided that the liability of relatives arose when a poor person was unable to maintain himself and had become chargeable to any city or town.

---

168. Mayor of New York v. Miln, 12 U.S. (11 Pet.) 357 (1837) (construing N.Y. Sess. Laws 1824, ch. XXXVII).

169. N.Y. Sess. Laws 1788, ch. 62.

170. N.Y. Sess. Laws 1788, ch. 31.

171. This provision was continued, distributed, and augmented in 1 N.Y. Rev. Stats. 802, § 1 & 819, § 1 (3d ed. 1846).

172. N.Y. Sess. Laws 1788, ch. 62. Procedures were later detailed and modified in 1 N.Y. Rev. Stats., ch. XX, tit. 1, at 621–40 (2d ed. 1835).

The property of an absconding husband or parent might be taken for the support of the abandoned wife or children.[173] As in 7 James I, chapter 4, a separate statute dealing with disorderly persons provided punishment in the house of correction for parents or husbands abandoning or threatening to abandon their wives and children to public support.[174] As originally prescribed by 18 Elizabeth I, both parents of an illegitimate child were made responsible for its support in the manner determined by the justices of the peace. The reputed father was liable to arrest and imprisonment until he gave security to indemnify the town should the bastard become its charge. If the "lewd mother" or "putative father" deserted, real or personal property left behind could be sequestered for the child's maintenance.[175]

The statute of apprentices[176] was not, as in the case of 5 Elizabeth, chapter 4, part of an overall system of labor control and apportionment, though methods of enforcing the terms of the indenture were carefully provided. The rights of the parties were specified in greater detail, and clauses were included for protection of the welfare and provision of the general education of the apprentices. The importance of the apprenticeship device in "the emigration of poor persons from Europe [which] hath conduced greatly to the settlement of this state" was recognized in a series of exemptions. Overseers of the poor with the consent of justices of the peace were authorized to bind out as apprentices or servants "according to their degree and ability" children who became chargeable to the public, whose parents became chargeable to the city or town, or who begged for alms. Included was the phrase in 43 Elizabeth, chapter 2, "where they shall see convenient," which had been interpreted to empower overseers and justices to assign children to unwilling masters. Refusal to be apprenticed was punishable in the house of correction or in the common jail.[177] Overseers of the poor were made guardians of pauper children bound out by them; it was their

---

173. N.Y. Sess. Laws 1788, ch. 62. For cases illustrating abuses by local officials without adequate proof of departure or likelihood that wife and children would become chargeable see People *ex rel.* Read v. Overseers, 23 Barb. 236 (N.Y. Sup. Ct. 1856); Downing v. Rugar, 21 Wend. 178 (N.Y. Sup. Ct. 1839); Bowman v. Russ, 6 Cow. 234 (N.Y. Sup. Ct. 1826); BRANSCOMBE, THE COURTS AND THE POOR LAWS IN NEW YORK STATE 1784–1929, at 77–79 (U. CHI. SOC. SERV. MON. 1943).

174. N.Y. Sess. Laws 1788, ch. 31.

175. N.Y. Sess. Laws 1788, ch. 14.

176. N.Y. Sess. Laws 1788, chs. 15, 62.

177. N.Y. Sess. Laws 1788, ch. 15.

duty generally to supervise the execution of the indenture's terms and to see that the child was not mistreated.[178]

The principal features of the Elizabethan poor law system, thus adopted by New York at the beginning of its statehood with modifications adapting them to local conditions, remained intact until and after their incorporation in the Field Draft Codes of the 1850's and the 1860's. While the state legislature tinkered continuously with the poor law, especially with its settlement and removal provisions, the legislative changes were generally minor. In the 1820's changes of somewhat greater importance were instituted. Removal of paupers to other counties was forbidden.[179] Grandparents and grandchildren were eliminated from the list of relatives legally liable for support.[180] The state began to assume responsibility, financial and otherwise, for the creation of institutions for particular groups thought to need special care.[181] In 1824 after a public uproar and an official investigation, the state initiated a system of county poorhouses,[182] and within a decade fifty counties had erected such institutions.[183] Outdoor relief was virtually abolished; all poor were to be sent to the poorhouse "unless the sickness of the pauper prevent." All vagrants if "proper object[s] for such relief" were to be sent there unless "notorious offender[s]." At the discretion of the justice of the peace with the concurrence of the superintendent, disorderly persons might also be sent there instead of to jail. The justice's warrant need only state "generally, that such person has been duly convicted of being a disorderly person without more particular specification of the offense." Children under fifteen found begging were also to be sent to the poorhouse until able to support themselves. Vagrants and disorderly persons were to be kept at hard labor, and all other inmates were to labor to the extent of their ability. The superintendents of the poorhouses, with

---

178. N.Y. Sess. Laws 1788, ch. 62. This provision was continued, substantially the same, in 2 N.Y. Rev. Stats., pt. II, ch. 8, tit. IV, art. 3, §§ 26–43, at 90–92 (2d ed. 1835).

179. See N.Y. Sess. Laws 1824, ch. CCCXXXI, § 8.

180. See N.Y. Sess. Laws 1821, ch. CXVII, § 4, as amended by N.Y. Rev. Stats., ch. XX, § 1, at 62 (2d ed. 1835).

181. For the insane see N.Y. Sess. Laws 1827, ch. CCXCIV; for destitute and delinquent children see N.Y. Sess. Laws 1825, ch. CVII; N.Y. Sess. Laws 1824, ch. CXXVI; for the deaf and dumb see N.Y. Sess. Laws 1832, ch. CCXXIII; N.Y. Sess. Laws 1822, ch. CCXXXIV; for the blind see N.Y. Sess. Laws 1831, ch. CCXIV.

182. See N.Y. Sess. Laws 1824, ch. CCCXXXI. The statute was mandatory in sixteen counties, permissive in the other thirty-eight.

183. See BRANSCOMBE, THE COURTS AND THE POOR LAWS IN NEW YORK STATE 1784–1929, at 30–31, 35 (1943). In 1849 the county supervisors were authorized, at their discretion, to reinstate the town administration of aid. N.Y. Sess. Laws 1849, ch. 194, § 4.10; BRANSCOMBE, *op. cit. supra* at 40.

the consent of a majority of the judges of the county court, were empowered to establish "such prudential rules . . . for the well ordering of the same, and the employment, relief, management and government of the persons therein placed . . . and the correction of the refractory, disobedient and disorderly, by solitary confinement therein, and feeding them on bread and water only, as they shall deem expedient."[184]

Charles Warren described the period from 1830 to 1860 as one of "legal development in State and Federal law greater than any . . . in the legal history of the country." He depicts the transformation of this era as characterized by an increasing recognition and protection of individual rights under the law: the emancipation of married women; the safeguarding of infants, the insane, and criminals; prison reforms; and the establishment of milder forms of criminal punishment.[185] The history of the poor law is one of stark contrast; it underwent no such transformation and hardly felt the impact of progressive forces and surrounding developments. From 1820 to 1840 the gradual abolition of property qualifications for voting and for holding office, given by Warren as one principal reason for the radical changes, signified no meaningful change in the status of the poor. Indeed, at the very threshold of this period the state of New York, in common with most of the rest of the country, drastically expanded and made largely mandatory its poorhouse system and invested the system's governors with a fresh supply of custodial, coercive, and punitive powers.

The Elizabethan poor law system, emerging from its historical context of a controlled economy, a subjugated laboring class, and a paternalistic, autocratic monarchy into the context of a free economy, a labor force with growing legally recognized rights, and a democratic system of government, continued to embody the law of the poor as the law of a distinct and subordinate class. In a land

---

184. N.Y. Sess. Laws 1849, ch. 194, § 5. For power to punish paupers and vagrants in the almshouse of New York City see N.Y. Sess. Laws 1822, ch. XIII.

185. WARREN, A HISTORY OF THE AMERICAN BAR 446 (1911). In his list of subjects in course of transformation, Warren included the emancipation of the wife and the greater protection of infants and insane. He particularly referred to the breakdown of the common-law legal identity of husband and wife through giving married women unrestricted authority to hold property, to contract, to convey, and otherwise to act as a *feme sole*. In the case of the insane, he spoke of the development of the rule that insanity is a defense to a charge of murder as laid down in M'Naghten's Case, 10 Cl. & Fin. 200, 8 Eng. Rep. 718 (H.L. 1843), in England; in Commonwealth v. Rogers, 48 Mass. (7 Met.) 500 (1844), in Massachusetts; and in Freeman v. People, 4 Denio 2 (N.Y. Sup. Ct. 1847), in New York. WARREN, A HISTORY OF THE AMERICAN BAR 471–72 (1911). With regard to the protection of infants, Warren does not support his assertion.

where free movement and the open frontier were determinative forces in shaping the nation, the poor were still bound to the places of their misfortune, held immobile by rigid rules of settlement and removal, and locked in poorhouses attempted escape from which resulted in solitary confinement and bread and water. Denominated paupers and vagabonds, they were at one with fugitives from justice in the Articles of Confederation.[186] Judicially stigmatized by the highest court in the land as carriers of a moral pestilence, they were subject to the social opprobrium and personal restrictions applicable to those with physical pestilence. All the relevant world was transforming or transformed. The poor law system continued its steady course—except where it retrogressed.

### *The Common Law in New York*

Just as New York's reception of the poor law followed a common pattern, so did its reception of the common law.[187] The first state constitution continued as the law of the state "such parts of the common law of England, and of the statute law of England and Great Britain, and of the acts of the legislature of the colony of New York, as together did form the law of the said colony on the 19th of April, . . . [1775]."[188] The legislature was given full power to revise and alter any of these. The parts of the common law and colonial legislation in effect on April 19, 1775, and not subsequently altered and other legislation in force in 1821 and 1846 were perpetuated by the constitutions of those years unless repugnant to the constitutions themselves.[189] Again legislative alteration was authorized. In connection with this provision in the 1846 constitution the legislature was directed at its first session to appoint a three-man code commission which became largely dominated by David Dudley Field and a substantial part of the product of which was adopted by the California Legislature in 1851 and 1872.

In New York, as in other states, the common law of England did not remain a static body of rules and procedures, even when

---

186. Articles of Confederation art. 4.
187. For a recent summary see Hall, *The Common Law: An Account of Its Reception in the United States,* 4 Vand. L. Rev. 791 (1951). See generally 1 Crosskey, Politics and the Constitution in the History of the United States 578–609 (1953); 1 Powell, Real Property § 59 (1949, Supp. 1963).
188. N.Y. Const. § 35 (1777).
189. N.Y. Const. art. I, § 17 (1846); N.Y. Const. art. VII, § 13 (1821). *But see* the Statutory Construction Law 1892–1896, 1 N.Y. Rev. Stats. § 30, at 117, which provided: "A statute of England or Great Britain shall not be deemed to have had any force or effect in this state since May 1, 1788. Acts of the legislature of the colony of New York shall not be deemed to have had any force or effect in this state since December 29, 1828."

not changed by the legislature. Although the courts were not mentioned by the constitution as possessing amendatory power, regarding themselves as charged with the special function of interpreting and developing the common law they continued the process of creative application which historically had characterized all stages of the common law. The New York courts freely adverted to post-Revolutionary judicial decisions in England, to post-Revolutionary English statutes, and to the judicial decisions of other American states.[190]

Pursuant to these powers, trends, and doctrines the courts of New York and other states—and to a minor extent the legislatures as well—struggled with the development of the law of family relations, and during the first half of the nineteenth century there was both some movement and some progress in the field of family law other than that of the poor. The courts continued to rely on the master-servant analogue of the parent-child relationship, which still infests family law and hinders its development,[191] but cracks and fissures began to appear through which could be seen a new theory on which to establish the parent's relations with third persons regarding the child and his claims to the child's services and earnings. Something more than loss of services crept into case discussions of the parent's right to recover for the seduction of the daughter.[192] Emancipation, which might be inferred by the courts from the circumstances and created by operation of law as well as explicitly arranged by the parent, began to moderate the parent's right as a master to the services and earnings of the child.[193]

With respect to the status of the earlier common-law doctrine of custody Bishop tells us that the father was "in some sense, the guardian of his minor children, though in precisely what sense the books seem not to be agreed."[194] During the first half of the nine-

---

190. E.g., Holcomb v. Hamilton, 1 Cole. & Cai. Cas. 67 (N.Y. Sup. Ct. 1799); Matter of Murphy, 294 N.Y. 440, 63 N.E.2d 49 (1945); People v. Appraisers, 33 N.Y. 461 (1870); Williams v. Williams, 8 N.Y. 525, 540–60 (1853); Morgan v. King, 30 Barb. 16 (N.Y. 1850); Bogardus v. Trinity Church, 4 Paige Ch. 178 (N.Y. 1833); Myers v. Gemmel, 10 Barb. 537 (N.Y. Sup. Ct. 1851).

191. See generally MADDEN, PERSONS AND DOMESTIC RELATIONS §§ 117–41 (1931).

192. See Knight v. Wilcox, 18 Barb. 212 (N.Y. Sup. Ct. 1854) (emotional distress is factor in determining damages).

193. Armstrong v. McDonald, 10 Barb. 300 (N.Y. Sup. Ct. 1851); Conover v. Cooper, 3 Barb. 115 (N.Y. Sup. Ct. 1848); Burlingame v. Burlingame, 7 Cow. 92 (N.Y. Sup. Ct. 1827); 2 KENT, COMMENTARIES *193–94 (4th ed. 1840).

194. 2 BISHOP, MARRIAGE & DIVORCE § 527 (5th ed. 1873); see IV Comyns, Digest 267 (4th ed. 1822): "So, the father and mother of an infant, who is not an heir apparent, shall be guardian to him, till his age of fourteen years, by reason of nurture. 8 Ed. 4. 7. b. 3 Co. 38. . . . Guardian by reason of nurture is for the education or governance of an infant,

teenth century in New York and other states, this was the developing status of custody: the father was entitled prima facie to the
custody of his children of both sexes during their entire minority;
the right of the father to custody might be forfeited for misconduct
or unfitness on his part involving the interests and welfare of the
children; the right of the father to custody was likewise subordinate to the interest of the public in the well-being and allegiance
of the children;[195] in some circumstances the mother might acquire
custody during the lifetime of the father, and her rights after his
death as against his testamentary disposition of the children were
also increasing.[196]

The parent's obligation for support in other than poor law cases
underwent the greatest change. Its course is at once characteristic
of common-law evolution and illustrative of the judicial search for
a basis on which both to rationalize and to reason about family
relationships. In developing the obligations of parental support,
the New York courts traced the line between poor law and common law, working their way through great confusion and uncertainty into a complete separation between the family law of the
poor and that of the rest of the community.

In two cases the New York Supreme Court confronted problems involving the common-law obligation of parental support.[197]
In one the duty of the parent to maintain his minor offspring was
said to be "a perfect common law duty" and in the other "a natural
obligation." In the first case though the duty was said to be perfect
at common law, no remedy was mentioned for its breach, and a
duty without a corresponding right of enforcement leaves the duty
less than perfect. In the second a third-party supplier of necessaries
was said to be able to recover from the parent on the theory that,

---

who has no other guardian, till his age of discretion. 8 Ed. 4. 7. b. . . . And the father or
mother by reason of the nurture shall have trespass against a stranger, who takes the infant."
TYLER, INFANCY & COVERTURE 245 (1st ed. 1868), relying on English cases, says: "With
respect to the guardianship of the father, it may be safely asserted that there is a right inherent in the parent, recognized by positive law, and in no degree dependent on the discretion of chancellors or judges, to act as guardian of all his children, not only during the
time of guardianship for nurture, but till the age of twenty-one."
    195. See People *ex rel*. Barry v. Mercein, 8 Paige Ch. 46 (N.Y. 1839); Mercein v.
People *ex rel*. Barry, 25 Wend. 64 (N.Y. Ct. Err. 1840); People *ex rel*. Barry v. Mercein,
3 Hill 399 (N.Y. Sup. Ct. 1842); People *ex rel*. Nickerson v. ———, 19 Wend. 16 (N.Y.
Sup. Ct. 1837); People *ex rel*. Ordroraux v. Chegarary, 18 Wend. 637 (N.Y. Sup. Ct. 1836);
2 KENT, COMMENTARIES *194, *205–07, *220–21; 2 STORY, EQUITY JURISPRUDENCE § 1341,
at 595–96 (10th ed. 1870).
    196. See Wood v. Wood, 5 Paige Ch. 596, 3 N.Y. Ch. 844 (1836); In the Matter of
Wollstonecraft, 4 Johns. Ch. 80 (N.Y. 1819).
    197. Edwards v. Davis, 16 Johns. R. 281 (N.Y. Sup. Ct. 1819); Van Valkinburgh v.
Watson, 13 Johns. R. 480 (N.Y. Sup. Ct. 1816).

since the parent was under a duty, the third-party supplier had conferred a benefit on him. Therefore the law implied a promise on his part to pay. In neither case did the court cite any judicial authority squarely in point but relied on Reeves's *Domestic Relations* and on Blackstone. But Reeves had relied on Blackstone, and Blackstone merely said that the duty of support was a natural one and only enforceable through the poor law. In both New York cases the statement was dictum—in the first because the decision related to the responsibility of an adult child for the support of his parents and in the second because the third-party supplier of an item to an infant child was not allowed to recover since the father was adequately maintaining the child. In Kent's *Commentaries* a similar statement of parental duties appears.[198] He cites more authorities but none of them any better.

In 1844, again in dicta, Chancellor Walworth stated that the parent "undoubtedly" was bound to support minor children and that the rule applied to a widowed mother as well as to the father, though the Chancellor would not intervene "to control parental discretion" to require the widow to furnish a twenty-year-old son in perfect health, capable of supporting himself by his own industry, the means of obtaining a professional education. Where the parent was liable the remedy, Chancellor Walworth said, was not by petition in chancery but by proceedings under the poor law statute, by an application to the general sessions for an order upon the parent, or "where there is a clear and palpable omission of duty," by getting the necessaries from the third party, who could then sue for compensation.[199] In 1851 Judge Augustus Hand reviewed the whole matter and concluded that it was "not so clear" how the parental obligation was to be enforced and therefore whether such an obligation existed in law.[200]

Finally, in 1863 the New York Supreme Court squarely held that a third-party supplier of necessaries could recover from the delinquent parent in an action at common law. Moreover, the recovery was allowed for necessaries supplied not only a minor son but also a "daughter who, although a few years past her majority, was unmarried and a member . . . [of the father's] family, and who . . . was an invalid unable to support herself by her labor."[201]

---

198. 2 KENT, COMMENTARIES *189–93.
199. In the Matter of Ryder, 11 Paige Ch. 185, 188 (N.Y. 1844).
200. Raymond v. Loyl, 10 Barb. 483 (N.Y. Sup. Ct. 1851).
201. Cromwell v. Benjamin, 41 Barb. 558, 561 (N.Y. Sup. Ct. 1863).

The basis was made quite clear. It was not the right to custody, property interests in the child, or reciprocal rights to services and earnings. It was parentage plus the voluntary assumption of obligation implicit in the act of begetting. To the court the basis of the action depended upon principles analogous to those imposing liability upon the husband for the support of the wife: "by virtue of the marital relation, and in consequence of the obligations assumed by him upon marriage."[202]

The reasons for the rule of parental liability for the support of minor children in civil family law and how they differed from those for the same liability in the family law of the poor are revealed by the three types of situations in which the rule evolved: In the first the parent sought an allowance for the child's support from the child's estate; in the second it was necessary to determine whether adequate consideration existed for parental transfers of property or money to the infant for services rendered; in the third a tailor, storekeeper, other tradesman, or physician supplied necessaries to the child without the knowledge or against the order of the parent and sought compensation from the parent. In the first situation the courts often asserted the liability of the parent while approving the allowance from the estate. The decisions were largely a matter of comparing the opulence of the parent and the child.[203] Since no argument arises unless the child has an estate, the child in this situation is not likely to be a poor person within the meaning of the poor laws. In the second the assertion of the parental duty facilitates protection of the father's creditors, especially antecedent creditors, against transfers to children with or without fraudulent intent. The rights of other heirs may also be at stake.[204] In the third-party supplier situation, the courts again seemed most concerned about interests outside the family. The child might well be eligible for poor relief. Thus the father's common-law liability to this extent duplicated that created by the poor

---

202. *Id.* at 560.
203. 2 KENT, COMMENTARIES *191.
204. See Swartz v. Hazlett, 8 Cal. 118 (1857). Indeed, it is in this case, in which the rights of antecedent creditors are protected, that we find one of the most glowing statements of the duty of the father to support: "Can the parent then divest himself of this duty by giving the child his own time? Suppose the child is taken sick, and the parent has means, is he not bound to take care of him, even after he has given him his time? How, and in what way, and under what system of morals, can a parent absolve himself from that responsibility? And if that responsibility continues, the power over the child must also continue. The responsibility and the power must stand or fall together. The duty of the parent to feed, clothe, and educate the child, must be commensurate with the power to control and govern." *Id.* at 125.

law. As a means of securing food and clothing for the deprived, allowing suits by suppliers is an indirect and ineffective method; it cannot compare with the continually operating administrative machinery of the poor law. It is less effective than suits directly between the child and parent and has somewhat the same impact on family relations. Though to some extent common-law liability was supplementary to poor law liability, the principal object was to supply a remedy to third-party suppliers who could not recover from poor law officials or make use of the responsible relatives machinery. Recompense for their outlays would have to be gained through the courts.[205]

While in civil family law the New York courts gradually evolved a limited rule of parental liability and a civil remedy to enforce it, they did all in their power to prevent an amalgamation with the family law of the poor or an interlocking administration. In 1826 the Supreme Court declared that a person under no obligation who voluntarily cared for a poor couple in his own home could not recover expenses from poor law officials.[206] "It was a commendable humane act,"[207] but the cost incurred did not result from any authorization by poor law officials or any negligence on their part. This principle applied to physicians who treated illness and injury, unless they had previously been authorized by an overseer or an order of a justice, even in emergency cases where previous authorization was not always feasible.[208]

Judicial reasoning about third-party suppliers of necessaries to minors was held inapplicable when the necessaries were supplied

---

205. This rule of liability has elicited a great deal of criticism. Taking into account parental control of the child and freedom to determine his circumstances and standard of living, Bishop thought that to allow the child to pledge the father's credit against his consent would encourage disobedience in those who had not arrived at the years of discretion. The wife likewise was to be obedient but in a little different sense, and she had arrived at the years of discretion. 2 BISHOP, MARRIAGE AND DIVORCE 443 (5th ed. 1873). Lord Kenyon noted that, since the question of necessaries was a relative fact governed by the fortune or circumstances of the infant, dangers existed of collusion between the children and the tradesmen in procuring extravagances and in confusing apparent and actual necessity. Ford v. Fothergill, 1 Esp. 211, 170 Eng. Rep. 331 (K.B. 1794) (confusing apparent and actual necessity); Simpson v. Robertson, 1 Esp. 17, 170 Eng. Rep. 266 (K.B. 1793) (dangers of collusion). Madden emphasizes the danger in removing from the father discretion in determining what is sufficient, necessary, and proper for the child and conferring that discretion on a third person—perhaps an intermeddling stranger—whose judgment may be confirmed by a jury in a suit against the father. MADDEN, PERSONS AND DOMESTIC RELATIONS §§ 110–11, at 386 (1931). See generally TYLER, INFANCY & COVERTURE 99–121 (1st ed. 1868).

206. Minklaer v. Rockerfeller, 6 Cow. 276 (N.Y. Sup. Ct. 1826).

207. *Id*. at 280.

208. See Flower v. Allen, 5 Cow. 654 (N.Y. Ct. Err. 1825); Gourley v. Allen, 5 Cow. 644 (N.Y. Ct. Err. 1825); BRANSCOMBE, THE COURTS AND THE POOR LAWS IN NEW YORK STATE 1784–1929, at 66 (1943).

to destitute parents and an adult child was sued for reimbursement. In *Edwards v. Davis*[209] the third-party supplier was told that the liability of the child for the support of the parent was not known to the common law and that, therefore, the poor law statutory procedure and remedy were exclusive. Clearly the analogy from marital relations of the voluntary assumption of the support obligation, which was applied to the parent-child relation, has less relevance to the child-parent relationship.

The courts equally insisted upon separation of the poor law from the civil law of domestic relations when poor law officials sought to use equitable and common-law procedures to recover from the husband for aid rendered the wife. These officials did not occupy the position of third-party suppliers of necessaries who were entitled to recover in the wife-husband relationship. Since the poor law did not include the husband among the legally responsible relatives, poor law officials could not proceed against him to compel support of his wife. The judges thought this omission due to the fact that the husband was liable at common law. Under the poor law the husband's property was subject to the support of the wife if he absconded but not otherwise. In considering the petition of poor law officials to recover against the husband for care given his insane spouse as a pauper, Chancellor Walworth had before him a case in which the care supplied had not been authorized under the poor law. However, he indicated that had the opposite been true the petition would still have been denied. The petitioners might have a suit at common law, but if they did not, the court of equity had "no general jurisdiction . . . to enforce the performance of a moral obligation, which the law will not recognize as a sufficient foundation for an action."[210]

When the poor law officials tested the chancery intimation that they might have an action at common law, the supreme court turned them away with a sharp pronouncement: "[I]t would be extremely dangerous to confer upon the superintendents of the poor, in their official capacity, the right to interpose in cases of difficulties between husband and wife, and thus involve the county in the controversy, and array its power against one of the parties."[211] In effect the poor law officials would have to adjudicate whether the husband was at fault, whether the wife left him wrongfully,

---

209. 16 Johns. R. 281 (N.Y. Sup. Ct. 1819).
210. Pomeroy v. Wells, 8 Paige Ch. 406, 411, 4 N.Y. Ch. 481, 483 (1840).
211. Norton v. Rhodes, 18 Barb. 100, 101 (N.Y. Sup. Ct. 1854).

whether he was adequately supporting her in the circumstances, and similar intermediate legal questions upon which the ultimate legal liability of the husband depended. That third-party suppliers other than poor law officials had to make these same determinations and that the courts and juries would review their correctness in a suit to recover from the husband were not allowed to outweigh, in the court's mind, the danger of official intrusion. The wife of a man able to support her and legally bound to do so was not among the poor for whom the superintendents were authorized to care. The statement that the poor law officials could not properly determine the wife to be an eligible pauper for their purposes seems clearly in error.

Chancellor Kent was in many ways Blackstone's counterpart for the first half of the nineteenth century in New York and in the rest of the established American states. Famous historians dispute the state of the law as it came under Kent's review—Roscoe Pound saying that at the end of the eighteenth century "the law was so completely at large in New York that the genius of a Kent was needed to make the common law the law of that state"[212] and Julius Goebel saying that New York started out with an elaborate code in 1665 and that by the opening years of the eighteenth century the law rapidly became professionalized.[213] Like Blackstone's, Kent's capacity for systematic statement often exceeded the amount of system in the law, though the technique of adding footnotes to cover developments as succeeding editions of *Commentaries* appeared tended to becloud the reader's perception of system. In the words of one critic, Kent was better qualified to be "a commentator whose work is mainly retrospective" than the architect of a new and improved jurisprudence.[214] The remark would apply as well to Blackstone. They were equally enamored of the common law and extolled its virtues uncritically.

Whatever may be said of the character and quality of Kent's *Commentaries*, the portion dealing with the New York and American law of the parent-child relationship closely paralleled Blackstone's treatment of the same subject. He too started with the natural duties of the parent to the child: "maintaining and educating them during the season of infancy and youth, and in making

212. Pound, Spirit of the Common Law 116 (1912).
213. Goebel, *King's Law and Local Custom in Seventeenth Century New England*, 31 Colum. L. Rev. 416, 420 n.9 (1931).
214. Butler, The Revision of the Statutes of New York and the Revisers 9 (1889).

reasonable provision for their future usefulness and happiness in life, by a situation suited to their habits and a competent provision for the exigencies of that situation."[215] "The wants and weaknesses of children render it necessary that some person maintain them, and the voice of nature has pointed out the parent as the most fit and proper person."[216] The parental duty is enforced by "the strength of natural affection." "A father's house is always open to his children. The best feelings of our nature establish and consecrate this asylum."[217] In consequence of the natural duty of support and education, the father is entitled to the custody of his children and to the value of their labor and services. In Kent as in Blackstone, custody is not the source or summation of rights but the consequence and instrument of a duty to maintain and to rear. "The father (and on his death the mother) is generally entitled to the custody of infant children, inasmuch as they are their natural protectors, for maintenance and education."[218]

Kent emphasized that the responsible-relatives provisions of the poor laws were "intended for the indemnity of the public against the maintenance of paupers."[219] Despite their encompassing sweep and pentrating impact, he thought them a "feeble and scanty statute provision."[220] He approved of the relaxation of common-law rigors in several states by which bastards might inherit through their mothers as resting upon the principle that the relation of parent and child "which exists in this unhappy case, in all its native and binding force, ought to produce the ordinary legal consequences of that consanguinity."[221]

## *The Field Draft Codes in New York*[222]

The instruction given Field and his fellow code commissioners by the constitution of 1846 "to reduce into a written and systematic code the whole body of the law of this State, or so much and such parts thereof as to the said Commissioners shall seem practicable and expedient . . . and [to] specify such alterations and amendments therein as they shall deem proper"[223] imposed on them a

---

215. 2 KENT, COMMENTARIES *189.
216. *Ibid.*
217. *Id.* at *190.
218. *Id.* at *203.
219. *Id.* at *191.
220. *Ibid.*
221. *Id.* at *213.
222. For a brief history of the Field Codes in New York see Reppy, *The Field Codification Concept,* in DAVID DUDLEY FIELD CENTENARY ESSAYS 17, 30 (Reppy ed. 1949).
223. N.Y. CONST. art. 1, § 17 (1846).

task which they mildly described as "untried and difficult."[224] No
complete codification of English or American common law had
ever been attempted, as they quite correctly insisted.[225] But a good
start had been made in the famous New York statutory revision
of 1828 which largely reconstructed the law of real property and
which Charles Warren characterized as "the first modern American code."[226] To the task of collecting, scientifically organizing,
and restating the existing common and statutory law was added
the duty of law reform. Indeed, law reform had been the principal
motivation. The movement for codification in New York, as well
as elsewhere, must be seen as an integral part of the political and
economic liberalism of the times.[227]

The reforming purpose was clearly manifest in the completed
draft codes. In preparing the Penal Code, for example, the commissioners stated that they kept these objects in view: "first, to bring
within the compass of a single volume the whole body of the law
of crimes and punishments; second, to supply deficiencies and
correct errors in the present definitions of crimes; third, to make
the relative degrees of punishment more nearly equal to the relative degrees of crime; and fourth, to define and punish acts de-
serving of punishment, but not punishable by the existing law."[228]
In the introduction to the Draft Civil Code, the commissioners
identified three major changes in the law—giving men and women
equal rights in their property and children, providing for the adop-

---

224. N.Y. CODE COMM'RS, DRAFT OF A CIVIL CODE FOR THE STATE OF NEW YORK viii
(Final Draft 1865) [hereinafter cited as DRAFT N.Y. CIV. CODE].

225. *Ibid.*

226. WARREN, A HISTORY OF THE AMERICAN BAR 424 (1911). A writer in the New
York Daily Times of that day says that the revision of the laws "in three volumes, in 1828,
known as the 'Revised Statutes' . . . [was] a revision far more thorough, philosophical
and radical than either of the others [referring to the statutory revisions of 1801 and 1813],
making great changes in the Statutes and coming nearer to Jeremy Bentham's idea of a
Code than any body of Statutes in force in any of the states ruled by the common law."
Reprinted in app., 18 Barb. 666 (Sup. Ct. 1855). This statement must be read in the light
of the strong opposition of conservative lawyers to the movement for codification. The
revisers themselves insisted that they were not preparing a code "in the sense of substituting
positive written definitions and enactments for the law as existing in the common law and
equity systems and as interpreted and applied by the Courts," yet they did organize, classify,
and revise the entire body of statutes of the state. See BUTLER, *op. cit. supra* note 214, at 22
(1889).

227. Warren attributes the movement to five factors: "First, the old, underlying an-
tagonism of the American public towards the Common Law, as being of English origin;
second, the ever-active jealousy, entertained by laymen in a democracy, towards lawyers,
as a privileged class and a monopoly, and the consequent desire to make the law a layman's
law; third, the increase in the number of law reports deemed, even then, to be 'vast and
unwieldy'; fourth, the success of the *Code Napoleon* in Europe; fifth, the influence of
Jeremy Bentham." WARREN, *op. cit. supra* note 227, at 508. Compare the repeated claim
that no change was intended in POMEROY, THE "CIVIL CODE" IN CALIFORNIA (1885).

228. DRAFT N.Y. CIV. CODE v.

tion of children, and assimilating real property to personalty, especially with respect to the rules of succession—and some 120 changes of lesser importance.[229] Reforms accomplished in the selection of competing existing rules and the foreclosure of undesired alternatives have never been counted. Expressing the reformers' futile hope of confining all lawmaking to the elected representatives of the people and acting in the spirit of Cnut commanding the sea not to rise, Field and his colleagues grandly bade the courts and the common law to change their nature in a section declaring, "In this state there is no common law in any case where the law is declared by the five Codes."[230]

The plan finally consummated in 1865 employed five codes:[231] a Code of Civil Procedure, a Code of Criminal Procedure, a Political Code, a Penal Code, and a Civil Code. The Codes of Civil and Criminal Procedure covered practice and pleading, remedies in civil and criminal judicial tribunals, and the law of evidence.[232] The Code of Criminal Procedure embraced the system of procedure in "special proceedings of a criminal nature" as well as in criminal actions.[233] The Political Code, dealing with government, defined the people of the state, listed political rights and duties, marked out the territory of the state and its civil divisions, and prescribed the structure of state and local government and the functions of state and local public officers. The Penal Code defined the crimes punishable under the law of the state and fixed the punishment. The Civil Code encompassed "the law of civil rights and obligations affecting all the transactions of men with each other

---

229. *Id.* at xxxi.
230. *Id.* § 6.
231. In New York the Code of Civil Procedure was adopted in 1848 and a Code of Criminal Procedure and a Penal Code in 1881. The Political and Civil Codes were not adopted.
232. The constitution of 1846, in addition to providing for the codification of the substantive law, provided for the appointment of a commission "to revise, reform, simplify, and abridge the rules of practice, pleading, forms and proceedings of the Courts of Record of this State . . . ." Art. VI, § 24. The legislature, in carrying out this provision, directed the commission "to provide for the abolition of the present forms of actions, and pleadings in cases at common law; for a uniform course of proceeding in all cases whether of legal or equitable cognizance, and for the abandonment of all Latin and other foreign tongues, . . . and of any form and proceeding not necessary to ascertain and preserve the rights of the parties." N.Y. Sess. Laws 1847, ch. 59, § 8. David Dudley Field, David Graham, and Arphaxed Loomis served on the Commission. The Code of Civil Procedure produced was adopted by the New York Legislature in 1848. A version of this code was adopted in California in 1850 and 1851, partly through the work of Stephen Field, the brother of David Dudley. Clark, *Code Pleading and Practice Today*, in David Dudley Field Centenary Essays 55, 56 (Reppy ed. 1949).
233. N.Y. Code Comm'rs, Draft of a Code of Criminal Procedure pt. 6 (Final Draft 1850) [hereinafter cited as Draft N.Y. Code Crim. Proc.].

in their private relations" and contained divisions dealing with persons, property, and obligations.[234] The organizational pattern is important: the distribution among the codes of the branches of family law reveal the understanding which the Field Code drafters had of its nature. The poor law, including the family law of the poor, was allocated to the Political Code and the Code of Criminal Procedure. The poor law was not regarded as dealing with the rights and relations of persons among themselves; it was not part of the private, civil law of persons. It was defined in terms of the functions of public officers and therefore placed in the Political Code and in terms of the procedures by which those officers might govern the poor and their relatives and therefore placed in the Code of Criminal Procedure.

Accordingly the Political Code contained provisions empowering county supervisors to acquire real property necessary for the support of the poor[235] and "to abolish or revive the distinction between town and county poor,"[236] provisions including among county charges "the sums necessarily expended . . . in the support of county poor houses" and of county indigent cases[237] and the costs incurred by the justices of the peace "under the laws for the relief and settlement of the poor of such county,"[238] and provisions empowering the electors of the towns at their annual town meetings to raise money for the support of the poor[239] and to determine the number of overseers of the poor.[240] Since the poor are a custodialized and controlled part of the people, they find a prominent place in the Political Code's list of the state's powers over persons. The state has the power to punish for crime, to imprison for the protection of the public peace or individual health or safety, and to imprison to enforce civil remedies.[241] The enumeration of state powers over persons then continues, "4. To establish custody and restraint for the persons of idiots, lunatics, drunkards and other persons of unsound mind; 5. To establish custody and restraint of

---

234. N.Y. Code Comm'rs, Ninth Report to the Legislature 1 (1865).
235. N.Y. Code Comm'rs, Draft of a Political Code for the State of New York § 882(3) (Final Draft 1860).
236. *Id*. § 882(15).
237. *Id*. § 938(14).
238. *Id*. § 938(13).
239. *Id*. § 964(12).
240. *Id*. § 964(4). If a proposition for the support of the poor was not acted on at the regular annual meeting, a special meeting might be called for that purpose. Vacancies among overseers of the poor were to be filled at special meetings also. See *id*. § 968. See also *id*. §§ 983, 1000, 1006, 1012, 1016, 1035.
241. *Id*. §§ 248 (1)–(3).

paupers, for the purposes of their maintenance; 6. To establish custody and restraint of minors unprovided for by natural guardians, for the purposes of their education, reformation and maintenance . . . .''[242]

The Code of Criminal Procedure contains elaborate provisions on vagrants,[243] disorderly persons,[244] bastards,[245] and responsible relatives of the poor.[246] The provisions are dominantly procedural;[247] for example, the titles on vagrants and disorderly persons deal with apprehending them, detaining them, committing them to poorhouses, procuring materials and compelling them to work, and binding them out. In the case of relatives responsible for poor persons, the proceedings relate to summoning the relatives, determining amounts of payment, distributing the burden among them, reviewing the orders and enforcing the payment, and seizing and selling the property of absconding parents and husbands and applying the income to the maintenance of children and wives. These are not procedures in criminal actions but rather "special proceedings of a criminal nature."[248] Yet, they also define "vagrants,"[249] "disorderly persons,"[250] and those liable for the support of poor persons[251] and bastards.[252] These definitions appear almost as incidental appendages to the procedure; the character of the provisions derives from the nature of the proceedings. Departing from the general pattern of placing powers and duties of officers and of governmental units in the Political Code, the Code of Criminal Procedure section imposing liability on the father and mother for the support of a bastard child declares that if they neglect or are unable to do so "it must be supported by the county, city or town in which it is born, as provided by special statutes."[253] In the case of

242. *Ibid.*
243. DRAFT N.Y. CODE CRIM. PROC. pt. VI, tit. VII.
244. *Id.* tit. VIII.
245. *Id.* pt. VI, tit. VI.
246. *Id.* pt. VI, tit. IX.
247. The title dealing with bastards is headed "Proceedings Respecting Bastards," and its three chapters deal with proceedings before the magistrate to inquire into bastardy, to issue warrants against the putative father, to place him under sureties, to commit him for failure to give undertakings, to order filiation, and to order the mother to support, *id.* pt. VI, tit. VI, ch. I, with appeals from orders of the magistrates, *id.* pt. VI, tit. VI, ch. II, and with enforcement of undertakings for the support of the bastard or the mother or for appearance on appeal, *id.* pt. VI, tit. VI, ch. III.
248. *Id.* pt. VI, tit. V (Code Comm'rs' Note).
249. DRAFT N.Y. CODE CRIM. PROC. § 973.
250. *Id.* § 983.
251. *Id.* § 998.
252. *Id.* § 925.
253. *Ibid.*

poor persons with legally liable relatives, the duty of town and county to support them is presupposed rather than declared.[254]

Since the subject was viewed as dealing with the functions of public officers administering legislation controlling a subordinate class of the population, no need existed for much of the poor law to find its way into the Penal Code; very little of it did. Intentional abandonment of a child under the age of six years by a parent or one to whom it is "confided for nurture or education" is defined as a crime.[255] The parent's willful omission to supply necessaries enumerated in the Civil Code was made a misdemeanor.[256] However, the Penal Code, while defining all of the crimes punishable in the state and prescribing their punishment, did not deal with begging, vagrancy, being a disorderly person, fornication, or bastardy. These matters were left to the special proceedings set out in the Code of Criminal Procedure.

In the Draft Civil Code, the Field commissioners were dealing primarily with judicial decisions and the common law, in contrast with the dominantly statutory materials which were the basis of the Political Code and the Code of Criminal Procedure.[257] Though the common law of New York embodied in its own judicial decisions was, of course, the principal source, many rules were drawn from other jurisdictions. The cases cited in the supporting notes were often those of other American states and England. In addition to restating and classifying firmly established common-law rules, the commissioners clarified many that were uncertain, chose between competing rules, filled in gaps, and made some very striking innovations. All of this applies with special force to the family-law portion of the Draft Civil Code.

Although efforts were made in the code to place men and women more nearly upon an equal footing with respect to their rights in children and in property, equality was far from achieved. A new, judicial, method of adoption of children was established, conferring upon the adoptive parent all of the rights and responsibilities of the natural parent. While maintaining the separation of

---

254. *Id*. pt. VI, tit. IX.
255. N.Y. Code Comm'rs, Draft of a Penal Code for the State of New York § 332 (Final Draft 1865).
256. *Id*. § 333.
257. Warren describes the Field Draft Civil Code of 1865 as "the first real code in the broad and correct sense of the term, prepared in this country." Warren, A History of the American Bar 533 (1911). Note Sir Frederick Pollock's characterization of it as "about the worst piece of codification ever produced." Kleps, *Revision and Codification of California Statutes 1849–1953*, 42 Calif. L. Rev. 766, 778 n.45 (1954).

poor law and civil law, the commissioners drew from the poor law one of its principal features, responsibility of relatives for the support of their poor kinsmen, and placed it in the Civil Code: "It is the duty of the father, the mother, and the children, of any poor person who is unable to maintain himself by work, to maintain such persons to the extent of their ability."[258] In a note to the section, the commissioners explained: "the provisions of the Poor Laws declare the duty of parents and children to support each other . . . but it is held that the obligation on the part of the children is purely statutory, and no other remedy exists except that provided by proceedings under those laws . . . ." "On the part of parents, the obligation is not now merely statutory." "It is the object of this section to recognize the obligation as a ground of legal liability independent of those provisions."[259] It followed that a third-party supplier of necessaries could recover from an adult child, and now in addition "the promise of an adult child to pay for necessaries previously furnished" was binding.[260] Why the obligation should be recognized as an independent ground of legal liability is not stated. The emphasis on the right of recovery of a third-party supplier and the particular reference to the *Benjamin* and *Davis* cases indicate that providing an additional remedy for third-party suppliers was the goal to be achieved.

Language of the Civil Code section was not identical with that of the poor law; though the same relatives—parents and children of the poor person—were liable, in the poor law not every poor person's relatives were liable—only the relatives of "a poor person who is insane, blind, old, lame, impotent or decrepid" so as to be unable by work to maintain himself.[261] The enforcement machinery of the poor law remained distinct. There is no suggestion that the Civil Code section penetrated the wall of separation previously established. Under the poor law, since the amount of liability was approved by the overseers of the poor, the overseers also judged what was necessary and the standards of need to be met. Under the Civil Code section, necessity would be finally determined by the court or a jury.[262]

---

258. Draft N.Y. Civ. Code § 97; Cal. Civ. Code § 206. Since this and other Draft Civil Code sections to be discussed were adopted almost verbatim in California, the New York and California sections will be cited in pairs.
259. Draft N.Y. Civ. Code § 97, Comm'rs' Note.
260. Draft N.Y. Civ. Code § 97; Cal. Civ. Code § 206.
261. Draft N.Y. Code Crim. Proc. § 998.
262. Two sections crossed the line and made a civil remedy available to poor law offi-

The poor law imposition of support liability on both parents of illegitimate children was not similarly transferred to the Civil Code. Indeed, the Civil Code seems to place liability exclusively on the mother.[263] The relatives-of-poor-persons section may be read as duplicatory of the sections dealing with parents of minor children, including the mothers of illegitimates, or on the contrary as yielding to them in view of their specificity. The latter view is also indicated by a difference in standards. In the sections specifically dealing with parents and minor children, the liability is to supply not only support but also education and to do both "according to their circumstances"[264] or "suitable to their circumstances,"[265] a distinction of wealth and rank not taken with respect to the poor and their relatives.

The commissioners further formulated and systematized a series of rules settling previously vexing questions about custody, control, care, upbringing, services, earnings, and estates of children. Most striking is the degree to which these elements are organized around and dependent on the right to custody. Not only do these rights and duties converge in custody, but custody is their starting point.

To whom does custody belong and of what does it consist? It belongs to the parents.[266] This is unqualifiedly declared: "The father of a legitimate unmarried minor is entitled to its custody."[267] Nothing is said about the father's fitness, competence, age, finances, morals, politics, knowledge, religion, or residence. Nothing is said about the best interests of the child. The only fact to be established, whether by presumption or investigation, is that the claimant is the father. A limitation is placed on his power to dispose of the custody—he may not transfer it to any person except the mother "without her written consent if she is living and capable of consent."[268] This affects the father's authority to terminate his custody; it does not affect his right to it. Circumstances in which the mother may become entitled to custody of legitimate unmarried minor

---

cials. One provided that the supervisor of the town (supervisors of the county in California) might, in the case of a publicly chargeable child, "claim provision for its support from the parent's estate by civil action." DRAFT N.Y. CIV. CODE § 96; CAL. CIV. CODE § 205. The same officials by civil action might bring abuse of parental authority to judicial cognizance. DRAFT N.Y. CIV. CODE § 94; CAL. CIV. CODE § 203.

263. DRAFT N.Y. CIV. CODE §§ 89, 91; CAL. CIV. CODE §§ 196, 200.
264. DRAFT N.Y. CIV. CODE § 98; CAL. CIV. CODE § 207.
265. DRAFT N.Y. CIV. CODE § 89; CAL. CIV. CODE § 196.
266. DRAFT N.Y. CIV. CODE §§ 90, 91; CAL. CIV. CODE §§ 197, 200.
267. DRAFT N.Y. CIV. CODE § 90; CAL. CIV. CODE § 197.
268. DRAFT N.Y. CIV. CODE § 90; CAL. CIV. CODE § 197.

children are stated: "If the father is dead, or is unable, or refuses to take the . . . [custody], or has abandoned his family, the mother is entitled thereto."[269] The circumstances stated do not deal with the fitness or competence of the father to rear the child or with the interests of the child but with his ability or willingness to take custody. Again, if the identified circumstances are present, the mother's right is absolute without regard to the child's interests. Equally absolute are the mother's primary rights: "The mother of an illegitimate, unmarried minor is entitled to its custody . . . ."[270]

The services and earnings of the child went along with custody.[271] So did the obligation to educate and support. "The parent entitled to the custody of the child must give him support and education suitable to his circumstances."[272] As the father had primary right to the custody of the legitimate child, he had primary responsibility for its support. As the mother's right to its custody was in most circumstances residual and secondary, so was her obligation to support. If the support and education which the father was able to give were inadequate, the mother was under a duty to "assist him to the extent of her ability."[273] Since the obligation to support was dependent on the right to custody and since the mother had the right to custody of illegitimate children, she had the responsibility for their support. Moreover, she had it entirely and alone.[274]

Under the New York Draft Penal Code the obligation to support and custody were implicitly interdependent. It made a parent's

---

269. *Ibid.*

270. DRAFT N.Y. CIV. CODE § 91; CAL. CIV. CODE § 200.

271. DRAFT N.Y. CIV. CODE §§ 90, 91; CAL. CIV. CODE §§ 197, 200. In addition, see CAL. CIV. CODE § 169, declaring that "The earnings and accumulations of the wife, and of her minor children living with her or in her custody, while she is living separate from her husband, are the separate property of the wife."

The right to the services, earnings, and control of the child could be relinquished by the parent to the child whether the parent was solvent or insolvent. Abandonment is presumptive evidence of such relinquishment. DRAFT N.Y. CIV. CODE § 102; CAL. CIV. CODE § 211. In the absence of a thirty-day notice from the parent to the employer of a minor child, the wages may be paid to the minor. DRAFT N.Y. CIV. CODE § 103; CAL. CIV. CODE § 212. An adult child continuing to serve the parent and to be supported by him is not entitled to compensation in the absence of an agreement, nor is the parent liable for support. DRAFT N.Y. CIV. CODE § 101; CAL. CIV. CODE § 210.

272. DRAFT N.Y. CIV. CODE § 89; CAL. CIV. CODE § 196. This section is qualified by the provision that the court "may direct an allowance to be made to the parent of a child, out of its property, for its past or future support and education, on such conditions as may be proper, whenever such direction is for its benefit." DRAFT N.Y. CIV. CODE § 92; CAL. CIV. CODE § 201. "The parent, as such, has no control over the property of the child." DRAFT N.Y. CIV. CODE § 93; CAL. CIV. CODE § 202.

273. DRAFT N.Y. CIV. CODE § 89; CAL. CIV. CODE § 196.

274. A third person supplying necessaries to a child in good faith might recover for them but only from a parent neglecting to provide them for a child "who is under his charge." DRAFT N.Y. CIV. CODE § 98; CAL. CIV. CODE § 207.

willful omission without lawful excuse "to perform any duty imposed upon him by law, to furnish necessary food, clothing, shelter and medical attendance" a misdemeanor. The duty itself was imposed by the law contained in the Civil Code sections. The point is made explicit by Field's notes to his draft section of New York Penal Code Section 333 which refers to Draft Civil Code sections imposing parental duty of support as explaining the Penal Code phrase "to perform any duty imposed upon him by law."

Having settled the right to custody in the parents or in one of them and having determined the content or incidents of the concept, provision was made for its termination and for some considerations of judges when awarding it. "The authority of a parent ceases: 1. Upon the appointment by a court of a guardian of the person of a child; 2. Upon the marriage of the child; or, 3. Upon its attaining majority."[275] "[T]he child may be freed from the dominion of the parent" by the courts if there is "abuse of parental authority . . . ."[276] The rule of equity is laid down, and a hierarchy of preferences among potential guardians established for courts awarding the custody of a minor or appointing a general guardian. The court is to be guided by "what appears to be for the best interest of the child, in respect to its temporal and its mental and moral welfare"[277] and by the preferences of the child if it is of sufficient age to form an intelligent preference.[278] "3. Of two persons equally eligible in other respects, preference is to be given as follows: (1) to a relative; (2) to one who was indicated by the wishes of a deceased parent; (3) to one who already stands in the position of a trustee of a fund to be applied to the child's support."[279]

The law of family relations as it had developed before English settlement in North America, with its separate and different branches dealing with the poor and with the rest of the community, became fully established in New York by the beginning of statehood and retained its essential characteristics during the three-quarters of a century that followed. Though the controlled econ-

---

275. DRAFT N.Y. CIV. CODE § 95; CAL. CIV. CODE § 204.
276. DRAFT N.Y. CIV. CODE § 94; CAL. CIV. CODE § 203.
277. DRAFT N.Y. CIV. CODE § 127; CAL. CIV. CODE § 246 (1872).
278. DRAFT N.Y. CIV. CODE § 127; CAL. CIV. CODE § 246 (1872).
279. DRAFT N.Y. CIV. CODE § 127; CAL. CIV. CODE § 246 (1872). The right of custody does not include an unqualified right to change the residence of the child, which is subject to the power of the court "to restrain a removal which would prejudice the rights or welfare of the child." DRAFT N.Y. CIV. CODE § 104; CAL. CIV. CODE § 213.

omy and system of subjugated labor in which it had originated had largely disappeared in New York, though it was out of harmony with the conditions of abundant land, open frontiers, and free movement in the new nation, though liberal reform in related institutions was the hallmark of the age, the family law of the poor and the Elizabethan poor law system of which it was an integral part remained, in nineteenth-century New York, virtually static in the form achieved in England by the first decade of the seventeenth century. As in England, so in New York, this subject was taken within the exclusive jurisdiction of the legislature, which lavished attention upon it: imposing upon county finances and administration the mandatory duty of caring for the impotent poor, the able-bodied pauper, the idle, and the disorderly—a duty increasingly discharged through a system of combined poorhouses, workhouses, and houses of correction; minimizing public costs through enforcing liability on relatives of the poor, deserting family heads, and both parents of bastard children; and fixing county responsibility by rigorous regulation of settlement and removal. Bespeaking its legislative origin, its administrative execution, its political nature, its fiscal ingredients, and its penal implications, David Dudley Field distributed the various provisions of the poor law in his Draft Political Code among the powers of government and the functions of public officers and in his Draft Code of Criminal Procedure among special proceedings of a criminal nature.

The New York history of the family law of the rest of the community is in sharp contrast. Received formally as part of the common law and informally as part of the judicial process of selective incorporation, its administration and development, though occasionally influenced by legislative action, were left to the courts. Systematically, they erected a wall of separation between it and the family law of the poor, the presence of which, nevertheless, helped to determine its character and shape its provisions. Case by case, decade by decade, responding to the transforming forces of the age, civil family law underwent a gradual process of growth and deliberate reform, capped by Field's codification in 1860 which was both a summary and an amendment. Bespeaking its common-law origin, its judicial administration, its civil nature, and its private interpersonal relationships, Field distributed its various provisions in the Draft Civil Code encompassing "the law of civil rights and obligations affecting all the transactions of men with each other in their private relations." As expressed in the Draft Civil Code, civil family law improved the relative position of the wife and mother with respect to property and children, created a judicial procedure for the adoption of children, augmented parental rights to custody, integrated other parental rights and duties within this concept, and conferred on third-party suppliers of necessaries to poor persons, young and old, a right of action against parents and children, thus providing a civil remedy for an obligation previously existing only under the poor law.

As embodied and altered in the Field Draft Codes, New York's dual system of family law made its way across the nation to be considered by code commissioners and legislators in the State of California.

# 4

# Adoption
# of the Dual System
# in California

## The California Codes of 1872

When Dean Roscoe Pound said at the 1948 David Dudley Field
Centenary celebration that California adopted all of Field's codes,[280]
he was stating what many have said before and since, but he was
speaking only in the most general terms. Partly in response to the
general forces moving toward legislative reform and legal codification but more particularly because of the wild and uncertain state
of its laws arising from the peculiarities of its history, California did
adopt a set of codes in 1872.[281] All five of the Field code titles were
embraced within the four California Codes—a Code of Civil Procedure,[282] a Penal Code, a Political Code, and a Civil Code—and the

---

280. Pound, *David Dudley Field: An Appraisal*, in DAVID DUDLEY FIELD, CENTENARY
ESSAYS 3, 10 (1949).

281. Kleps, *The Revision and Codification of California Statutes 1849–1953*, 42 CALIF.
L. REV. 766 (1954); Parma, *The History of the Adoption of the Codes of California*, 22 L.
LIBRARY J. 8 (1929). See also LINDLEY, CALIFORNIA CODE COMMENTARIES (1872). Lindley's summary of the situation is somewhat exuberant but not entirely inapt: "California
had the Spanish or Mexican law—the law of a conquered people. Her Constitution was
made of shreds from the Constitutions of the older states. Her early Statutes were patch-
work from the Statutes of the States from whence the constitution-makers and early legislators had emigrated. She had a sort of spontaneous formation arising from a congregation
of a vast army of gold hunters from all parts of the world.

"In 1850, the Mexican law was overcome by the adoption of the 'Common Law of
England.' It was soon ascertained by the Judiciary that this phrase meant Common Law
of the United States—the Common Law of over thirty different states, with different modifications and rules upon the same subject. Her legislation, since, has been the most special,
incongruous and ponderous that ever disgraced a civilized people. Such was the condition
and such the necessity, when the California Commission undertook the *integration*, after
the models of the New York Codes." *Id.* at 26.

282. The Code of Civil Procedure was a revision of the Practice Acts of 1850 and 1851,
Cal. Stat. 1850, ch. 142, at 428; Cal. Stat. 1851, ch. V, at 51; ch. 29, at 212, which, in turn,
had been revisions of the New York Code of Civil Procedure and, in part, of the New York
Code of Criminal Procedure. See Kleps, *supra* note 281, at 766 n.4. The 1851 act "To

California drafters acknowledged great indebtedness to Field's drafts.[283] The California Codes, however, stood in varying relationships to the form and content of those drafts—all drawing some of their substance and specific language from them but varying significantly, though in different degrees, from the model.[284] In the area of our interest, the departures are dominant except with respect to the law of parent and child in the Civil Code.

The California Penal Code of 1872 is at once a criminal code,[285]

---

Regulate Proceedings in Criminal Cases" became Part II of the Penal Code of 1872. The California Code of Civil Procedure is exclusively that; its four major divisions deal with courts of justice, civil actions, special proceedings of a civil nature, and evidence. It contains little of direct bearing on our topic aside from a provision authorizing the father, in some circumstances the mother, and the guardian to sue for the seduction of the daughter or ward in the absence of any loss of services and aside from some provisions diverging from related sections of the Civil Code.

Compare these two sections for an example of the divergence: "1757. If any minor, having a father living, has property, the income of which is sufficient for his maintenance and education in a manner more expensive than his father can reasonably afford, regard being had to the situation of the father's family and to all the circumstances of the case, the expenses of the education and maintenance of such minor may be defrayed out of the income of his own property, in whole or in part, as judged reasonable, and must be directed by the Probate Court . . . ." Cal. Code Civ. Proc. of 1872, § 1757 (now CAL. PROB. CODE § 1504); "201. The proper Court may direct an allowance to be made to the parent of a child, out of its property, for its past or future support and education, on such conditions as may be proper, whenever such direction is for its benefit." Cal. Civ. Code of 1872, § 201. *Compare* Cal. Code Civ. Proc. of 1872, § 1751, *with* Cal. Civ. Code of 1872, § 246 (now CAL. PROB. CODE §§ 1406, 1407, 1410).

283. See Lindley's statement quoted *supra* note 281 and his statement in *id.*, app. at iii: "Much of the work had been accomplished by the New York Commission and was ready for our use." See also note 284 *infra*.

284. In the Introduction to their Draft Political Code, dated January 1872—all four codes were adopted in March 1872—the California Code Commissioners described their work as follows: "[W]e contented ourselves in the main with an adherence to existing laws. The Penal Code, Code of Civil Procedure, and Political Code embody existing laws, arranged in a convenient and logical form. Some slight additions have been made to give completeness to certain subjects; and the practice in civil actions, *after* judgment, has been simplified. We had but few laws that related to the civil rights of 'persons and things'—such as the laws relating to the tenure, transfer, and mortgage of property; corporations, descents, and distributions; wills, notes, and bills of exchange, etc. All of these we have substantially retained, but they have been taken into what we present as the 'Civil Code.'

"That code is chiefly the work of the New York Commission. We took the New York Civil Code, and in place of the corresponding chapters, inserted our own laws, modified the rest of it to harmonize with our system, and recommend its adoption as a whole. . . . If any valid objections are urged to it, we have our own laws, that make part of the bill for a 'Civil Code' as we have presented it, so well in hand that they can be drawn from the bill in a few hours, and, if adopted, would make a Civil Code of about one hundred and fifty pages, and thus the whole work would be in fact a revision." CALIFORNIA CODE COMMISSIONERS, THE REVISED STATUTES OF CALIFORNIA, IN FOUR CODES: POLITICAL, CIVIL, CIVIL PROCEDURE, POLITICAL CODE v (1872) [hereinafter cited as Cal. Pol. Code of 1872]. Lindley, *op. cit. supra* note 283, one of the Code Commissioners, makes it plain, and comparison of the various codes quickly confirms, that this statement down-plays the reliance on the Field drafts, but it does so only in degree. That many of our precode statutes were taken bodily or in part from New York is also worth noting. California code sections and the Field sections may thus go back to a common source in instances in which the California sections are not copied from Field.

285. Part I deals with crimes and punishments. It is derived from two principal sources: The Crimes and Punishment Act of 1850, Cal. Stat. 1850, ch. 99, at 229, and the Field Penal Code, N.Y. CODE COMM'RS, DRAFT OF A PENAL CODE FOR THE STATE OF NEW YORK (Final Draft 1865) [hereinafter cited as DRAFT N.Y. PEN. CODE].

a code of criminal procedure,[286] and a code of state and county penal institutions.[287] From the Field Draft Penal Code, California adopted the definitions of the crimes of abandoning children, of willfully failing to support them,[288] and of child stealing, which made guilty "Every person who maliciously, forcibly or fraudulently takes or entices away any child under the age of twelve years, with intent to detain and conceal such child from its parent, guardian, or other person having lawful charge of such child . . . ."[289] Penal sanctions were thus given to the greatly strengthened notions of custody expressed in the Civil Code. Continuing the traditional parallel, the California Penal Code also made punishable aiding apprentices to run away or harboring them.[290]

Though the Penal Code contained a title on "Special Proceedings of a Criminal Nature,"[291] it said nothing about bastards, vagrants, disorderly persons, responsible relatives of the poor, or the property of absconding parents or husbands. Nowhere in the California Codes did these topics receive treatment similar to that in New York. Vagrancy, however, was declared a crime outright and made punishable by a county jail sentence not exceeding ninety days.[292] The New York pattern assimilating the treatment of vagrants and paupers by sending both to the poorhouse was rejected. Likewise rejected was the scheme of the famous statute on the subject adopted by Iowa[293] and Oregon[294] which bound the vagrant out to labor with a private employer and required use of the wages for family support and payment of debts. Idleness was described

---

286. Part II is derived from Cal. Stat. 1850, ch. 119, at 275, and Cal. Stat. 1851, ch. 29, at 212, both based on the Field Code of Criminal Procedure, N.Y. CODE COMM'RS, DRAFT OF A CODE OF CRIMINAL PROCEDURE (Final Draft 1850) [hereinafter cited as DRAFT N.Y. CODE CRIM. PROC.].

287. Part III, tit. I, §§ 1573–95 (state prisons), and Part III, tit. II, §§ 1597–614 (county jails), are based on earlier state statutes, *e.g.*, Cal. Stat. 1858, ch. CCXCI; Cal. Stat. 1851, ch. 23, §§ 17–42.

288. DRAFT N.Y. PEN. CODE § 332, CAL. PEN. CODE § 271; DRAFT N.Y. PEN. CODE § 333, CAL. PEN. CODE § 270.

289. DRAFT N.Y. PEN. CODE § 337, Cal. Pen. Code of 1872, § 278. See also N.Y. CODE COMM'RS, DRAFT OF A CIVIL CODE FOR THE STATE OF NEW YORK § 132 (Final Draft 1865) [hereinafter cited as DRAFT N.Y. CIV. CODE], Cal. Civ. Code of 1872, § 48 (abduction and seduction) (now CAL. CIV. CODE § 49).

290. Cal. Pen. Code of 1872, § 646 (based on Cal. Stat. 1858, ch. CLXXXII, § 17); *cf.* Cal. Civ. Code § 275 (1931) (defining the same crime and making it a misdemeanor in somewhat different language).

291. Cal. Pen. Code of 1872, pt. II, tit. XII.

292. Cal. Pen. Code of 1872, § 647. This section was drawn from earlier California statutes, the first enacted in 1855. Cal. Stat. 1855, ch. CLXXV, at 217, as amended, Cal. Stat. 1863, ch. DXXV, § 1, at 770, Cal. Pen. Code of 1872, § 647.

293. Iowa Terr. Laws 1838–1839, at 486.

294. Ore. Terr. Laws 1845, at 16.

in various of its postures, but its focal point was the ability to work and the failure to do so, particularly as tested by failure to seek work "for the space of 10 days" and refusal to labor "when employment is offered."[295] Healthy beggars who solicited alms as a business were covered by the Penal Code section which, however, did not include, as the earlier law did, those "who travel with written statements of their misfortunes."[296] Along with the willfully idle were included the dissolute: lewd persons who lived in or about houses of ill fame, common prostitutes, and common drunkards. And along with the idle and the dissolute were included the suspicious: associates of known thieves who wander about the streets late at night or who lodge in barns, sheds, and outhouses without permission.[297] The Penal Code did not carry forward the provision of the earlier law that convicted vagrants were to be put "at any kind of labor that the Board of Supervisors of the county may direct," provided that the vagrant "shall be secured whilst employed outside of the County Jail, by ball and chain of sufficient weight and strength to prevent escape."[298]

The California Political Code departed widely from the Field draft. A comparison of organization and content reveals that, while the Field draft was clearly used as a model and while some chapters and sections were copied directly or nearly so, numerous others were not in the Field draft at all or existed there in substantially different form. Local government, particularly its welfare functions, was built upon a different framework and embodied different conceptions. In the Field Draft Political Code, the basic poor law obligation—long encompassed in the statutory poor law system, major parts of which had been incorporated in the Code of Criminal Procedure—was presupposed rather than articulated, and some duties were distributed to local officials. In California a uniform grant of power had yet to be made to the counties, and the welfare system authorized by the code turned out to be a "feeble and scanty" provision by comparison with that existing in New York. The

---

295. Cal. Pen. Code of 1872, § 647.
296. Cal. Stat. 1855, ch. CLXXV, § 1. California Indians were exempted, presumably on the ground that they were adequately covered by separate statute. Cal. Stat. 1850, ch. 133.
297. Cal. Pen. Code of 1872, § 647.
298. Cal. Stat. 1855, ch. CLXXV, § 4. Under § 1613 of the Penal Code, "persons confined in the County Jail under a judgment of imprisonment rendered in a criminal action or proceeding, may be required by an order of the Board of Supervisors to perform labor on the public works or ways in the county."

counties were authorized but not required to supply assistance in the form of "care and maintenance." The care of indigent sick was emphasized, though the otherwise dependent poor were included.[299] Inferentially, the principal form of assistance was to be care in hospitals which the counties were authorized "to erect, officer and maintain" and in connection with which a county farm might be established.[300] Nothing is said about settlement and removal, about responsible relatives, or about bastardy and those involved in it. County per capita and ad valorem taxes were authorized to meet the costs.[301]

These Political Code provisions were almost entirely a recapitulation of existing California law, repeating and making more uniform and generally applicable ideas and phrases contained in the limited county supervisors act of 1852,[302] the numerous special statutes relating to individual counties passed during the 1850's,[303] and the State Hospital and Infirmary Acts of 1855[304] and 1860.[305] In one particular—that declaring the rights of the state over persons within its jurisdiction—the Field draft was copied exactly. Along with the right to punish for crime, to imprison for the protection and safety of the public and of individuals, and to enforce civil remedies, the state was declared to have the right to establish custody and restraint of persons of unsound mind, of paupers for the purposes of their maintenance, and of minors unprovided for by natural guardians for the purposes of their education, reformation, and maintenance.[306] The legal foundation for the harsh and punitive aspects of the Elizabethan poor law system was thus explicitly laid.

Of the four codes adopted by California in 1872, the one which

---

299. Cal. Pol. Code of 1872, § 4046(5).

300. Cal. Pol. Code of 1872, § 4046(6).

301. Cal. Pol. Code of 1872, § 4046(5). See also Cal. Pol. Code of 1872, § 4344(8) (expenses for support of county hospitals and county charges); Cal. Pol. Code of 1872, § 4408(20) (common councils of cities empowered to erect and maintain poorhouses and hospitals). Identical language appeared in the act to incorporate cities, Cal. Stat. 1850, ch. 30, § 11. Section 1239(2) provided that a person cannot gain or lose residence while kept in an almshouse. This provision had existed in California from its beginning. See CAL. CONST. art. II, § 4 (1841); Cal. Stat. 1850, ch. 38, § 11.

302. Cal. Stat. 1852, ch. XXXVIII.

303. These are summarized in tenBroek, *California's Welfare Law—Origins and Development*, 45 CALIF. L. REV. 241, 275–78 (1957).

304. Cal. Stat. 1855, ch. LVII.

305. Cal. Stat. 1860, ch. CCXLVII.

306. N.Y. CODE COMM'RS, DRAFT OF A POLITICAL CODE FOR THE STATE OF NEW YORK § 248 (Final Draft 1860) [hereinafter cited as DRAFT N.Y. POL. CODE], Cal. Pol. Code of 1872, § 37.

copied most from the Field draft, which most greatly expanded the existing body of statutory and judicial law of the state, and which has been most vigorously criticized is the Civil Code. In the general field of family law, important differences existed between the code as adopted and the Field draft. The new code accommodated California's far more liberal provisions on divorce[307] and the state's distinctive system of community and separate property, part of the Spanish heritage of the state which to a limited extent had been sanctified in the Treaty of Guadalupe Hidalgo of 1848,[308] in the Protocol of Querétaro,[309] and in the state's 1849 constitution.[310] In that part of the family law with which we are primarily concerned—the law of the child as it touches on his relations with his parents, on public programs and private charities, and on third persons generally—the Field draft was accepted practically as it stood, with its exaggerated doctrine of custody as an integrative principle, with its elaboration of the reciprocity of parental rights and responsibilities, with its improved but still very unequal status of women and mothers, with its separate and very unequal status of illegitimates, with its single section declaring the general responsibility of relatives after the manner of the poor law, and with its long-declared but only recently established New York common-law remedy against the parent for third-party suppliers of necessaries to children, whether minors or dependent adults.

However, the Field draft provision on preference among persons to be awarded custody or guardianship was markedly changed: "a parent" led the list in Civil Code section 246 as against "a relative" in Field's draft; next came a relative, then one indicated by the wishes of a deceased parent, followed by one having charge of the child's support money, and concluding with "one of good moral character."[311] By the code amendments of 1873–1874, the fifth group was deleted, and the second, "a relative," moved to fourth place. These priorities were to determine the selection between "two persons equally eligible in other respects."[312] Not only was the Field draft provision considerably altered, but the relationship of

307. Cal. Stat. 1851, ch. 20.
308. Arts. VIII, IX.
309. Protocol of Querétaro 2d (1848).
310. Cal. Const. art. XI, § 14 (1849); see tenBroek, *California's Welfare Law—Origins and Development*, 45 Calif. L. Rev. 241, 242–43 (1957).
311. Cal. Civ. Code of 1872, § 246.
312. N.Y. Draft Civ. Code § 127, Cal. Civ. Code of 1872, § 246, amended by Code Amendments 1873–1874, at 196.

Civil Code section 246 to the quite differently worded section 1751 on the same subject in the Code of Civil Procedure was not indicated. Section 1751 was a reformulation of section 5 of the Guardians Act of 1850[313] and provided that "The father of the minor, if living, and in case of his decease the mother, while she remains unmarried, being themselves respectively competent to transact their own business and not otherwise unsuitable, must be entitled to the guardianship of the minor."

These were the California Codes of 1872, their sources, content, and treatment of family law. The areas in which California least depended on the New York drafts were those traditionally occupied by the legislature, the realm of political, economic, and broad social questions and the control of public and private institutions. This is principally the subject matter of the Political Code, and provision for the poor is a prime example. The poor law system of New York —drawn lock, stock, and barrel from the Elizabethan poor law system, embodied in the statutes of New York at great length, full of public stresses and pressures, incessantly tinkered with by the legislature, abounding in special procedures of a criminal nature, and distributing authority and duties to governmental bodies and officials, placed by the Field Commission in the Code of Criminal Procedure and in the Political Code or simply left in its earlier statutory form and presupposed by the codes—was omitted from the codes adopted in California in 1872. Out of its own history, California collected bits and pieces of earlier statutes and, conformably to their nature and to the nature of the Political Code, placed them among powers vested in the county boards of supervisors. On the other hand, with some historically necessary and some other modifications, California adopted outright the Field Draft Civil Code, dominantly a codification of the common law rather than of statutes and dealing with the civil rights and personal relationships of individuals, subjects traditionally left by the legislature to the courts and regarded by the courts as their special province.

Civil family law, including the law of the child, is a prime example. As drafted by Field and adopted in California, the Civil Code contained many civil family rules which conflicted with the family law of the poor as it existed in England and in New York: the paramount right of the parents to custody of the legitimate and

---

313. Cal. Stat. 1850, ch. 115.

the illegitimate child, the connection between the obligation to support and custody, the dual and differing obligations of the parents to support legitimate children, the mother's sole obligation to support illegitimate children, the inclusion of education in the obligation to support, and the relation of support to the wealth and position of the family exemplified by the requirement that it be "suitable to his [the child's] circumstances." At the same time, while this conflict existed and while, with a few minor exceptions, the Civil Code maintained the wall of separation between the family law of the poor and the family law of the rest of the community, the code's system of family law was prepared in contemplation of the contemporaneous existence of another system of family law for the poor. Neither in provision nor in administration did the Civil Code arrangement care for the needs of destitute persons in poor families, whether children or adults. Civil Code section 206 imposing civil liability on the relatives of the poor, concededly designed to establish the obligation of support independently of the poor law, was to provide a judicial remedy for persons outside the family who supplied necessaries, not to relieve poverty of one family member at the cost of another. It was an addition to the poor law, not a substitute for it. Again, whether the items supplied by the third party were necessary presumably was to be judged in the light of the wealth and position of the family, not in the light of the minimum standards of absolute necessity established by poor law officials.

One of the striking things about the history of these California provisions is that, in the twenty-nine year interval between the adoption of the codes in 1872 and the adoption of the Elizabethan poor law in 1901, the Civil Code provisions operated in the absence of their usual counterpart. The poor law system that was supplementary, complementary, and presupposed did not exist in the state. The welfare system which did exist, left intact by the codes, was quite different. It did not involve a general assumption of public responsibility for all classes of the poor, imposed as a mandatory requirement upon the units of local government, and it therefore lacked local settlement, removal, and responsibility-of-relatives provisions. Prior to 1901, the unique state program for aid to needy children stood almost alone as a productive source of separate rules for the family law of the poor. In many respects, these were of the same general character as those emanating from the Elizabethan

[907]

poor law, though the creative potency of the aid-to-needy-children program was not as high and the emphasis of the rules was somewhat different.

### The Courts, the Legislature, and the Civil Code in California[314]

California's experience with the family-law provisions of the Civil Code, with special attention to that part relating to parent and child, may be stated and illustrated by comparing it with the reasons given by Field for codification. The most noteworthy feature of that experience has been that the principal advantages of codification envisioned by Field have never been realized. Field saw the codes as a means of transferring the lawmaking function to the legislature and thereby of carrying into effect the democratic principles of American government and the general reform movement then under way, of making more possible the continual adaptation of the law to the changing conditions of society, of destroying the rigidity and removing the anachronisms of the common law, and of better protecting the rights and liberties of the people. "The question," said Field, ". . . is between written and unwritten law; that is to say, between law written by the lawgiver, and law not thus written; between law promulgated by that department of government which alone has the prerogative of making and promulgating the laws; and the law not so promulgated."[315] Under his theory of the constitution, it was the function of the judges "to administer the laws as they find them."[316] It was not their function to make the laws; that function had been assigned to the legislature, elected by the people for that purpose. English and American judges had shown themselves incapable of exercising the lawmaking art. "Nothing is more conspicuous in this history of jurisprudence than the tenacity . . . [with which they had clung to precedents] even though the reason for them has ceased and their mischiefs have become palpable."[317] "In almost every instance where an improvement has been made in the laws, it has come from the legislature."[318] The code "not only adapts itself to the

---

314. Leading articles upon this topic are Harrison, *The First Half-Century of the California Civil Code*, 10 Calif. L. Rev. 185 (1922); Kleps, *supra* note 281; Palmer & Selvin, *The Development of Law in California*, 1 West Ann. Cal. Codes—Const. 1 (1954); Parma, *supra* note 281; Pound, *supra* note 280, at 3.
315. *Introduction* to Draft N.Y. Civ. Code xiv.
316. *Id.* at xxxi.
317. *Id.* at xxvi.
318. *Id.* at xxvii.

present wants of society better than the existing common law,"[319] but it facilitated future progress. It would place before the legislature and the people "the whole body of the laws in an accessible and compact form, by which the relation of the several parts to each other and to the whole can be better seen, a defect in any part sooner discovered, and the particular amendment indicated which ought to be made."[320] The Field code, moreover, repudiated the maxim that statutes in derogation of the common law are to be strictly construed, by which the judges had buttressed the primacy and preserved the integrity of the common law against legislative efforts to provide remedies and make improvements.

In Field's view, thus, on the side of the codes were popular sovereignty, legislative lawmaking, flexible adaptation to change, and protection of the rights and liberties of the people. On the other side were arguments for a privileged judicial oligarchy, possessing a near monopoly of legal knowledge and administering laws of their own recollection or creation, full of anachronisms and incapable of adjustment to change.[321] It was argued that this system was suited to "countries where the conflicts between the different orders in a state render a written definition of their relative rights a difficult or an impossible task . . . ."[322] It was not suited to our country in which "we have no orders in the state; no classes of society clashing with each other." "[With us,] the will of the people is supreme law; that will is fitly expressed by their written constitution and their written laws. It should seem indeed to have no other fit expression."[323]

It is a conspicuous fact in the history of jurisprudence in California that the enactment by the legislature of the Civil Code did not change the character of that document as a restatement of the common law; nor did it change the function of the courts, as primarily responsible for the administration, interpretation, and continued evolution of the law. The Civil Code was not by enactment transported into the province of legislative concern and supervision.

---

319. *Id.* at xxv.
320. *Id.* at xxvi.
321. Field said, "The knowledge of the law is confined to a particular class; it is the interest of that class that it should be so confined; they keep the law scattered through thousands of books, where nobody can find it but themselves; they say to the people that from its very nature it must be so scattered; and they have had such influence with the people as to make most of them believe it." 20 Am. L. Rev. 1 (1886). The sealed books that now contain the laws "can be opened by codification and only by codification." *Id.* at 2.
322. Report of the Code Commissioners to the N.Y. Legislature viii (1865).
323. *Ibid.*

In a formal legal sense, it became part of the state's statutory law and as such was binding on the courts in a way different from that of the common law which it restated. But when we look beyond form to reality, no transformation was wrought. The legislature did little more than publish the Civil Code and give it publicity. The legislature did not create it or give it legal force but merely added to the legal force it already possessed. It did not determine the character of the code; that was imparted by judges and lawyers. It did not by enactment declare an intention actively to take over the field. Thereafter as theretofore the legislature was content to allow the judges to proceed almost with a free hand, only occasionally exerting its influence by remedial provison, usually related to some other area of more active legislative concern. In the area of the law of parent and child, most of the few legislative changes in the provisions of the Civil Code as adopted in 1872–1874 were a product of legislative interest in the family law of the poor extended beyond special statutes and the Welfare and Institutions Code, where the main body of that law was located.

The reasons for this history of the Civil Code in California are clear. First, attitudes of the legislature had not changed. Legislative passivity toward the subject matter of the Civil Code, momentarily interrupted by pressure from an active fragment of the bar and the spur of a general reform movement, was bound to resume its natural course and to prevail. Earlier pleading and practice conditions had grown so bad that the bar as a whole thought reform necessary; that plus the presence of Stephen J. Field seems to account for the Practice Acts of 1850 and 1851. The story of the other codes, however, appears to be quite different. No evidence exists of general pressure from the bar in California. For years efforts at statutory revision, sponsored by governors and a few interested lawyers, had come to naught. In New York the personality, purpose, and ability of David Dudley Field and a small band of attorney adherents had worked wonders, but in the end the Civil Code succumbed to the organized and articulate conservatism of the bar. Without the stimulus of Field's New York work and of the Field drafts, codification in California might well not have occurred in the nineteenth century.

California did not produce a David Dudley Field; it did produce, however, Charles Lindley, who was energetic, able, and devoted to codification. As a Code Commissioner, Lindley reports that he pushed through the plan of codes as against a lesser form of revision contemplated by the statute creating the commission.[324] But in a statement regrettably sparse in names, organizations, and particular events, Lindley characterized as "burlesque" the proceedings which "disgraced the pretended examination of the Codes by the . . . Legislature."[325] The codes moved through the legislature with a strange dearth of public controversy and debate and with unusual speed—Lindley thought, with unseemly haste. Trying to slow up action as premature, he complained bitterly that "the adroitness and energy of the management in carrying the work through the Legislature challenges the admiration of the most skillful manipulators."[326] If California did not have its David Dudley Field, neither did it have a James C. Carter who spoke for and aroused the organized bar, prevented adoption of the Civil Code in session after session of the New York Legislature, and prevailed only by a gubernatorial veto. California did have John Norton Pomeroy, distinguished law teacher and scholar, but he entered the fray after the codes were adopted and fought a mutilative rather than a preventive battle, although reasonably effectively.[327] Thus, basically the subject matter of the Civil Code did not engender conflicting and contending forces, political pressures and activity, broad and controversial questions of public law, or balancing of social and economic factors—all of which stimulate and are reflected in legislative examination, debate, and action. The absence of these in the past had assured this realm to the judges, with only sporadic and remedial intrusions by the legislature. Their continued absence operated with the same effect, unchanged by adoption of the code. Nothing

324. LINDLEY, CALIFORNIA CODE COMMENTARIES, app. at iii (1872). He felt impelled to transcend the legislative instructions, he tells us, because his "convictions were so full and clear" as to the necessity of codification, because "much of the work had been accomplished by the New York Commission and was ready for our use," and because "it was the time to make codes if they were ever to be made." For various reasons, including turmoil in the commission, his having fallen into a minority, and dissatisfaction with the way the work was going, Lindley resigned from the commission before the work was completed, but he continued an active role from the sidelines.

The San Francisco Chronicle, Jan. 7, 1872, p. 1, col. 3, reports: "Much surprise was caused this morning at the announcement . . . that Lindley resigned. From a perusal of his letters to the governor it appears that the labors of the Commission from the beginning of the term have been wanting in harmony, and moreover that the official notice to the Legislature by the Commissioners that the revision had ended and the Codes complete was not participated in by Mr. Lindley although his name was without his consent, attached to the notification. It is surmised that Mr. Lindley's untiring labors on the Commission have produced *temporary insanity*; many of his friends so declare." (Emphasis added.)

325. LINDLEY, *op. cit. supra* note 324, app. at vii.

326. *Id*. at v.

327. Ironically, too, Pomeroy's attacks on California's Civil Code helped to defeat adoption of Field's draft in New York.

had happened to change the attitudes and interests of the courts. Whatever the elements of reform in the Civil Code, it was still largely a summary of case law. The way thus lay open for the courts to rely on the common law to discover the meaning of the code, to govern its interpretation, and to shape its development. As Dean Pound points out, the judges and practitioners in California assumed "the [Civil] Code to be merely declaratory of what they had already learned and knew and had practiced."[328] This assumption was greatly strengthened by Professor Pomeroy's systematic analysis of the code and his formulation of an "unvarying rule" of construction: read the code as declaratory of the common law; interpret every provision as intended to be a mere statement of unchanged common-law doctrines with all of their consequences; construe all new, previously unused, and ambiguous phraseology as not designed to change the preexisting settled rules—do all this "unless from the unequivocal language of the provision a clear and certain intent appeared to alter the common law rule."[329] Pomeroy sponsored this approach, in part at least, for reasons exactly opposite from those advanced by Field for codification. The common-law doctrines, he wrote,

> while embodied in the code, under the authority of the legislature, would still retain the elasticity, the power of expansion and of adaptation to new facts and circumstances, and the comprehensiveness which belong to them in their original form as portions of "unwritten" common law,—or law promulgated by judicial decisions.[330]

> The peculiarity of statutes, on the other hand, is their rigidity. Statutory rules once enacted cannot be readily modified and expanded by the courts so as to cover new facts and relations not included within their expressed terms.[331]

Nothing could better illustrate the fluidity of statutes as interpreted by a skilled lawyer and therefore the ingenuousness of Pomeroy's conclusion than his own analysis of the Civil Code. And few things could better deflate Pomeroy's overt exuberance about the wisdom and adaptability of the common law than the judicial application of the common law of parent and child declared in the Civil Code.

---

328. Pound, *supra* note 280, at 12.
329. Pomeroy, *The Civil Code in California*, 3 & 4 West Coast Reporter 50 (1884 Reprint).
330. *Id*. at 55.
331. *Id*. at 53.

The California courts did in the main accept Pomeroy's approach to the code.[332] It must be admitted that "a clear and certain intent" to the contrary does not appear from any "unequivocal language" of the code itself. The Civil Code starts with a plain rule that seems to preclude Pomeroy's doctrine. "The rule of the common law," says section 4, "that statutes in derogation thereof are to be strictly construed, has no application to this Code. The Code establishes the law of this State respecting the subjects to which it relates, and its provisions are to be liberally construed with a view to effect its objects and to promote justice."[333] Legislative intent was made only a little less clear by the simultaneous reenactment in the Political Code of the statute of 1850 adopting the common law of England "so far as it is not repugnant to or inconsistent with . . . the Constitution or laws of the State of California . . . ."[334] The common law would not displace the law of the code respecting the subjects to which the code related, but questions of repugnancy and inconsistency would have to be decided. The door to judicial freedom, thus opened a crack, was flung wide by Civil Code sections 5 and 20. According to section 5, the provisions of the code, "so far as they are substantially the same as existing statutes or the common law, must be construed as continuations thereof, and not as new enactments."[335] So it is acknowledged that the law established by the code is at least in part declaratory of the common law, making it necessary for judges to determine that part by a liberal test of substantial similarity. Moreover, the judges were certainly free to conclude, as they did, that the common law so continued was the elastic common law adapted to the habits and conditions of our society then and in the future. No wonder that the Code Commissioners, when they took this section from a Massachusetts statute of 1858,[336] noted that it was "of doubtful propriety, though drawn from high

---

332. See cases cited in Harrison, *supra* note 314.

333. Cal. Civ. Code of 1872, § 4 (Haymond & Burch ed.). The Code Commissioners explain this section as follows: "The common law rule is correctly stated in the first sentence of this section. . . . However sound may be the arguments in favor of this rule, when applied to ordinary acts of the Legislature, it is apparent that it would be improper to apply it in all its severity to a system of laws intended, in a great measure, to take the place of the common law, and having in view, as its leading object, the furtherance of justice and a disregard of technical strictness. The provisions of such a system ought to be construed in the same manner, and with like force and effect, as they would be were the principles enunciated resting in the unwritten law, and it was to this end that the section has been made part of each of the Codes." Cal. Civ. Code of 1872, § 4, Code Comm'rs' Note.

334. Cal. Pol. Code of 1872, § 4468; Cal. Stat. 1850, ch. 95.

335. Cal. Civ. Code of 1872, § 5.

336. Mass. Rev. Laws 1858, ch. CLXXXII, § 9.

authority."[337] Thus restored to a customary common-law position by section 5 of the same code that contained section 4, the judge could only be baffled by section 20: "No statute, law, or rule is continued in force because it is consistent with the provisions of this Code on the same subject . . . ."[338] Whether consistent with its provisions, all earlier statutes, laws, and rules were repealed "unless expressly continued in force,"[339] by the code. But those statutes, laws, and rules "substantially the same"[340] as code provisions were continuations of them and were therefore "expressly continued in force."[341]

Beyond the persistence of preexisting legislative and judicial attitudes about the content of the Civil Code, two other factors required judicial freedom in the interpretation of the Civil Code. One was the incompleteness and defects of the code. Pomeroy's conclusion seems inescapable:

> Our civil code, regarded as a comprehensive system of statutory legislation, covering the entire private jurisprudence of the state, as a scientific or practical arrangement and statement of the principles, doctrines and rules constituting that jurisprudence . . . is . . . full of defects, imperfections, omissions and even inconsistencies, which must, so far as possible, be supplied, removed and harmonized by the courts, for it is useless to expect any real aid from the legislature.[342]

The second and complementary factor involved the relationship of the code to a multitude of special statutes already in existence and thereafter enacted. While the codes provided that they were to be read as continuations of earlier statutes on the same subject and for the repeal of all statutes not thus continued, no lost of repealed statutes was provided. Judicial determination of the statutes repealed by implication was a spectre which haunted the future. Moreover, the legislature which adopted the codes enacted numerous statutes which were not incorporated in the codes and many of which conflicted with them, thus as Lindley said, "commencing the destruction of the *system* simultaneously with its adoption."[343] Ralph

---

337. See Cal. Civ. Code § 5, ed. note (Deering ed. 1935).
338. Cal. Civ. Code of 1872, § 20.
339. *Ibid.*
340. Cal. Civ. Code of 1872, § 5.
341. Cal. Civ. Code of 1872, § 20.
342. Pomeroy, *supra* note 329, at 6. With this evaluation Lindley fully concurred: "However crude their condition, premature their adoption, tardy their publication, piecemeal or sudden their operation," "The Codes are accomplished facts." LINDLEY, *op. cit. supra* note 324, at 7. A revisory commission at the next session of the legislature introduced 400 pages of amendments to the code.
343. *Ibid.*

Kleps has explained how difficulties were caused "by the failure to repeal the legislation preceding the 1872 codes, by ambiguities in the commissioner's publication of *Statutes Continued in Force*, and as time passed, by the failure to integrate current legislation into the code system."[344] These difficulties were especially numerous and acute with respect to the law of parent and child.

## Judicial Interpretation of the California Civil Code

Judicial interpretation of the Civil Code sections dealing with the relationship of parent and child has not been uniform and harmonious, and the interpretive problems vary greatly as different sections and different groups of sections are considered. When the family is intact and enjoying domestic tranquility, no problems of the relationships of custody, care, control, education, support, and the right to earnings and services exist. These factors are either indistinguishably intermingled or apportioned and distributed by personality and other forces operating within a family unit. Legal authority and distinctions are seldom of controlling importance, undoubtedly accounting for the fact that no controversies between mother and father over the custody of children in an undivided family have ever reached the California appellate courts.

The 1872 Civil Code reflected common-law ideas about the make-up of the family and the distribution of authority and rights within it. The husband and father had the dominant role: he was head of the family,[345] he might choose the place of abode,[346] and he had custody of the legitimate children[347] and virtually of the wife, too, though Field thought his sections liberally relaxed the rigorous control previously vested in the husband over the wife, her property, and the children.[348] Under another family-relation concept derived from a different source, the Spanish Civil Law, but manifesting the same theme, the husband also had the management and control of the community property with as absolute a power of disposition, other than testamentary, as he had of his separate estate.[349] One

344. Kleps, *The Revision and Codification of California Statutes 1849–1953*, 42 Calif. L. Rev. 766, 779 (1954).

345. Cal. Civ. Code of 1872, § 156; Draft N.Y. Civ. Code § 76.

346. *Ibid.*; see Cal. Civ. Code of 1872, § 103; Hardenbergh v. Hardenbergh, 14 Cal. 654 (1860) (dictum) (he might even choose to live in California in the early days).

347. Cal. Civ. Code of 1872, § 197; Draft N.Y. Civ. Code § 90.

348. See Draft N.Y. Civ. Code § 90, Code Comm'rs' Note.

349. Cal. Civ. Code of 1872, § 172, amended in 1891, Cal. Stat. 1891, ch. 220, § 1, to preclude gift without consent and also in 1917, Cal. Stat. 1917, ch. 583, § 1, limiting the husband's power of disposition of the community property, personal and real.

might conjecture with Professor Armstrong that, while this legal rule vesting in the father the dominant custodial right may have played some part in the settlement of family arguments, "it is to be doubted that its role weighed heavily against other factors."[350] In 1913 the legislature amended the code equalizing the custodial rights of parents.[351] One might be less of a feminist than Barbara Armstrong and still join her in the belief that the principal importance of the legal change was a feeling of "gratification . . . at the replacement on our statute books of a Victorian and pre-Victorian statement by one in keeping with contemporary thought and custom."[352]

A quite different situation is portrayed by the treatment of the parent-child relationship when the family is disrupted or broken by divorce and the parents claim rights to or seek to escape responsibilities for the children. These sections immediately raise questions about custody as an integrative principle: the reciprocity of rights to control, services, and earnings on the one hand and the obligation of support and education on the other; the relative weight to be given the wishes of the parents as against an independent judicial judgment of the welfare of the children. The code sections are far from presenting a unified view or set of uniform standards.

Two sections govern disposition of custody between parents when the family is divided but marriage is still legally in existence. Drawn from an earlier California statute,[353] one section, 199, contains unclear and undefined ideas about natural rights of parents and children. It provides that, during marriage and without application of either parent for divorce, either spouse may bring an action for the exclusive control of the children and the court may then make such order "in regard to the support, care, custody, education, and control of the children . . . as may be just, and in accordance with the natural rights of the parents and the best interests of the children, and may at any time thereafter . . . vary . . . such order . . . as the natural rights and the interests of the parties, including the children, may require."[354] In section 214, drawn directly from the Field draft[355] and in part overlapping sec-

---

350. 2 Armstrong, California Family Law 961 (1953).
351. Cal. Civ. Code § 197.
352. 2 Armstrong, *op. cit. supra* note 350, at 961.
353. Cal. Stat. 1870, ch. CCXXVII, § 2.
354. Cal. Civ. Code § 199.
355. Draft N.Y. Civ. Code § 106.

tion 199, the best interests of the children are not thus counterbalanced with the natural rights of the parents, whatever they might be vis-à-vis each other, and the two sections accordingly seem to lay down conflicting or at least diverging rules for the same situation. The latter section applies "When a husband and wife live in a state of separation, without being divorced" and provides that the court might award the custody of the children to either parent "for such time and under such regulations as the case may require."[356] The court's decision must be guided by the best interests of the child's temporal, mental, and moral welfare, by the intelligent preference of the child, and by the "tender years" rule.[357]

Upon divorce discretion is vested in the courts to give such direction for the "custody, care, and education of the children . . . as may seem necessary or proper . . . ."[358] Standards by which to judge necessity or propriety are not supplied, and no mention is made of the natural interests of parents or of the best interests of children. In 1931 the legislature added to this section a provision about the best interests of the child, its intelligent choice, and its tender years.[359]

In interpreting these sections the appellate courts have largely ignored differences in standards or their complete absence and have tended, with some qualification, to follow a single path. The welfare of the children is prescribed as the test, and the trial court is permitted wide latitude in determining what would best promote that welfare in the particular case:

> The good of the child is regarded as the controlling force in directing its custody . . . . The morals of the parents, their financial condition, their subsequent marriage, the age of the child, and the devotion of either parent to its best interests are all factors to be weighed and considered by the

---

356. Cal. Civ. Code § 214.

357. Cal. Civ. Code of 1872, §§ 214, 246. Section 214 refers to § 246, which was repealed by Cal. Stat. 1931, ch. 281, § 1700, and reenacted as Cal. Prob. Code §§ 1406–09. Notwithstanding the repeal, § 214 continued to refer to § 246 and still does even though in 1955 a new § 246 was enacted which sets forth factors to be considered in awarding support.

358. Cal. Civ. Code of 1872, § 138. Section 138 was amended in 1905 to read "custody, care, education, maintenance and support . . . ." The amendments of 1951 bring the statute to its present form by (1) omitting "care, education, maintenance and support" in the first sentence; (2) omitting "in respect to its temporal and its mental and moral welfare" in subdivision (1). For complete changes see Cal. Stat. 1951, ch. 1700, § 6.

359. Cal. Civ. Code § 138. This unconfined discretion was withheld in the case of a marriage annulled on the ground of force or fraud; the court was required to award the children to the innocent parent. Cal. Civ. Code of 1872, § 84. This provision was deleted by Cal. Stat. 1951, ch. 230. The custody of the children was thus to be used to reward innocence and punish guilt.

court. All such applications are addressed to the sound legal discretion of the court below, and its conclusion will not be disturbed here, except it should clearly appear that its discretion has been abused.[360]

In custody determinations between the parents in the absence of divorce proceedings, the courts have relegated Civil Code section 199, with its requirement of attention to the natural rights of the parents, to a subordinate and almost unnoticed position and have emphasized instead the provisions of Civil Code section 214, with its incorporated mandate that the decision is to be guided by the temporal, mental, and moral welfare of the child.[361] In cases of prior divorce or present action for it, the courts have exercised their freedom to dispose of the custody of the children under the code injunction to do what is "necessary or proper" by proclaiming the best interests of the child to be the governing standard. The code sections presumptively preferring the father or mother on a basis of the child's age have been melted into the common rule. The presumption is to operate, "other things being equal,"[362] although the courts seldom find them so. In any event, the presumption, say the courts, cannot be understood as disregarding the best interest of the child. "The trial court, when faced with two fit parents must give consideration to the best interests of the children, and in determining that fact has a broad discretion in deciding whether other things are equal."[363]

Generally, the parent at fault in an action for separate maintenance, divorce, or annulment has not been held ineligible for the custody of the children. Although innocence or guilt has apparently played a role in some instances,[364] in the main the rule stated

360. Crater v. Crater, 135 Cal. 633, 634–35, 67 Pac. 1049, 1050 (1902). See also Taber v. Taber, 209 Cal. 755, 756–57, 290 Pac. 36, 37 (1930): "In the first instance it is for the trial court to determine, after considering all the evidence, how the best interests of the child will be subserved. The question is to be determined solely from the standpoint of the child, and the feelings and desires of the contesting parties are not to be considered, except in so far as they affect the best interests of the child."

361. See Guardianship of Cantwell, 125 Cal. App. 2d 866, 271 P.2d 168 (1st Dist. 1954); Campbell v. Campbell, 103 Cal. App. 2d 848, 230 P.2d 433 (2d Dist. 1951); Cole v. Superior Court, 28 Cal. App. 1, 151 Pac. 169 (3d Dist. 1915).

362. "As between parents adversely claiming the custody or guardianship, neither parent is entitled to it as of right; but other things being equal, if the child is of tender years, it should be given to the mother; if it is of an age to require education and preparation for labor or business, then to the father." Cal. Civ. Code of 1872, § 246(2) (now CAL. CIV. CODE § 138(2)). As to guardianship see CAL. PROB. CODE § 1408.

363. Clayton v. Clayton, 117 Cal. App. 2d 7, 11, 254 P.2d 669, 671 (4th Dist. 1953). See also Munson v. Munson, 27 Cal. 2d 659, 166 P.2d 268 (1946); Morgan v. Morgan, 103 Cal. App. 2d 776, 230 P.2d 130 (4th Dist. 1951); Priest v. Priest, 90 Cal. App. 2d 185, 202 P.2d 561 (2d Dist. 1949); Booth v. Booth, 69 Cal. App. 2d 496, 159 P.2d 93 (1st Dist. 1945); Phillips v. Phillips, 48 Cal. App. 2d 404, 119 P.2d 736 (3d Dist. 1941).

364. See 2 ARMSTRONG, *op. cit. supra* note 350, at 972–73.

in the *Cozza* case[365] seems to have prevailed. In that case the trial court awarded custody to the mother while granting the husband a divorce on the ground of cruelty. The supreme court found no impropriety in this disposition:

> There is nothing in the fact that a mother has been guilty of cruelty toward her husband which compels the court in awarding him a decree on that ground to also award the custody of the children to him. The weightiest and most natural considerations looking exclusively to the welfare of the children—their tender years, her conceded affection and love for them, the mental and moral and even material advantages which they will derive by being left with her . . . make it highly important that the court should so decree . . . .[366]

During marriage and upon divorce the code authorizes the court's order to encompass support, care, custody, education, control,[367] and maintenance.[368] The courts have always construed these provisions to list elements which may be distributed as the courts see fit and thus to permit the allocation of custody to one parent and the obligation of support to the other.[369]

Little can be learned from the interparent custody cases about the rules to be applied when the contest is between one or both parents and a stranger. As used by the courts, "stranger" includes all relatives other than parents as well as outsiders. But the developed judicial attitudes and the code sections are quite different in the two situations. When parents quarrel over their rights to or responsibilities for the children, with few exceptions the courts declare that they will be guided by the children's best interests, moderate and equalize parental rights by making the claims of both subject to this test, and diminish the integrative function of custody by separating the right to custody and the obligation of support. When the contest is between one or both parents and a stranger, the courts have (1) adhered to and amplified the primary role of custody in parent-child relations, (2) elaborated and strengthened a

---

365. In the Matter of the Adoption of Cozza, 163 Cal. 514, 126 Pac. 161 (1912).

366. *Id.* at 526, 126 Pac. at 166. See also Lampson v. Lampson, 171 Cal. 332, 153 Pac. 238 (1915) (custody of two-year-old child given to defendant wife found guilty of desertion); Lawatch v. Lawatch, 161 Cal. App. 2d 780, 329 P.2d 603 (2d Dist. 1958); Morgan v. Morgan, 103 Cal. App. 2d 776, 230 P.2d 130 (4th Dist. 1951); In the Matter of De Leon, 70 Cal. App. 1, 232 Pac. 738 (3d Dist. 1924); 3 WITKIN, SUMMARY OF CALIFORNIA LAW 2439–40 (1960).

367. CAL. CIV. CODE § 199.

368. Cal. Civ. Code of 1872, § 138, as amended, Cal. Stat. 1905, ch. 49, § 1 (now CAL. CIV. CODE § 138).

369. See Lewis v. Lewis, 174 Cal. 336, 163 Pac. 42 (1917); People v. Schlott, 162 Cal. 347, 122 Pac. 846 (1912).

doctrine of paramount parental right to guardianship and custody of children, (3) subordinated the independent judicial determination of the children's best interests, and (4) developed the principle that the child is a chattel.

The California Supreme Court has said that custody "embraces the sum of parental rights with respect to the rearing of a child, including its care. It includes the right to the child's services and earnings . . . and the right to direct his activities and make decisions regarding his care and control, education, health and religion."[370] So also does custody embrace the sum of parental duties. The Civil Code is explicit that the parent entitled to custody is under an obligation to provide support and education.[371] Thus, third persons supplying necessaries to a child in good faith may recover[372] from a parent neglecting to provide them "for his child who is under his charge." Does the negative proposition follow—that he who does not have custody need not support? This is the form in which the issue often reaches the courts, and the courts have held affirmatively.[373]

So far, judicial decision has closely followed the literal command of the code plus a reasonable, if not a palpable, inference from it. Not so, however, when we come to questions about the character of parental rights to custody, the nature of parental interest in the child, and the degree to which courts will exercise independent judgment upon what disposition of the child will best serve his well-being. These find their most emphatic expression in the remarkable language of the old but still leading case of *In re Campbell*, the spirit and rhetoric of which persist in modern California judicial opinions:

> Under the general law, and independently of the provisions of the codes, the father has a natural right to the care and custody of his child (2 Kent's Commentaries, 205; Schouler on Domestic Relations, secs. 245–48); and this right is recognized by the provisions of our codes (Civ. Code, sec. 197; Code Civ. Proc., sec. 1751); which are to be regarded as but a re-expression of the principles of the common law governing the subject. (Civ. Code, sec. 5.) The father's right, at least so far as the services of the child are concerned, is strictly a property right, for the loss of which—as in the case of servants generally—an action could at common law be maintained; and in other respects the right, though not com-

370. Burge v. San Francisco, 41 Cal. 2d 608, 617, 262 P.2d 6, 12 (1953).
371. CAL. CIV. CODE § 196.
372. CAL. CIV. CODE § 207.
373. See Selfridge v. Paxton, 145 Cal. 713, 79 Pac. 425 (1905); Calegaris v. Calegaris, 4 Cal. App. 264, 87 Pac. 561 (1st Dist. 1906).

monly spoken of as such, is of essentially the same nature as the right of property. For though the subject of the right is not salable, it is valuable, and of all species of property the most valuable to the parent. Hence it is a mistake to suppose that the right of the father is merely fiduciary. It is that; but it is also—like the right of the child in the father—a right vested in him for his own benefit, and of which it would be a personal injury to deprive him. The right must therefore be regarded as coming within the reason, if not within the strict letter, of the constitutional provisions for the protection of property. (Beatty, C. J., in *Ex parte Miller*, 109 Cal. 662.)

The father's right is, however, coupled with the obligation to support and educate the child (Civ. Code, sec. 196), and is also qualified and strictly limited by the fact that the child itself is a human being, and as such vested with rights for which it is entitled to protection. . . .

Accordingly, by the provisions of section 1751 of the Code of Civil Procedure, it is made the duty of the court to appoint the father or mother of the minor, "if found by the court competent to discharge the duties of guardianship." But under this provision, and under the general law, the *prima facie* presumption is that the parent is competent; and hence the court is not authorized to appoint another as guardian, unless it finds to the contrary. Hence the section is to be construed as if it read that the father or mother is to be appointed "if not found by the court incompetent" . . . .[374]

The opinion's emphasis on Civil Code section 197 and Code of Civil Procedure section 1751 as "but a re-expression of the principles of the common law" which governed the subject in the absence of statutory provision laid one foundation for continued adherence to the case's rule of paramount parental right after section 1751 was repealed.[375] It aided the rule in withstanding such persistent attacks as that of the *Casad* case,[376] which maintained that the rule had been "disapproved by the legislature in the repeal of section 1751" and that therefore the *Campbell* opinion "is merely an interesting treatise on the subject of an obsolete law."[377]

---

374. 130 Cal. 380, 382–83, 62 Pac. 613, 614 (1900).
375. Cal. Stat. 1931, ch. 281, § 1700.
376. Guardianship of Casad, 106 Cal. App. 2d 134, 234 P.2d 647 (3d Dist. 1951).
377. *Id.* at 149; 234 P.2d at 656. See also Guardianship of Smith, 42 Cal. 2d 91, 102–03, 265 P.2d 888, 895 (1954) (Schauer, J., dissenting): "The holdings of *In re Campbell* (1900), 130 Cal. 380 [62 Pac. 613], and *In re Mathews* (1917), 174 Cal. 679 [164 Pac. 8] (see also *Estate of Wise* (1918), 179 Cal. 423, 426 [177 Pac. 277]) . . . are both based upon the specific language of the first sentence of former section 1751 of the Code of Civil Procedure. That sentence was, however, repealed in 1931, and not reenacted, although the other provisions of the section were reenacted as sections 1406 and 1410 of the Probate Code. It thus appears that the Legislature, in recognition of what seems to me to be the protest expressed by this court in *In re Mathews, supra*, and *Estate of Wise, supra*, against statutes construed to require that the property right of a parent in a child be considered superior to the best interest and welfare of the child, wisely decided to, and did, remove such requirement from the law of this state."

However, statutory authority is still claimed for the rule of paramount parental right. In the codes of 1872, four sections—Civil Code sections 197, 200, and 246 and Code of Civil Procedure section 1751—dealt with the factors determinative of the right to custody. Civil Code sections 197 and 200 declare the parents' right to the custody of their children but contain no suggestion that parental right is qualified by the best interests of the children or terminated by the unfitness of the parents. Code of Civil Procedure section 1751 dealt specifically with guardianship, proclaiming that the parents, "being themselves respectively competent to transact their own business, and not otherwise unsuitable," were entitled to be appointed guardians.[378] Civil Code section 246 dealt with custody awards as well as with guardianship; here again the parental right was one of preference, not of absolute right, and the parent was to be "preferred" only if he was one "of two persons equally entitled to the custody in other respects." What other respects; what other persons? Under Civil Code sections 197 and 200 there were no other persons than the parents and no other respects than parentage in which to be equal. Apparently, the other respects in which others might achieve equal or impliedly superior right under section 246 were equivalent to the "best interests" of the child laid down in the first part of section 246 as a guide for awarding custody or appointing guardians. Thus sections 197 and 200 settled title to custody on the parents absolutely, section 1751 gave them a preference as long as they were found by the court to be competent, and section 246 allowed them to have the child if its best interests would not be better served by giving it to some other person. Following the *Campbell* opinion, the courts emphasized section 1751, parental competency, and guardianship matters, usually without reference to Civil Code sections 197 and 200; preferred section 1751's competency to section 246's child's interest; and further diminished the role of section 246 by employing the *Campbell* presumption of parental fitness, which required an affirmative finding of unfitness before avoiding the parental right. Notwithstanding the importance earlier attributed to section 1751, its repeal did not change the judicial assertion of code sanction for the rule of paramount parental

---

378. Cal. Code Civ. Proc. 1872, § 1751, amended by Cal. Stat. 1891, ch. CXXIII, to read: "The father or the mother of a minor child under the age of fourteen years, if found by the Constitution competent to discharge the duties of guardianship, is entitled to be appointed a guardian of such minor child, in preference to any other person . . . ."

right. Since that repeal, the courts have given Civil Code sections 197 and 200 greater prominence and have suggested that section 246 was permanently affected by its earlier association with section 1751. Accordingly, they have held that section 197 and 246 should be "construed" together[379] and that Probate Code section 1407 is "substantially the same" as former Civil Code section 246 (3) and Code of Civil Procedure section 1751.[380] The more the statutes change, therefore, the more they remain the same, and the doctrine of the *Campbell* case, whether as common law or as legislative enactment, has the steady adherence of the supreme court of the state.[381]

The enduring rule of the *Campbell* case is that parents have a paramount right to their children unless they are affirmatively found to be unfit. The claims of other relatives and of strangers based on any grounds, including the best interests of the children, must give way to this right. In reaffirming the *Campbell* rule, the supreme court said in the *Roche* case that the law presumes "in the absence of either evidence or findings showing the contrary" the parents are fit persons.[382] The courts have applied the rule in custody as well as guardianship proceedings, in modification orders as well as in original orders. They have sustained it against evasion; it "may not be thwarted by the artifice of giving a fit parent bare legal control while denying actual physical care and custody."[383] Accordingly, the order of a trial judge giving joint control to both parents but physical care to the grandparents was reversed.

One of the two bases of the *Campbell* opinion for the rule of paramount parental right—that "the father's right . . . [to] the services of the child . . . is strictly a property right . . . and in other respects the right . . . is of essentially the same nature as the

---

379. Roche v. Roche, 25 Cal. 2d 141, 152 P.2d 999 (1944).

380. Stewart v. Stewart, 41 Cal. 2d 447, 452, 260 P.2d 44, 47 (1953).

381. See Guardianship of Smith, 42 Cal. 2d 91, 265 P.2d 888 (1954); Stewart v. Stewart, *supra* note 380; Roche v. Roche, 25 Cal. 2d 141, 152 P.2d 999 (1944); Stever v. Stever, 6 Cal. 2d 166, 56 P.2d 1229 (1936); Wilkinson v. Wilkinson, 105 Cal. App. 2d 392, 233 P.2d 639 (3d Dist. 1951); Becker v. Becker, 94 Cal. App. 2d 830, 211 P.2d 598 (2d Dist. 1949); Guardianship of Sloot, 92 Cal. App. 2d 296, 206 P.2d 862 (3d Dist. 1949); Robertson v. Robertson, 72 Cal. App. 2d 129, 164 P.2d 52 (3d Dist. 1945); Juri v. Juri, 61 Cal. App. 2d 815, 143 P.2d 708 (3d Dist. 1943); *In re* White, 54 Cal. App. 2d 637, 129 P.2d 706 (3d Dist. 1942); Guardianship of McCoy, 46 Cal. App. 2d 494, 116 P.2d 103 (2d Dist. 1941); Guardianship of DeRuff, 38 Cal. App. 2d 529, 101 P.2d 521 (2d Dist. 1940); Eddleman v. Eddleman, 27 Cal. App. 2d 343, 80 P.2d 1009 (4th Dist. 1938); Newby v. Newby, 55 Cal. App. 114, 202 Pac. 891 (2d Dist. 1921).

382. Roche v. Roche, *supra* note 381, at 143, 152 P.2d at 999, citing Stever v. Stever, *supra* note 381.

383. 25 Cal. 2d at 144, 152 P.2d at 1000.

right of property"[384]—has gradually lost its prominence but not necessarily its life. Five years after the *Campbell* decision, the United States district court in San Francisco declined to give credence to the idea that the right of the parent must "be regarded as coming within the reason, if not within the strict letter, of the consitutional provisions for the protection of property."[385] The thesis that a child is a chattel is no longer asserted in support of the rule by its friends but only charged against it by its enemies, being treated disparagingly in supreme court dissenting opinions and in majority opinions in the district courts of appeal manifesting displeasure with the rule.[386]

The second basis of the *Campbell* opinion—that "the father has a natural right to the care and custody of his child"—has been accepted generally and prevails among the judges who support the rule. For this basis the *Campbell* opinion relies on Chancellor Kent.[387] Beyond Kent stood his model Blackstone who acknowledged Puffendorf and Montesquieu as sources of this doctrine.[388] But this is one of the naturalistic principles of the Roman civil law received by the common-law writers.[389] According to the civil-law principle the right of the parent is not "essentially the same nature

---

384. *In re* Campbell, 130 Cal. 380, 382, 62 Pac. 613, 614 (1900). The *Campbell* opinion's citation of *Ex parte* Miller, 109 Cal. 662, 42 Pac. 428 (1895), was not altogether in point. The reference was the dissenting opinion in which Mr. Chief Justice Beatty only claimed that "The natural right of a parent to the custody and society of his child is certainly equal in dignity and importance to any right of property, and ought not to be taken away with less deliberation than would be required if the controversy were over a cart or a horse." *Id.* at 662, 42 Pac. at 428.

385. See Wadleigh v. Newhall, 136 Fed. 941 (N.D. Cal. 1905), quoting *In re Campbell, supra* note 384.

386. Thus Mr. Justice Schauer, dissenting in *Roche v. Roche*, said: "The majority opinion cites cases which in turn rely upon In re Campbell, . . . the leading case upon the subject . . . . [In that case,] the child is regarded somewhat as a chattel and the property interest therein of the parent is made paramount to the best interests of the child." 25 Cal. 2d at 144–45, 152 P.2d at 1000. In *Stewart v. Stewart* Mr. Justice Schauer wrote, in a dissent, that the matter should be determined on the basis of the best interests of the children "and not any theory of Divine—or mercenary—parental right." 41 Cal. 2d at 454, 260 P.2d at 49. In his dissent in Guardianship of Smith, 42 Cal. 2d 91, 103, 265 P.2d 888, 896 (1954), Mr. Justice Schauer reemphasized the same theme: "To place this property right conception of a parent's claim to children over and above the welfare of the children seems to me to be a throwback of generations if not of centuries." *Ibid.* In Shea v. Shea, 100 Cal. App. 2d 60, 65, 223 P.2d 32, 34 (1950), the First District Court of Appeal wrote in an opinion very critical of the paramount parental right rule, "California has, in effect, adopted the harsh rule that the right of a fit and proper parent to have the custody of his child is somewhat in the nature of a property right and paramount to the welfare and best interests of the child." Guardianship of Casad, 106 Cal. App. 2d 134, 234 P.2d 647 (1951), refused to follow the *Campbell* doctrine.

387. *In re* Campbell, 130 Cal. 381, 382, 62 Pac. 613, 614 (1900), citing 2 KENT, COMMENTARIES *203.

388. 1 BLACKSTONE, COMMENTARIES 447 (Cooley ed. 1899).

389. See Radin, *The Rivalry of Common-Law and Civil-Law Ideas in the American Colonies,* in 2 LAW, A CENTURY OF PROGRESS 1835–1935, at 404 (1937).

as the right of property." It is not "a right vested in him for his own benefit" but is conferred in order to enable him to discharge his natural duties of maintenance and protection, duties "laid on [him] by nature herself," "implanted by Providence in the breast of every parent, augmented by the parent's voluntary assumption of responsibility through the act of begetting."[390] This is exactly the doctrine taken by Kent: "The wants and weaknesses of children render it necessary that some person maintain them, and the voice of nature has pointed out the parent as the most fit and proper person."[391] The natural duties of the parent to maintain and educate the child during infancy and youth and to make reasonable provision for his future usefulness and happiness are discharged because they are natural and are prompted by "the strength of natural affection."[392]

The common-law concept is to be contrasted. It goes back to feudal principles of custody and a proprietary right in the person, marriage, and land of the heir.[393] Less distantly, it goes back to the pecuniary relationship of master and servant as an analogue.[394] Because these original relationships were proprietary and pecuniary, the common-law emphasis is on parental right rather than on parental duty imposed by nature and expressed in the civil law. If Kent and Blackstone, Puffendorf and Montesquieu are authority for the parental-right doctrine, then it is a very different doctrine from the one asserted in *Campbell*, both as to right to custody and as to its content. In the *Campbell* opinion and in the Civil Code these contradictory origins and doctrines are thrown together without a conscious attempt at selection or system.

Contemporary cases speak of the natural right of the parent in the same way that earlier cases spoke of the property right, exalting the right and subordinating the duty, referring to the right almost in the Lockean sense of natural rights with overtones of absoluteness and inalienability. "One of the natural rights incident to parenthood, a right supported by law and sound public policy, is the right to the care and custody of a minor child, and this right can

---

390. 1 Blackstone, *op. cit. supra* note 388, at 447.
391. 2 Kent, Commentaries *189.
392. 2 *id.* at *190.
393. 1 Pollock & Maitland, History of English Law Before the Time of Edward I, at 303 (1895).
394. See Blackstone, *op. cit. supra* note 388, at 450; 1 Hawkins, Pleas of the Crown 458–59 (1716); Plucknett, A Concise History of the Common Law 545 (5th ed. 1956); Radin, *supra* note 389, at 503.

only be forfeited by a parent upon proof that the parent is unfit to
have such care and custody."[395] At times, however, some semblance
to Kent's and Blackstone's theories creep in: "In the case of a child
of tender years, experience has taught that in the vast majority of
cases there is no one who will give such complete and selfless devotion, and so unhesitatingly and unstintingly make the sacrifices
which the welfare of the child demands, as the child's own
mother."[396]

Mr. Justice Traynor, in his concurring opinion in *Guardianship
of Smith*,[397] restated the parental right doctrine in terms of preference rather than right, recast the concept of parental fitness in terms
of the best interests of the child, and placed the rule upon its best
possible modern footing:

> The objection to the rule that custody must be awarded to the parent
> unless he is unfit carries the harsh implication that the interests of the
> child are subordinated to those of the parent when the trial court has
> found that the best interests of the child would be served by giving his
> custody to another. The heart of the problem, however, is how the best
> interests of the child are to be served. Is the trial court more sensitive than
> the parent to what the child's best interests are, better qualified to de-
> termine how they are to be served? It would seem inherent in the very
> concept of a fit parent that such a parent would be at least as responsive
> as the trial court, and very probably more so, to the best interests of the
> child. The rule requiring that custody be awarded to such a parent in
> preference to a stranger does not operate to subordinate the interests of the
> child to those of the parent; it merely serves to define the area of the
> parent's responsibility for the welfare of the child. The court's statu-
> tory duty to be "guided by what appears to be for the best interests of the
> child in respect to its temporal and mental and moral welfare" (Prob.
> Code sec. 1406) encompasses the view that the child's welfare is part of
> the responsibility of a fit parent.[398]

Thus, while the "child-is-a-chattel" explanation of paramount
parental right has been subordinated, the rhetoric of fundamental
parental right continues, though a judicial tendency is emerging
to indicate that paramount parental right is simply shorthand
for the proposition that parents generally are more likely than

---

395. Wilkinson v. Wilkinson, 105 Cal. App. 2d 392, 398, 233 P.2d 639, 642–43 (3d
Dist. 1951), quoting *In re* White, 54 Cal. App. 2d 637, 640, 129 P.2d 706, 708 (3d Dist.
1942).

396. Wilkinson v. Wilkinson, *supra* note 395, at 424, 233 P.2d at 644, quoting with
approval Robertson v. Robertson, 72 Cal. App. 2d 129, 135, 164 P.2d 52, 56 (3d Dist.
1945).

397. 42 Cal. 2d 91, 265 P.2d 888 (1954).

398. *Id*. at 94, 265 P.2d at 891 (concurring opinion).

strangers to give children the care they need because of the nature of parenthood. However difficult to explain, whatever the analogues and beliefs about natural impulses, the rule of the *Campbell* case is the law of the state. The parents, unless found unfit by the court, have a paramount right to the custody of their children, a rule given full importance by the treatment of custody as a summation of rights and duties to children.

# 5

# The Development of
# Public Aid Programs and
# the Family Law
# of the Poor

In the extent, character, and chronology of state government relief payments, in the inauguration and evolution of particular programs and of relationships between state, county, town, and private agencies, in the concentration on almshouses and their retention long after their decline elsewhere in the country, in the late reception of the Elizabethan poor law system, and in some aspects of the plan for the care of needy children, the development of California's welfare system was eccentric. Partly as a result of these unusual circumstances and partly in response to their common causes, California was slow in developing a distinct system of family law for the poor, and some of its traditional stages were inverted, but its ultimate formation was not thereby prevented or its characteristic features affected. The assumption of public responsibility for the support of the destitute manifested the same concomitants and produced the same effects as in English and American experience elsewhere.

The explanation for California's atypical welfare development lies in its Spanish-Mexican inheritance and in the peculiar conditions of Anglo-American settlement. The first was effective principally in the southern half of the state, the second in the northern. Curiously, they combined to require a welfare system dominated by the state and to retard the adoption of a full-fledged Elizabethan poor law system. Since the Spanish and English were both parts of a common Western European civilization, their political and their institutional systems, including welfare, contained common elements and similar features. However, there were significant variations. The Spanish employed a mixed system of private, religious, town, and central government responsibility for care of the needy, with varying emphasis, program by program and place by place, on the contributions of the different welfare agencies but with a pronounced role of the Church throughout. The central concept of the Elizabethan poor law had not been achieved. The Spanish had no comprehensive system of poor laws establishing general government responsibility to aid the poor, fixing the extent and character of the aid to be granted, determining the conditions of eligibility, and assigning powers and duties to particular governmental units for administering aid. As a result of the absence of an assumption of public responsibility, the Spanish system contained few provisions about the financial obligation of relatives legally liable for the support of their dependent kin; and as a result of the failure to impose public responsibility on units of local government, the Spanish paid little attention to settlement and removal rules to determine eligibility for aid. The Spanish evolved a pattern of care for dependent, delinquent, and homeless children through apprenticeship, informal placement in private families, and upbringing in orphanages, predominantly religiously sponsored and oriented. This was also true of the Elizabethan poor law system, but in it greatest emphasis was on apprenticeship, while the Spanish system emphasized church-supported orphanages and informal distribution to families.[399]

Gold-rush settlement in the northern part of the state drastically affected the makeup and distribution of the population, the circumstances of life, the needs to be met, and the statewide character of measures required to meet them; virtual irrelevance of a family law of the poor resulted. There were few families; single males predominated. Newcomers generally did not settle in established communities; they did not come to clear the wilderness or till the soil. They moved about feverishly in the mining areas and the neighboring towns. County and town government, adjusted to localized and largely agrarian existence, encompassed only a small part of the lives and activities of the new Californians. Their needs could only be met by a government with territorial jurisdiction as great as the area which they traversed in their shifting and semi-nomadic habits and occupations. Settlement rules, designed for settled societies, and relatives' responsibility, designed for societies organized into families, were strikingly inapplicable.

As a result of travel conditions, overland or by water, and of

---

399. See generally tenBroek, *California's Welfare Law—Origins and Development*, 45 CALIF. L. REV. 241 (1957).

living conditions upon arrival, widespread deficiency diseases and communicable maladies presented the first and most pressing health and welfare problem,[400] which scarce private charities[401] and partially formed town and county governments, singly or in combination,[402] were hopelessly incapable of solving. The state legislature necessarily stepped into the breach with a rapidly changing series of regulation and relief measures, including quarantine and other health measures in San Francisco,[403] the creation of state hospitals at Sacramento[404] and San Francisco,[405] principal points of entry, and at Stockton,[406] a center for moving to and from the mines, and medical care and other assistance to overland travelers before and while crossing the Sierra Nevadas.[407] As emergency pressures subsided and local government units and private charities were increased and strengthened, direct state programs largely gave way to mixed state-county[408] or state-private operations. In 1855 a plan was initiated providing state subsidies to counties for the support and care of the indigent sick.[409] Administration was left entirely to the counties, including decisions about the character and extent of support and medical care to be provided, the conditions of eligibility, and whether such support and care were to be supplied in hospitals or at home.[410] The 1855 act was expanded in 1860 to include other groups.[411] The counties were

---

400. HARRIS, CALIFORNIA MEDICAL HISTORY 67–99 (1932); PRASLOW, THE STATE OF CALIFORNIA: A MEDICO-GEOGRAPHICAL ACCOUNT 15, 46, 55–56, 58 (Cordes transl. 1939); SOULE, GIHON & NISBET, THE ANNALS OF SAN FRANCISCO 587–91 (1855); TYSON, DIARY OF A PHYSICIAN IN CALIFORNIA 70 (1850).

401. See, *e.g.*, San Francisco Alta, Dec. 22, 1841, p. 1, col. 4 (announcing the formation of the Public Association for the Relief of Destitution and Distress); *id.*, Dec. 22, 1851, p. 2, col. 5 (announcing the formation of the French Benevolent Society); 7 BANCROFT, HISTORY OF CALIFORNIA 705–07 (1890).

402. See San Francisco Alta, Feb. 4, 1850, p. 2, col. 3. Governor Burnett and Albert Priest had each donated one thousand dollars to the City Council of Sacramento, Governor Burnett for charitable purposes and Mr. Priest for the relief of the sick and distressed. See HARRIS, *op. cit. supra* note 400, at 101–03, 108–16.

403. Cal. Stat. 1850, ch. 66, repealed Cal. Stat. 1851, ch. 69; Cal. Stat. 1850, ch. 64, repealed Cal. Stat. 1851, ch. 50; Cal. Stat. 1852, ch. LXVI, § 1; Cal. Pol. Code of 1872, § 2993; Cal. Stat. 1853, ch. XXII, at 35, Cal. Pol. Code of 1872, § 3045; PRASLOW, *op. cit. supra* note 400, at 22–23. For a later act with equally sweeping quarantine and other health provisions to be effected in San Francisco see Cal. Stat. 1869–1870, ch. CCCCXC.

404. Cal. Stat. 1851, ch. 127.

405. Cal. Stat. 1850, ch. 65.

406. Cal. Stat. 1851, ch. 129.

407. Cal. Stat. 1852, ch. XXXV; ELDREDGE, HISTORY OF CALIFORNIA 256–58 (1901); FANKHAUSER, FINANCIAL HISTORY OF CALIFORNIA Table IV (1913).

408. Cal. Stat. 1855, ch. LVII.

409. *Ibid.*

410. The boards of supervisors were required to make a semiannual report to the state comptroller on the expenditure of the state funds. Cal. Stat. 1855, ch. LVII, § 2.

411. Cal. Stat. 1860, ch. CCXLVII, § 20, amended to except certain counties, Cal. Stat. 1870, ch. CCXLV. See generally Johnson v. County of Santa Clara, 28 Cal. 545 (1865).

empowered, "whenever in their opinion such a measure would
be advantageous," to establish "infirmaries for the relief of the
indigent," which were to care for the destitute infirm whatever
the source of their infirmity, "the indigent laboring under con-
tagious diseases,"[412] and every "poor person who is blind, lame, old,
sick, impotent, or decrepit, or in any other way disabled or enfeebled, so as to be unable by his or her work, to maintain themselves . . . ."[413] This county authority was in effect confirmed by
the County Government Act of 1872, embodied in California Political Code section 4046, and subsequent county government
acts.[414] In the two decades following 1860, state subsidies were
given to a number of general hospitals, to homes for aged women,
to the San Francisco Municipal Home for the Care of the Inebriate,
to the Howard Benevolent Society for general purposes and for
the care of flood victims, and to the Los Angeles Free Dispensary.[415]

The 1879 constitution gave mandatory direction and fresh im-
petus to welfare trends already under way: it segregated and specialized programs, accelerated establishment of state institutions,
withdrew state financial aid to some groups, and prescribed the
form of state grant to others. It forbade any withdrawals from the
state treasury or gifts of property "for the use or benefit of any corporation, association, asylum, hospital, or any other institution not
under the exclusive management and control of the state as a state
institution."[416] Special subsidies to particular institutions, private
or public, and general subsidies to counties fixed on a uniform basis
according to population were thus ended. Excepted from the constitutional ban were institutions conducted for the support and
maintenance of certain classes of children or aged persons in indigent circumstances.[417] Legislative grants of aid in these cases
were required to be "by a uniform rule, and proportioned to the
number of inmates."[418] Counties, cities, and towns providing for

---

412. Cal. Stat. 1860, ch. CCXLVII, § 11.
413. Cal. Stat. 1860, ch. CCXLVII, § 20.
414. County Government Act of April 27, 1880, reenacting Cal. Pol. Code of 1872,
§ 4046; Cal. Stat. 1880, ch. CCXLIV, § 14; Cal. Stat. 1883, ch. LXXV; Cal. Stat. 1897,
ch. CCLXXVIII, § 25. The County Government Act of April 27, 1880, containing and
amending Cal. Pol. Code of 1872, § 4046, was held to violate procedural requirements of
the 1879 constitution. See Leonard v. January, 56 Cal. 1 (1881).
415. See, *e.g.*, Cal. Stat. 1877–1878, ch. DCLIII; Cal. Stat. 1871–1872, ch. DVIII;
Cal. Stat. 1869–1870, ch. DXX; Cal. Stat. 1867–1868, chs. XLVI, CCCCXLVI; Cal. Stat.
1862, chs. CCCXVIII, CCCXVII, CCLXXXI.
416. CAL. CONST. art. IV, § 22 (1879).
417. *Ibid.*
418. *Ibid.*

the support of these children or aged were "entitled to receive the same pro rata appropriations as may be granted to such institutions under church or other control."[419]

## State Institutions

While the 1879 constitution permitted unrestricted state support to persons cared for in an "asylum, hospital, or any other institution . . . under the exclusive management and control of the state as a state institution . . . ,"[420] at the time few groups were eligible for this aid, and the categories have never been significantly enlarged, though the number of state institutions has greatly increased. Blind and deaf children were provided residential schools,[421] blind adults a home, sheltered shops,[422] and an orientation center,[423] and veterans of United States wars and their dependents two homes.[424] State institutional care, however, has

---

419. *Ibid.*
420. *Ibid.*
421. The residential school created in 1860 for the education and training of deaf, dumb, or blind children, Cal. Stat. 1860, ch. CCXLVI, was continued after adoption of the constitution of 1879. The single institution was separated into two schools, one for the blind and one for the deaf, in 1923, Cal. Stat. 1923, ch. 70, and a second state residential school for the deaf was established at Riverside in 1946, Cal. Stat. (1st Extra. Sess.) 1946, ch. 152.
422. In 1887 the legislature provided for a State Industrial Home for the Adult Blind, Cal. Stat. 1887, ch. CXLVIII, to serve as a residential home for "aged and enfeebled" blind persons, Cal. Stat. 1887, ch. CXLVIII, art. III, § 10, as a working home for "the adult blind, who after having learned a trade or trades, desire to remain at the Home as workmen," and as an industrial training center for those "adult blind that may be admitted as inmates in some trade or trades, in order to enable them to contribute to their own support . . . ." Cal. Stat. 1887, ch. CXLVIII, art. II, § 1. Its features as a home steadily declined and finally ended in 1963, and those as a sheltered workshop have been expanded to include state sheltered day workshops in other cities. CAL. WELFARE & INST'NS CODE §§ 3300–74.
423. In 1951 the Oakland Orientation Center for the Blind was established as a residential institution to aid in the "vocational and personal rehabilitation of blind adults and to assist them in preparation for useful and remunerative work." CAL. EDUC. CODE § 6202. The Center was moved to El Cerrito in 1964.
424. By legislation in 1883, Cal. Stat. 1883, ch. XXXI, § 1, $150 per year, or so much thereof as together with other income received for the specific support of the veteran would provide a monthly income of $12.50, was provided for each indigent veteran of the Mexican or Civil wars living at the Yountville Home, an institution maintained by the private Veterans' Home Association. Three years' residence in the state immediately preceding admission to the Home was required. The legislature attempted to guard against possible unconstitutionality under art. 4, § 22, of the California constitution by providing that no person should be eligible "unless he would be entitled to receive such aid by virtue of the laws and Constitution of this State." Cal. Stat. 1883, ch. XXXI. By 1889 and 1897 statutes, the Napa Valley Yountville Home became a state institution, Cal. Stat. 1889, ch. CCLXVIII, Cal. Stat. 1897, ch. CI, held valid in Treadway v. Board of Directors, 14 Cal. App. 75, 111 Pac. 111 (3d Dist. 1910), as did the Santa Clara County Women's Relief Corps Home, designed to accommodate ex-Army nurses and destitute widows, wives, mothers, sisters, and daughters of honorably discharged Union veterans of the Civil War, Cal. Stat. 1889, ch. CLXXIII; Cal. Stat. 1897, ch. CCLXXIV, held constitutional in Board of Directors v. Nye, 8 Cal. App. 527, 97 Pac. 208 (3d Dist. 1908).

always been most important with respect to the group unscientifically and undiscriminatingly called the insane. By the time of the constitutional convention, two state institutions exclusively for the care of the insane had been founded, that at Stockton, converted from a general hospital to this special use in 1853,[425] and that at Napa, authorized in 1872 and put into operation in 1875.[426] In the decade following the adoption of the constitution, four additional asylums were established, one for the care and training of feebleminded children.[427] In 1897 a state supervisory and investigative lunacy commission was created, the government and management of state insane asylums were put upon a uniform basis, and commitment, care, and treatment were standardized.[428] From that point, the plan of state hospitals has expanded into what the courts characterize as "a broad and comprehensive program for the care, support, maintenance and treatment" of the "mentally irresponsible":[429] the mentally ill, insane, feebleminded, other incompetents not insane, epileptics, inebriates, dipsomaniacs, drug addicts, sexual psychopaths, and mentally abnormal sex offenders.[430]

From the beginning of planned state institutionalization of the insane, two classes of inmates were contemplated on the basis of their financial circumstances. The "indigent insane" were to be conveyed to and from the asylum, maintained during their residence in it, and buried at state expense, the statute expressly providing that "no record of debt shall be made against them" and that they "shall in all respects receive the same medical care and treatment from the institution and good and wholesome diet as other inmates."[431] Those who had sufficient property to meet the costs, or who had friends able and willing to do so, were expected

---

425. Cal. Stat. 1853, ch. CLXVII, § 67; Cal. Stat. 1853, ch. CXLVX; Cal. Stat. 1853, ch. CL, §§ 1, 4.

426. Cal. Stat. 1872, ch. CCCCLIII.

427. Agnews State Hospital, Cal. Stat. 1885, ch. XXXIII, opened 1888; Mendocino State Hospital, Cal. Stat. 1889, ch. XXIII, opened 1893; Southern California State Hospital, Cal. Stat. 1889, ch. CIX, opened 1893; California Home for the Care and Training of Feebleminded Children, Cal. Stat. 1885, ch. CLVI.

428. Cal. Stat. 1897, ch. CCXXVII. In In the Matter of Lambert, 134 Cal. 626, 632, 66 Pac. 851, 854 (1901), the California Supreme Court held that, since "an order for a commitment of a person to an insane hospital is essentially a judgment by which he is deprived of his liberty" and since the statute did not require that notice and opportunity to be heard be given the alleged insane person upon trial of the issue of his insanity, the commitment procedures violated constitutional requirements of due process.

429. Estate of Setzer, 192 Cal. App. 2d 634, 637, 13 Cal. Rep. 683, 685 (2d Dist. 1961) (dictum).

430. CAL. WELFARE & INST'NS CODE §§ 5000–7510.

431. Cal. Stat. 1853, ch. CXLIX, §§ 16, 17.

to be paying patients, the rate to be fixed by the trustees of the asylum.[432] Whether patients were required to pay apparently did not depend on the basis of the statutory grounds for referral to the asylum: insane criminals, unsafe to be at large by reason of insanity, or suffering under mental derangement.[433] The method of enforcing the obligation to pay against those able to do so was clarified almost immediately; the committing judge was directed to inquire into ability, to appoint a guardian of the inmate's property, and to order sale of so much thereof as was necessary to meet the asylum bills.[434] With slight variation these provisions for securing payment have remained in effect.[435] In view of the historic reasons for imposing liability on relatives, it would seem a short step from this device for minimizing public costs to a declaration of relatives' responsibility, and that step was soon taken. In 1869–1870 the husband, father, mother, and children of the insane person were made responsible for his maintenance; the committing judge was to inquire into their existence, whereabouts, and pecuniary ability, and if they resided within the state, to require a joint and several bond to insure that they would meet their obligations to the asylum.[436] With variation in detail, this provision has also remained in effect.[437]

## Aid to the Aged

Exercising the power continued in it by the 1879 constitution, article 4, section 22, the legislature enacted an Indigent Aged Act in 1883. Under it grants were made "to each and every institution in this State conducted for the support and maintenance of aged

---

432. Cal. Stat. 1853, ch. CXLIX, § 17.
433. Cal. Stat. 1853, ch. CXLIX, § 14.
434. Cal. Stat. 1854, ch. LXXXVI, § 2; Cal. Stat. 1863, ch. CCCXIII, § 15.
435. Cal. Stat. 1869–1870, ch. DCXXI, § 13; Cal. Stat. 1872, ch. CCCCLIII, § 18; Cal. Stat. 1875–1876, ch. CXXV; Cal. Stat. 1883, ch. LIV; Cal. Stat. 1885, ch. XXXIII; Cal. Stat. 1889, ch. XXIII; Cal. Stat. 1889, ch. CCXX; Cal. Stat. 1889, ch. CIX; Cal. Stat. 1897, ch. CCXXVII, added to Cal. Pol. Code § 2181 by Cal. Stat. 1903, ch. 364, § 1, amended by Cal. Stat. 1905, ch. 189, § 1; Cal. Stat. 1913, ch. 162, § 1, transferred to Cal. Welfare & Inst'ns Code § 6655 by Cal. Stat. 1937, ch. 369.
436. Cal. Stat. 1869–1870, ch. DCXXI, § 13.
437. Relatives-responsibility provisions were omitted from the 1872 act establishing the Napa asylum, Cal. Stat. 1872, ch. CCCCLIII, but the oversight was corrected in Cal. Stat. 1875–1876, ch. CXXXV, § 19, amended by Cal. Stat. 1883, ch. LIV; Cal. Stat. 1889, ch. CCXX, §§ 8, 9, which generalized the provision, changed the list of relatives to "husband, wife, children, other than minors, father or mother, living within this State of sufficient pecuniary ability, who are otherwise liable," made them liable in the order listed, and detailed the method of enforcement, Cal. Stat. 1897, ch. CCXXVII, § 6, added to Cal. Pol. Code § 2176, by Cal. Stat. 1903, ch. 364, transferred to Cal. Welfare & Inst'ns Code § 6650 by Cal. Stat. 1937, ch. 369.

persons in indigent circumstances"[438] in the amount of one hundred dollars per annum for each indigent person over the age of sixty[439] for whose specific support the institution received less than fifteen dollars per month from other sources.[440] By operation of what the state supreme court called the "self-executing" constitutional mandate placing county, city, and town support of "aged persons in indigent circumstances" upon the same footing with respect to state grants as institutions under church or other control,[441] the provisions of this statute were judicially held to be applicable to public as well as private institutional care of the aged. Thus broadened by constitutional mandate and judicial interpretation, the act remained in effect until 1895, when the rapidly mounting expenditures under it[442] and the frauds on the state practiced by some of the institutions[443] caused the legislature to repeal it.[444] The Aged Act and article 4, section 22, were further judicially construed[445] to provide assistance to counties caring for aged persons not in public or private institutions at all but in their own homes or the homes of others. Authorized by the County Government Act of 1883 and, after *Yolo County v. Dunn*,[446] in part financed by the state, county outdoor support of the aged became common. It continued to spread throughout the state and to expand within the counties even after the 1895 repeal of the Aged Act of 1883 which was the basis of state financial participation. From 1883 through the first quarter of the twentieth century, outdoor relief to the indigent aged was an established practice of all of the counties of the state except San Francisco and Solano. From 1895 to 1930 the state remained entirely out of the field of aged aid except for data collecting and reporting functions conferred upon the State Board of

---

438. Cal. Stat. 1883, ch. XCVI, § 1.

439. Cal. Stat. 1883, ch. XCVI, § 7(2).

440. Cal. Stat. 1883, ch. XCVI, § 7(3). The institution could not have fewer than ten inmates, Cal. Stat. 1883, ch. XCVI, § 7(1), had to own at least $15,000 worth of real property "devoted to the support and maintenance of aged persons in indigent circumstances," Cal. Stat. 1883, ch. XCVI, § 7(4), and was required to maintain specified account books and inmate records, Cal. Stat. 1883, ch. XCVI, § 3.

441. City & County of San Francisco v. Dunn, 69 Cal. 73, 74, 10 Pac. 191 (1886).

442. The amounts rose from $15,000 in 1883 to $543,921 in 1895. CAHN & BARY, WELFARE ACTIVITIES OF FEDERAL, STATE, AND LOCAL GOVERNMENTS IN CALIFORNIA, 1850–1934, at 172 (1936); [1894–1896] CAL. STATE CONTROLLER BIENNIAL REP. 69, statement 3.

443. *Report to the State Board of Examiners, 1894*, in 1895 CAL. STATE BD. OF EXAMINERS REP. 46–58.

444. Cal. Stat. 1895, ch. 12.

445. County of Yolo v. Dunn, 77 Cal. 133, 19 Pac. 262 (1888).

446. *Ibid.*

Charities and Corrections for county hospitals[447] and county outdoor relief.[448]

In 1930 the present system of state-county old age assistance was inaugurated.[449] Under it the counties directly administered the program,[450] the state carried out a supervisory role,[451] and the two shared the cost equally.[452] Specified conditions of eligibility included that the applicant have one year of county residence,[453] fifteen years of state residence,[454] and no husband, wife, parent, or child able and responsible under California law for his support.[455] Only minor changes were necessary to gain federal participation under the Social Security Act in 1937.[456] Since 1937 substantial changes have been wrought. As a practical matter, responsibility of relatives has been all but terminated through legislative establishment of a table of individual liabilities fixed according to income and number of dependents[457] and through liberalization of the table. The citizenship requirement has been withdrawn.[458] County residence has been eliminated.[459] State residence for five of the last nine years is still required,[460] but this requirement has been softened by administrative interpretation deemphasizing intent and stressing physical presence.[461] Property a recipient may own has been greatly increased,[462] though pursuant to a federal requirement, such property must be utilized to produce income, reasonably consistent with its value, to meet the recipient's needs.[463]

447. Cal. Stat. 1903, ch. CCCLXIII, § 3.
448. Cal. Stat. 1911, ch. 683, §§ 3, 5.
449. Cal. Stat. 1929, ch. 530.
450. Cal. Stat. 1929, ch. 530, § 6(b).
451. Cal. Stat. 1929, ch. 530, § 6(a).
452. Cal. Stat. 1929, ch. 530, § 15.
453. Cal. Stat. 1929, ch. 530, § 2(d).
454. Cal. Stat. 1929, ch. 530, § 2(c).
455. Cal. Stat. 1929, ch. 530, § 2(g). In addition, recipients had to have been citizens of the United States for 15 years, Cal. Stat. 1929, ch. 530, § 2(b); could not have more than $3,000 worth of real property, Cal. Stat. 1929, ch. 530, § 4; and had to be 70 years of age, Cal. Stat. 1929, ch. 530, § 2(a). The maximum grant was one dollar per day. Cal Stat. 1929, ch. 530, § 3.
456. Cal. Stat. 1937, ch. 405. The minimum age had to be dropped to 65, Cal. Stat. 1937, ch. 405, § 2(a), and state residence cut to five out of the last nine years, Cal. Stat. 1937, ch. 405, § 2(c).
457. Cal. Stat. 1937, ch. 375.
458. Cal. Stat. 1961, ch. 1960, § 1; Cal. Stat. 1957, ch. 2330.
459. Cal. Stat. 1957, chs. 2293, 2330, 2411; tenBroek, *Welfare in the 1957 Legislature*, 46 CALIF. L. REV. 331, 363 (1958).
460. WELFARE & INST'NS CODE § 2160(b).
461. CAL. DEP'T OF SOCIAL WELFARE, OAS MANUAL §§ A–111–17 [hereinafter cited as OAS MANUAL]; tenBroek, *supra* note 459, at 364–65.
462. Cal. Stat. 1961, ch. 1971; OAS MANUAL §§ A–130–38.40.
463. Cal. Stat. 1961, ch. 1971; OAS MANUAL §§ A–133.10, A–133.40; see Pearson v. State Social Welfare Board, 54 Cal. 2d 184, 5 Cal. Rep. 553, 353 P.2d 33 (1960).

In effect the legislature has built a floor to relief as well as a ceiling. Legislative provisions are so numerous and so detailed, powers and authority of administrators and workers are so specified and circumscribed, and rights and responsibilities of the recipients are so fully elaborated and identified that there is concrete meaning to the notion that aid for the aged is a statutory right.

## Aid to the Blind and the Disabled

The history of state financial aid to the blind and to the disabled is far shorter than that of the aged and involves different constitutional problems. Some blind have been cared for in state institutions since the first decade of our state existence,[464] as have those disabled by virtue of mental condition. The counties were authorized to care for other blind and disabled persons under the Infirmary Act of 1860[465] and the County Government Act of 1883.[466] The counties were required to do so—though unenforceably as a practical matter—by the Pauper Act of 1901. In 1919 the legislature made this county obligation specific[467] by authorizing a special county tax and fund for blind relief, defining needy blind persons,[468] fixing residence qualifications,[469] and specifying a maximum grant.[470] Following a 1928 constitutional amendment[471] removing any doubt about the authority of the state to grant aid to the needy blind, the legislature established a state-county program, similar in all important respects to that provided for the aged, which was rendered eligible for federal funds in 1937.[472] In 1941 California's unique aid-to-the-potentially-self-supporting-blind program was created.[473] The program is financed by the state and county and administered through the same agencies which administer the categorical public assistance programs but contains several federally unacceptable provisions designed to encourage and facilitate recipients' efforts of a sustained and serious character toward self-support.[474] California's state-county-federal program of aid to

---

464. Cal. Stat. 1860, ch. CCXLVI.
465. Cal. Stat. 1860, ch. CCXLVII, § 20.
466. Cal. Stat. 1883, ch. LXXV, § 25(5).
467. Cal. Stat. 1919, ch. 144, § 1.
468. Cal. Stat. 1919, ch. 144, § 2.
469. Cal. Stat. 1919, ch. 144, § 3.
470. Cal. Stat. 1919, ch. 144, § 4.
471. CAL. CONST. art. IV, § 22(3).
472. Cal. Stat. 1937, ch. 394.
473. Cal. Stat. 1941, ch. 765.
474. CAL. WELFARE & INST'NS CODE §§ 3400–82.

the permanently and totally disabled, established in 1957,[475] is the last of the so-called categorical programs to be created. Its constitutional foundation was laid by a 1928 amendment authorizing state assistance "to needy physically handicapped persons";[476] its fiscal foundation was laid, in part, by a 1950 amendment to the Federal Social Security Act authorizing grants-in-aid "for the purpose of enabling each State to furnish financial assistance, as far as practicable under the conditions in such State, to needy individuals eighteen years of age and older who are permanently and totally disabled."[477] As established in 1957, California's program for the disabled, administered by the same state-county machinery carrying out the other categorical aid programs, contained a combination of features selected from the aged, blind, and children's programs and included a rigorously restrictive definition of disability and confused provisions on the amount of the grant, standards of assistance, and responsibility of relatives. In the ensuing years, the legislation has been systematically liberalized, disability now being defined in relation to employability rather than simply in physical and social terms.[478] In 1961 responsibility of relatives was eliminated from the blind[479] and disabled programs,[480] and in 1963 the duration of state residence requirement was struck from the blind programs[481] and diminished in the disabled.[482]

## County Programs Under Permissive Authority

State institutions and the Aged Act of 1883[483] thus provided state care or state-subsidized care to groups of the aged, insane, feebleminded, deaf, dumb, blind, and veterans of United States wars. Remaining needy persons in these categories and the lame, sick, impotent, decrepit, disabled, or enfeebled were to be aided by the counties if they saw fit to do so. The County Government Act of 1883[484] authorized, but did not require, the counties "To provide for the care and maintenance of the indigent sick, or otherwise

---

475. Cal. Stat. 1957, ch. 2411, CAL. WELFARE & INST'NS CODE §§ 4000–192.
476. CAL. CONST. art. IV, § 22.
477. 65 Stat. 555 (1950), 42 U.S.C. § 1351 (1958).
478. Cal. Stat. 1963, ch. 510, § 19, CAL. WELFARE & INST'NS CODE § 4000(c).
479. Cal. Stat. 1961, ch. 1996, CAL. WELFARE & INST'NS CODE § 3011.
480. Cal. Stat. 1961, ch. 1998, § 2, CAL. WELFARE & INST'NS CODE § 4011.
481. Cal. Stat. 1963, ch. 510, § 11.8, CAL. WELFARE & INST'NS CODE § 3040.
482. Cal. Stat. 1963, ch. 510, § 26, CAL. WELFARE & INST'NS CODE § 4160.
483. Cal. Stat. 1883, ch. XCVI.
484. Cal. Stat. 1883, ch. LXXV.

dependent poor of the county."[485] "[W]ithin their discretion," the counties might do this by erecting and maintaining hospitals and poorhouses.[486]

The system of domiciliary care of the aged and otherwise infirm in state-subsidized county hospital-almshouses[487] spread and developed steadily for forty years, reaching a peak at the time of the repeal of the Aged Act in 1895[488] when there were combined hospital-almshouses in over fifty of the fifty-eight counties and separate hospitals and almshouses in three.[489] These institutions flourished in California long after their decline elsewhere in the country because of the high percentage of unattached males in the population, the higher percentage of foreigners, and the seasonal character of California's mining and specialized agriculture.[490]

In the twentieth century developments in the county programs established pursuant to the indigent sick and otherwise dependent poor law have given emphasis to the indigent sick and paid less and less attention to the otherwise dependent poor. The almshouse features of the county hospital-almshouses have gradually dropped away, and the hospitals, existing in California counties in a number far beyond the national pattern, have become such in the modern sense, establishments devoted exclusively to providing medical care for the ill and injured. Section 2400 of California Welfare and Institutions Code authorizing county supervisors to "establish almshouses and county farms, prescribe rules and regulations for their government and management, and appoint the necessary officers

485. Cal. Stat. 1883, ch. LXXV, § 25(5).

486. The counties were required to "appoint . . . some suitable person . . . to take care of . . . such hospitals and poorhouses" and "some suitable graduate in medicine to attend such indigent sick, or otherwise dependent poor." County Government Act, Cal. Stat. 1883, ch. LXXV, § 25. Similar provisions were contained in the County Government Act of 1897, Cal. Stat. 1897, ch. CCLXXVII, § 25(5). "Suitable graduate in medicine to attend the indigent sick" in the act of 1883 does not mean, it was judicially held, one with a medical degree from an academic institution but only one with a license to practice under the laws of the state. See People v. Eichelroth, 78 Cal. 141, 20 Pac. 364 (1889).

487. This system was inaugurated under the Indigent Sick Act of 1855, Cal. Stat. 1855, ch. LVII, and the Infirmary Act of 1860, Cal. Stat. 1860, ch. CCXLVII, and continued and augmented under article IV, § 22, of the 1879 constitution, the Aged Act of 1883, Cal. Stat. 1883, ch. XCVI, and the County Government Acts of 1872, Cal. Pol. Code of 1872, § 4046; 1880, Cal. Stat. 1880, ch. CCXLIV; and 1883, Cal. Stat. 1883, ch. LXXV.

488. Cal. Stat. 1895, ch. XII.

489. [1903–1904] CAL. BOARD OF CHARITIES AND CORRECTIONS BIENNIAL REP. 108–09 (1905).

490. See tenBroek, *California's Welfare Law—Origins and Development*, 45 CALIF. L. REV. 241, 289–92 (1957).

and employees thereof . . ." stands as an unrepealed and continuing reminder of an outmoded past.[491]

### The Pauper Act of 1901—The Elizabethan Poor Law

By the turn of the century California had become a part of the
nation. The peculiarities of local history, geography, and demog-
raphy—the Spanish-Mexican heritage, the Gold Rush settlement,
the separation of the state from older parts of the Union, the im-
balance of population between single males and families, the open-
armed reception of all classes as long as they were Anglo-Ameri-
cans—which had determined the character of welfare programs
in the state had ceased to exist or lost their potency. Excepting aid
to needy children, national patterns took over and were not thereafter seriously challenged or modified. Thus, fifty-one years after
statehood and twenty-nine years after it had adopted Civil Code
provisions which presupposed the existence of the Elizabethan
poor law system, California at last enacted that system with its traditional features intact in the form of the Pauper Act of 1901.[492]
The traditional features included a state-imposed, county-financed,
county-administered duty to relieve the poor, residence and other
requirements designed to exclude the indigent or potential indigent and to identify the county responsible for providing support,
and legal liability of an array of relatives for the support of their
destitute kinsmen.

The earlier, repeatedly reenacted County Government Act per-
missively authorizing the county to care for the "indigent sick"
was not repealed but continued in effect with the Pauper Act of
1901 and was significant in the depression of the 1930's in making
available to counties various methods of financing relief.[493] Though
"indigent sick" in the County Government Act was broadly construed[494] and indeed was later associated with "the otherwise de-

---

491. See also CAL. WELFARE & INST'NS CODE § 205: "The board may provide a farm
in connection with the county hospital or almshouse and may make regulations for working the same." A statement in Goodall v. Brite, 11 Cal. App. 2d 540, 54 P.2d 510 (4th
Dist. 1936), embodies legal logic rather than history: in Kern County the poor are cared
for in the county hospital; therefore, it is a combination county hospital and almshouse.
492. Cal. Stat. 1901, ch. CCX.
493. See San Francisco v. Collins, 216 Cal. 187, 13 P.2d 912 (1932). Bonds were
held to be authorized by Cal. Pol. Code § 4088 in addition to property or poll taxes under
Cal. Pol. Code § 4041.16.
494. See Infirmary Act of 1860, Cal. Stat. 1860, ch. CCXLVII.

pendent poor,"[495] the Pauper Act of 1901 was a landmark, not only
because of its mandatory character, but because of the sweep of its
coverage. The counties were directed to relieve "all pauper, incompetent, poor, indigent persons and those incapacitated by age,
disease, or accident, lawfully resident therein, when such persons
are not supported and relieved by their relatives or friends, or by
their own means, or by state hospitals or other state or private institutions."[496] Residence was loosely defined as "actual residence"
or the place where the person "was employed" or where he made
"his . . . home, or . . . headquarters"[497] for three months immediately before becoming chargeable;[498] on request from another
county, the county of residence was required to remove its paupers
and pay accrued expenses,[499] and the person or corporation who
brought a pauper into or left him in a county where he did not
reside, knowing him to be a pauper, was guilty of a misdemean-
or.[500] The list of liable relatives outstripped that of Elizabeth and
New York, reaching into the collateral line—"husband, wife, children (other than minors), father or mother, brother or sister,
grand-children, or grand-parents . . . ."[501] They were liable in
that order and to the extent of their pecuniary ability.[502] Payments
by them were to be made to the county treasury quarterly and in
advance,[503] and enforcement was to be by judicial proceedings instituted by the district attorney and conducted as all other "actions
for the recovery of money."[504] Moreover, the relatives were liable,
not only for relief supplied directly by the county through its hospitals, almshouses, or through outdoor relief, but also for assistance
provided by any "charity supported by public funds or aided in
part by public funds."[505] Under the supervision and control of the
district attorney who was authorized to proceed by lawsuit "or
otherwise," currently owned or after-acquired property of the

---

495. Cal. Pol. Code § 4307.7.
496. Cal. Stat. 1901, ch. CCX, § 1.
497. Cal. Stat. 1901, ch. CCX, § 2.
498. Cal. Stat. 1901, ch. CCX, § 4.
499. *Ibid.*
500. Cal. Stat. 1901, ch. CCX, § 3. The Infirmary Act of 1860, Cal. Stat. 1860, ch.
CCXLVII, had made it an offense to bring a poor or indigent person from one city or county
in the state to another and leave him there with the intent of making him chargeable, Cal.
Stat. 1860, ch. CCXLVII, § 17, and to bring such person or a lunatic into the state with
such intention, Cal. Stat. 1860, ch. CCXLVII, § 18.
501. Cal. Stat. 1901, ch. CCX, § 6.
502. *Ibid.*
503. *Ibid.*
504. Cal. Stat. 1901, ch. CCX, § 7.
505. Cal. Stat. 1901, ch. CCX, § 5.

chargeable pauper, "real, personal, or mixed," was to be devoted to his "entire or partial support."[506]

While numerous changes have been made in this program in the three-score years since its inauguration and while developments in the last decade or two portend its transformation if not its determination, yet as its basic features had survived the centuries in England and elsewhere in the United States, so in California they survived the impact of two world wars, the great depression of the 1930's, various population explosions, industrialization, and urbanization. Though in the overall governmental system the role of the counties has drastically declined and the creative and directive centers of welfare have shifted to state and national capitals, the counties have retained the duty of providing this form of relief with the exclusive power of administering and the sole responsibility of financing it. In discharging that duty and particularly in determining the conditions of eligibility and the form of relief and its standards, the discretion of the boards of supervisors has been left largely unfettered from state administrative interference and judicial control.[507] The manner in which that discretion has been exercised—through numerous episodes of political administration and personal favoritism, harsh and discriminatory policies, and inadequate and uneven aid[508]—in short, the Elizabethan manner of administering the poor law—has led to gradual and increasing, though still quite minimal, state control by correction of specific weaknesses or abuses. Accordingly the counties have been directed to investigate all applications for relief, to supervise persons on relief "by periodic visitation," to devise ways and means for bringing recipients to self-support, to keep "full and complete" records prescribed by the state,[509] to adopt standards of aid and to make

---

506. Cal. Stat. 1901, ch. CCX, § 6.

507. Patten v. County of San Diego, 106 Cal. App. 2d 467, 470, 235 P.2d 217, 219 (4th Dist. 1951): "The administration of county general relief given pursuant to section 2500 of the Welfare and Institutions Code is vested in the county board of supervisors. The Welfare and Institutions Code does not require that the county grant indigents any specific type of relief nor does it require the payment of any specific amount of money to indigents nor prescribe the time at which payments are to be made. These are matters within the discretion of the boards of supervisors and the court has no authority to interfere with the administrative determinations of a board of supervisors with respect to the granting of county general relief in the absence of a clear showing of fraud or arbitrary or capricious conduct."

508. See, *e.g.*, Cahn & Bary, Welfare Activities in California, 1850–1934, at 175 (1936); Lauren Hyde Associates, A Study of Selected Aspects of the Public Assistance Programs of the State of California (1962) (report to the Welfare Study Commission); [1914–1916] State Bd. of Charities & Corrections Rep. 63–68.

509. Cal. Stat. 1917, ch. 252.

them open to inspection,[510] and to moderate policies with respect to liens on the property of recipients.[511] Other amendments have been designed to clarify and confirm county power or to alter details of existing statutory provisions. The list of responsible relatives has been reduced to spouse, parent, and adult children.[512] The procedures for ascertaining and enforcing responsibility and ability to pay have been amplified and varied,[513] as have the methods for securing support from the recipient's own property;[514] residence has been redefined in standard terms, lengthened to require one year in the county and made three years in the state,[515] and the practice of removing nonresident indigents has been buttressed.[516]

In response to the stresses of the great depression, judges and legislators made explicit much that had been inherent, historical, and implied in the poor law program. They declared the unemployed as well as the unemployable within the mandatory duty and permissive authority of the Pauper Act and the act about indigent sick and dependent poor. "The statutes are neither in terms nor spirit," said the supreme court, "limited to the relief of chronic or permanent paupers, or any other class of poor persons, but extend to every person coming within the terms of the statute, dependent upon public assistance for the necessities of life."[517] Shortly thereafter the legislature added language to the Pauper Act specifying that the able-bodied indigent was eligible for relief as well as the person "incapacitated by age, disease or accident."[518] At the same time the legislature confirmed an established county practice of putting the able-bodied to work as a condition of granting relief.[519] The explanation was strictly Elizabethan: such work would keep "the indigent from idleness . . . assisting in his rehabilitation and the preservation of his self-respect,"[520] reduce the burden on the county by enabling the recipient to contribute to his own support,

510. Cal. Stat. 1957, ch. 1323, CAL. WELFARE & INST'NS CODE § 200.1.
511. Cal. Stat. 1963, ch. 2159, § 1, CAL. WELFARE & INST'NS CODE § 2601.5.
512. Cal. Stat. 1933, ch. 761, § 2.
513. Cal. Stat. 1933, ch. 761, § 2; Cal. Stat. 1941, ch. 1174, § 1.
514. Cal. Stat. 1933, ch. 761, §§ 6–9; Cal. Stat. 1939, ch. 241; Cal. Stat. 1941, ch. 683; Cal. Stat. 1945, ch. 636; Cal. Stat. 1959, ch. 1443; Cal. Stat. 1963, ch. 2159, CAL. WELFARE & INST'NS CODE § 2601.5.
515. Cal. Stat. 1927, ch. 239; Cal. Stat. 1929, ch. 252; Cal. Stat. 1931, ch. 110, § 2; Cal. Stat. 1937, ch. 369, art. 2; Cal. Stat. 1955, ch. 1178.
516. Cal. Stat. 1931, ch. 110, § 4; Cal. Stat. 1933, ch. 761, § 10(d); Cal. Stat. 1937, ch. 369, § 2502.
517. San Francisco v. Collins, 216 Cal. 187, 190, 13 P.2d 912, 913 (1932).
518. Cal. Stat. 1933, ch. 761, § 1.
519. *Ibid.*
520. *Ibid.*

and demonstrate "to the welfare authorities the sincerity and good faith of the applicant,"[521] however bad a test that might be of his necessity. The legal and social status of the pauper was judicially characterized, not to say stigmatized: "During the time a person is receiving relief" under the act of 1901, said the judges, "he is in a sense a ward of the county."[522] When injured in the performance of such "created"[523] or "made" work,[524] he is not an employee within the meaning of the state workmen's compensation laws, even though he is paid a definite sum per hour or per day.

Depression-stimulated questions about the constitutionality of the Elizabethan poor law system in California and persistent county claims of quasi-sovereign autonomy in the whole welfare field were judicially settled. Though counties are admittedly distinct units of local government under the California constitution and, in providing for the maintenance and care for the poor, discharge a largely discretionary function, they are not independent agencies of government exerting a constitutionally vested authority. They are governed by the general law of the state and act as an "agent of the state," carrying out "a matter of statewide interest" under the indigent statutes.[525] Moreover, since the purpose served is not private benefit but public health and welfare under the state's police power, the expenditure of public funds does not violate the constitutional prohibition against giving, lending, or pledging the credit of the state or any of its subdivisions in aid of any individual, association, or corporation or the making of any gift of public money or other thing of value to any individual, association, or corporation.[526] These doctrines were applied to general outdoor relief for the depression-era jobless, the funds for which were to be raised by a county bond issue,[527] and to a tax-supported county hospital serving persons not entirely destitute.[528] "Under the principles of humanitarianism," said the court in a much quoted passage, "and in the interest of a sound policy, we are compelled to

521. McBurney v. Industrial Acc. Comm'n, 220 Cal. 124, 128, 30 P.2d 414, 416 (1934).
522. *Id*. at 127, 30 P.2d at 416.
523. Cal. Stat. 1933, ch. 761, § 1.
524. 220 Cal. at 127–28, 30 P.2d at 416.
525. See San Francisco v. Collins, 216 Cal. 187, 191–92, 13 P.2d 912, 914 (1932); Madison v. City and County of San Francisco, 106 Cal. App. 2d 232, 244, 234 P.2d 995, 1003 (1st Dist. 1951).
526. See CAL. CONST. art. IV, § 31; County of Sacramento v. Chambers, 33 Cal. App. 142, 164 Pac. 613 (3d Dist. 1917).
527. San Francisco v. Collins, 216 Cal. 187, 13 P.2d 912 (1932).
528. See Goodall v. Brite, 11 Cal. App. 2d 540, 54 P.2d 510 (4th Dist. 1936).

hold that a patient in need of hospitalization, who cannot himself, or through legally liable relatives, pay the charges of a private institution, should be admitted to the county hospital because the care of such sick or injured promotes the public health and general welfare of the community in which he lives."[529] An eligible indigent included "an inhabitant of a county who possesses the required qualifications or residence, and who has insufficient means to pay for his maintenance in a private hospital after providing for those who legally claim his support."[530]

## Children's Public Aid Law

Along with the undifferentiated methods of caring for children as a part of the overall mass of the dependent sick or poor—some of which were state institutions, county institutions or outdoor relief, and mixed state, county, or town enterprises[531]—the state maintained a separate program of aid to needy children having a legal base, life, and characteristics of its own. This program began in 1855 and has continued without interruption to the present. It started as a state subsidy to private child-caring institutions.[532] Later, provisions of the 1879 constitution required equal state subsidy to counties, cities, or towns caring for needy children in county, city, or town institutions, in their own homes, or in other private homes.[533]

---

529. *Id.* at 549, 54 P.2d at 515. See also Patrick v. Rylie, 209 Cal. 350, 287 Pac. 455 (1930); Pasadena High School Dist. v. Upjohn, 206 Cal. 775, 276 Pac. 341 (1929); Veterans' Welfare Bd. v. Riley, 189 Cal. 159, 208 Pac. 678 (1922); Macmillan Co. v. Clarke, 184 Cal. 491, 194 Pac. 1030 (1920); County of Sacramento v. Chambers, 33 Cal. App. 142, 164 Pac. 613 (3d Dist. 1917).

530. Goodall v. Brite, 11 Cal. App. 2d 540, 550, 54 P.2d 510, 515 (4th Dist. 1936).

531. The indigent sick under the act of 1855, Cal. Stat. 1855, ch. LVII, and the "blind, lame . . . decrepit . . . disabled" under the Infirmary Act of 1860, Cal. Stat. 1860, ch. CCXLVII, § 20, might of course be children and often were. Some children were cared for in the county hospital-almshouses. 1895 STATE BD. OF EXAMINERS REP. 40–43; [1906–1908] STATE BD. OF CHARITIES & CORRECTIONS THIRD BIENNIAL REP. 198–99. The San Francisco almshouse was required to receive children and had from sixty to seventy-five during the 1870's. 2 WILLIS & STOCKTON, DEBATES AND PROCEEDINGS, CONSTITUTIONAL CONVENTION OF THE STATE OF CALIFORNIA 1878, at 791–92 (1881). Children were part of the class of "indigent sick, or otherwise dependent poor" whom the counties were given jurisdiction and power to care for under the county government acts of 1872, Cal. Pol. Code of 1872, § 4046; 1880, Cal. Stat. 1880, ch. CCXLIV, § 14; 1883, Cal. Stat. 1883, ch. LXXV, § 25(5); and 1897, Cal. Stat. 1897, ch. CCLXXVII, § 25(5). They were covered by the Pauper Act of 1901, Cal. Stat. 1901, ch. CCX, mandatorily imposing responsibility on the counties for all classes of the destitute. A few children were at the Women's Relief Corps Association Home at Evergreen, Santa Clara County. Cal. Stat. 1897, ch. CCLXXIV. Some feebleminded children, Cal. Stat. 1885, ch. CLVI, and some blind or deaf children, Cal. Stat. 1860, ch. CCXLVI, were enrolled in state institutions especially created for them.

532. Cal. Stat. 1855, ch. CXLVIII.

533. CAL. CONST. art. IV, § 22 (1879).

The form and amount of payment, the child-caring institutions and methods employed, the conditions of eligibility, the definition of need, and the procedures of administration have changed during our history as a state. The principle of state financial participation in the support of dependent children has not. That principle was not deflected from its main course when the state withdrew from aid to other groups, from aid to most classes of the poor under the constitution of 1879,[534] and from aid to the aged in 1895[535] or when the state devolved the duty upon counties in 1901 to care for all paupers not cared for in state institutions.[536] However, at no period has the program covered all needy children, nor for most of its history has it completely supported those covered, though the discrepancy between state payment and cost of maintenance has varied.

From 1855 to 1870 the state subsidy was a lump-sum grant to named private institutions.[537] The institutions to receive money and the amount of the grant to each were determined by the legislature.[538] From 1870 to 1880 per-inmate allocations were made to

534. *Ibid.*
535. Cal. Stat. 1895, ch. XII, § 1.
536. Cal. Stat. 1901, ch. CCX.
537. The grants in 1855 were of $5,000 each to the San Francisco Protestant Orphanage and the San Francisco Roman Catholic Orphanage. Cal. Stat. 1855, ch. CXLVIII.
538.    Roman Catholic Female Orphan Asylum, San Francisco:

| | |
|---|---|
| Cal. Stat. 1862, ch. CCLXXXII | $5,500 |
| Cal. Stat. 1863, ch. CCCXLVIII | 6,000 |
| Cal. Stat. 1863–1864, ch. CCCLXIX | 4,000 |
| Cal. Stat. 1865–1866, ch. DXXI | 15,000 |
| Cal. Stat. 1867–1868, ch. CCCCXLVI | 2,500 |
| Roman Catholic Orphan Asylum, Los Angeles: | |
| Cal. Stat. 1862, ch. CCLXXX | $1,000 |
| Cal. Stat. 1863, ch. CCCXLVIII | 2,000 |
| Santa Barbara Roman Catholic Female Orphan Asylum: | |
| Cal. Stat. 1863, ch. CCCXLVII | $1,000 |
| Cal. Stat. 1863–1864, ch. CCCLXIX | 2,000 |
| San Francisco Protestant Orphan Asylum: | |
| Cal. Stat. 1862, ch. CCLXXXII | $5,500 |
| Cal. Stat. 1863, ch. CCCXLVIII | 6,000 |
| Cal. Stat. 1863–1864, ch. CCCLXIX | 15,000 |
| Cal. Stat. 1865–1866, ch. DXXI | 15,000 |
| Cal. Stat. 1867–1868, ch. CCCCXLVI | 18,000 |
| Cal. Stat. 1869–1870, ch. DXX | 8,000 |
| Howard Benevolent Society: | |
| Cal. Stat. 1862, ch. CCCXVIII | $3,000 |
| Cal. Stat. 1863, ch. CCXLVIII | 2,000 |
| Cal. Stat. 1863–1864, ch. CCCLXIX | 2,000 |
| Cal. Stat. 1865–1866, ch. DXXI | 2,000 |
| Cal. Stat. 1867–1868, ch. CCCCXLVI | 4,000 |
| Cal. Stat. 1869–1870, ch. DXX | 5,000 |
| Magdalen Society of San Francisco: | |
| Cal. Stat. 1862, ch. CCLXXI | $5,000 |
| Cal. Stat. 1863, ch. CCLXII | 5,000 |

the child-caring institutions, supplemented until 1874 by lump-sum grants to some institutions.[539] The eligible institutions were "the . . . orphan asylums or institutions in this state, in which orphans are received and provided for," if "supported and sustained wholly or in part by charitable donations." Excluded were those established upon a "self-sustaining basis, where the inmates are required to pay for admission, support and maintenance."[540] Half orphans were included, though on a discriminatory basis. The rate was fifty dollars per year for each orphan, provided "that two half orphans shall . . . be counted as one orphan."[541] Abandoned

| | |
|---|---:|
| Cal. Stat. 1863, ch. CCXLVIII ................. | 3,000 |
| Cal. Stat. 1863–1864, ch. CCCLXIX ............. | 5,000 |
| Cal. Stat. 1867–1868, ch. XLVI ................. | 4,000 |
| Cal. Stat. 1869–1870, ch. DXX ................. | 8,000 |
| San Francisco Ladies' Protection & Relief Society: | |
| Cal. Stat. 1862, ch. CCCXVII .................... | $3,000 |
| Cal. Stat. 1863, ch. CCCXLVIII ................. | 3,000 |
| Cal. Stat. 1863–1864, ch. CCCLXIX ............. | 6,000 |
| Cal. Stat. 1865–1866, ch. DXXI ................. | 9,000 |
| Cal. Stat. 1867–1868, ch. CCCCXLVI ............ | 9,500 |
| Cal. Stat. 1869–1870, ch. DXX ................. | 5,000 |
| Cal. Stat. 1869–1870, ch. DXX ................. | 12,000 |
| Boys Orphan Asylum, San Rafael: | |
| Cal. Stat. 1863, ch. CCCXLVIII ................. | $2,000 |
| Cal. Stat. 1863–1864, ch. CCCLXIX ............. | 2,000 |
| Cal. Stat. 1869–1870, ch. DXX .................. | 2,500 |
| Sacramento Half Orphan Asylum: | |
| Cal. Stat. 1863–1864, ch. CCCLXIX ............. | $2,000 |
| Ladies Protestant Orphan Asylum, Sacramento: | |
| Cal. Stat. 1867–1868, ch. CCCCXLVI ............ | $3,000 |
| Cal. Stat. 1869–1870, ch. DXX ................. | 1,500 |
| Marysville Benevolent Society: | |
| Cal. Stat. 1867–1868, ch. CCCCXLVI ..............$ | 500 |
| Cal. Stat. 1869–1870, ch. DXX ................. | 1,000 |
| Catholic Foundling House: | |
| Cal. Stat. 1867–1868, ch. CCCCXLVI ............ | $4,500 |
| St. Vincent's Roman Catholic Female Orphan Asylum, Santa Barbara: | |
| Cal. Stat. 1867–1868, ch. CCCCXLVI ............ | $1,000 |
| Roman Catholic Orphan Asylum, Grass Valley: | |
| Cal. Stat. 1867–1868, ch. CCCCXLVI ............ | $3,000 |
| St. Joseph's Orphan Asylum, Sacramento City and County: | |
| Cal. Stat. 1867–1868, ch. CCCCXLVI ............ | $2,000 |
| Female Orphan Asylum, Los Angeles County: | |
| Cal. Stat. 1867–1868, ch. CCCCXLVI ............ | $2,000 |
| Episcopal Church Home Association: | |
| Cal. Stat. 1869–1870, ch. DXX ................. | $2,000 |
| Stockton Ladies Benevolent Society: | |
| Cal. Stat. 1869–1870, ch. DXX ................. | $1,000 |
| San Francisco Lying-In Hospital and Foundling Asylum: | |
| Cal. Stat. 1869–1870, ch. DXX ................. | $1,000 |

539. For such grants covering the years 1870–1872 see Cal. Stat. 1869–1870, ch. DXX; for 1872–1874 see Cal. Stat. 1871–1872, ch. DVIII.

540. Cal. Stat. 1871–1872, ch. DCXVI, § 1; Cal. Stat. 1869–1870, ch. CCCXXVI, § 1.

541. Cal. Stat. 1871–1872, ch. DCXVI, § 4. The rates were raised as follows: 1874, $75 for each whole orphan, $50 for each half orphan, Cal. Stat. 1873–1874, ch. DCXLVIII, § 1; in 1876, whole orphans $100, half orphans and abandoned children, $75, Cal. Stat. 1875–1876, ch. CCCCXCII, § 1. In the next biennium the rates remained the same. Cal. Stat. 1877–1878, ch. DCLIII, § 1.

children were added in 1874 at fifty dollars each if they had been in the orphanage for at least a year.[542] The maximum age of eligible children was fourteen.[543] If the orphanage received ten dollars or more per month from any other source for the support of a child, state aid was unavailable for that child.[544] In 1878 the appropriation act first required orphanages to have twenty inmates or more to be eligible for state aid.[545]

Orphanages increased in size and number during the 1860's and 1870's,[546] and by December 1880, 2554 children in thirteen institutions received state subsidies of $146,736.[547] Doubtless the availability of state funds was a fostering factor, but some institutions received no state aid, and some children in aided institutions were ineligible.[548] Of the many church-connected orphanages, Catholic homes, responding to the needs of the many Irish and Mexican inhabitants, were in a clear majority. The growth of the orphanages was attributed by the state board of examiners, aside from state aid and the depression conditions of the 1870's, to the number of foreigners in the population and the rising incidence of divorce and intemperance. Four-fifths of the children in the asylums were of foreign parentage.[549]

---

542. Cal. Stat. 1873–1874, ch. DCXLVIII, § 1.
543. Cal. Stat. 1871–1872, ch. DCXVI, § 4; Cal. Stat. 1869–1870, ch. CCCXXVI, § 4.
544. *Ibid.*
545. Cal. Stat. 1877–1878, ch. DCLIII, § 1.
546. Stanton, *The Development of Institutional Care of Children in California from 1769 to 1925*, 25 Soc. Serv. Rev. 320, 323 (1951).
547. 1881 State Bd. of Examiners Rep. 9.
548. The following private child-caring institutions were founded in California before 1880: San Francisco Protestant Orphan Asylum, 1851; Mt. St. Joseph's Infant Orphan Asylum, San Francisco, Sisters of Charity (St. Vincent de Paul), 1852; San Francisco Ladies' Protection & Relief Society Home, 1852; St. Vincent's Orphan Asylum, San Rafael, 1855; St. Catherine's Home and Training School, San Francisco, Sisters of Mercy, 1857; St. Vincent's Institute, Santa Barbara, Sisters of Charity, 1858; Holy Cross Convent Orphan Asylum, Santa Cruz, Sisters of Charity, 1862; Grass Valley Orphan Asylum, Sisters of Mercy, 1863; Sacramento Protestant Orphan Asylum, 1867; Babies' Aid, San Francisco, 1868; Los Angeles Orphan Asylum, Sisters of Charity, 1869; Good Templars' Home for Orphans, Vallejo, 1869; St. Francis Orphanage, Watsonville, Franciscan Fathers, 1869; Oriental Home for Chinese Girls, San Francisco, S.F. Women's Home Missionary Society, M.E. church for Chinese dependent women, orphans, and slave girls, 1870; Infants' Shelter, San Francisco, 1871; Pacific Hebrew Orphan Asylum, San Francisco, 1871; Children's Home, Ladies Relief Society, Oakland, 1872; Chinese Mission Home, San Francisco, Presbyterian Church, U.S.A., Chinese and Japanese slaves and homeless girls, 1873; Boys and Girls Home School, San Francisco, Boys & Girls Aid Society, 1874; Youths' Directors, Roman Catholic, San Francisco, 1874; California Society for the Prevention of Cruelty to Children, San Francisco, 1876.
549. "[T]he parents being in a foreign country far from relatives and friends, are usually cramped in finances. When a case of whole orphanage occurs there is no recourse but these homes, and when half orphanage takes place the surviving parent, unable to provide sufficient support for their offspring, is also compelled to seek aid for a part, if not all the children, from the same source . . . . With regard to abandoned children, intemperance and divorce are prolific causes, and so numerous are the applications for admission of this class that the asylums would be filled to overflowing, to the exclusion of

The constitution of 1879 was designed to allow and give constitutional sanction to the system of state aid to private child-caring institutions as it existed from 1870 and made it clear that counties, cities, and towns supporting children were also entitled to state assistance. Thus, institutions for the support and maintenance of orphans, half orphans, and abandoned children were excepted from the general ban of article 4, section 22, against payment of state money or gift of state property "for the purpose or benefit of any corporation, association, asylum, hospital, or any other institution not under the exclusive management and control of the State as a State institution . . . ." Should the legislature exercise its discretionary power under the excepting proviso, the grant was required to be "by a uniform rule, and proportioned to the number of inmates," in the manner formulated by the legislature during the preceding decade.[550] Counties, cities, and towns providing for the support of these children were entitled to receive the same "pro rata appropriations as may be granted to such institutions under church or other control."

In response to the 1879 constitutional provision, the legislature in 1880 adopted a statute which followed the pattern developed in the preceding decade. The fixed but different rates used in 1878 were provided for orphans, half orphans, and abandoned children. Also retained were the fourteen-year age limit, exclusion of children for whom ten dollars a month were contributed from outside sources, and the requirement that eligible institutions have at least twenty inmates. The record and bookkeeping requirements were amplified. Two new provisions appeared: The first required institutions to submit to state inquiry into management as a condition to receipt of state funds; the second provided that, in addition to institutions, payments were to be made to "every county, city and

---

orphans, were not the greater part of them denied; those only of extreme destitution, and where known to be worthy, being entertained, and some refuse them altogether." 1881 STATE BD. OF EXAMINERS REP. 9. Some different causes were identified by the San Francisco Ladies' Protection and Relief Society, a recipient institution. "[W]ith the increase of population and commercial greatness has come an increase of all the saddening causes which throw helpless children and destitute women upon the charities of the world . . . . Some are deserted by an abandoned mother, or a vagabond father, and are outcasts. Some come by sudden sickness of parents, the death of a father or mother in poverty, rash speculation, the gaming table or the curse of drunkenness." Sixteenth Annual Report to the Legislature, Journals, Senate and Assembly, App. III, at 13 (1869–1870).

A measure of the times might be seen in the attitude toward inmates of the orphanages expressed by the secretary of the state board of examiners. "[T]hese waifs . . . by reason of hereditary traits are on a lower moral basis than the average American boy. . . ." 1889 STATE BD. OF EXAMINERS REP. 43.

550. CAL. CONST. art. IV, § 22 (1879).

county, city, or town maintaining . . . orphans, half orphans, or abandoned children."[551] With minor variations this statute remained intact until 1913.[552] In 1888 the California Supreme Court ruled that, as a constitutional matter, the appropriation to which the counties were equally entitled could be used for children "maintained" in their own homes.[553]

One of the purposes of the famous 1913 mothers' pension amendments to children's public aid law was control and curtailment of the orphanages. Utilizing powers incident to supplying money and inquiring into management, the state had demonstrated it was not helpless in this regard. Now, however, it procured a grant of more direct authority. The Board of Control was empowered to establish standards "for the proper maintenance and care of children" in the institutions.[554] By a second statutory provision state aid was no longer to be available to a child in an institution "for whom a bona fide offer of a proper home" had been made.[555] This applied to orphans and abandoned children as well as to half orphans; it was less a contributory support to mothers' pensions than an across-the-board method of reducing the population of the institutions and the attendant state expenses. In the absence of adequate followup and investigative staff, the bona fides of the offer and the propriety of the home were largely meaningless prerequisites.

Child-caring institutions receiving state aid in 1913 also became subject to a general licensing statute authorizing the State Board of Charities and Corrections to license "any institutions, boarding house, home or other place conducted as a place for the reception

---

551. Cal. Stat. 1880, ch. XLIX, § 1.

552. Foundlings were added as a specific class of abandoned children in 1883. Cal. Stat. 1883, ch. XXXII, § 9. "Other dependent illegitimate infants" were added in 1907. Cal. Stat. 1907, ch. 496, § 1. In the latter year the aid-to-orphans statute was incorporated in the Political Code.

553. Yolo County v. Dunn, 77 Cal. 133, 19 Pac. 262 (1888). The provision which excluded children who received $10 a month from other sources proved a trap for the state. The institutions showed a tendency to refuse to admit children free of any charge but accepted only contributions below the $10 limit. State officials sought to solve this by an accounting device. For example, children receiving $54 in six months were credited with $10 for each of five months instead of nine dollars a month for six. The state thus supplied aid for only one out of the six months. 1895 STATE BD. OF EXAMINERS REP. 48; 1893 *id.* at 40. The California Supreme Court invalidated the device as not conforming to the statute. Grand Lodge of the I.O.G.T. v. Markham, 102 Cal. 169, 36 Pac. 423 (1894). Since the legislature did not see fit to change the formula, as recommended by the board of examiners, the arrangement itself constituted continuing pressure for state control of institution admission policies and determinations of need.

554. Cal. Stat. 1913, ch. 323, § 3.

555. Cal. Stat. 1913, ch. 323, § 5.

and care of children."[556] Conducting such institutions, homes, or places without a license was a criminal offense.[557] The Board of Charities and Corrections was empowered "to inspect and report upon the conditions prevailing in all such institutions," to prescribe the conditions upon which the licenses would be granted, and to make "such rules and regulations as it may deem best for the government and regulation . . . of the licensed establishments."[558]

The other main purpose of the 1913 amendment to the orphans' aid law—to strengthen state control over the counties—was likewise embodied in two provisions. Mothers of half orphans denied aid by the counties were given a direct appeal to the State Board of Control, and the counties were obligated to carry out board decisions.[559] The role of the counties as administrative agents of the state, long asserted as a general constitutional proposition, was now legislatively prescribed in the field of welfare, and the amendment provided a sanction which could be invoked by the recipients. In addition, the State Board of Control was armed with three children's agents who were to "visit the homes and the institutions" aided by the state "to obtain such information as the board may need in carrying out the provisions of this chapter."[560]

The important change in the state-aid law in 1921 reflected the change in the constitution approved in 1920.[561] Hitherto, the constitutional categories of eligible children—orphans, half orphans, and abandoned children—consisted of children deprived of parental support or care by reason of the death or desertion of one or both parents. The 1920 modification of the constitution and the 1921 modification of the statute admitted children in homes in which the family was still intact but in which the breadwinner had become unable to work. The statutory language revealed the pressure

---

556. Cal. Stat. 1913, ch. 69, § 1.
557. Cal. Stat. 1913, ch. 69, § 3.
558. Cal. Stat. 1913, ch. 69, § 2.
The Board of Charities and Corrections indicated that it had licensed 62 child-caring institutions, 38 receiving state aid, 26 not, 2 pending; 394 family boarding homes for children; 200 maternity hospitals and homes; 9 rescue homes licensed to do maternity work; 10 child-placing agencies; and 10 day nurseries. [1914–1916] STATE BD. OF CHARITIES & CORRECTIONS BIENNIAL REP. 19. Child-placing agencies were licensed under a statute of 1911. Cal. Stat. 1911, ch. 509, § 1. The other listed establishments were licensed under the statute of 1913.
559. Cal. Stat. 1913, ch. 323, § 1. True, the only person given the right of appeal was the mother, but the critical factor was the allowance of the appeal to the state.
560. Cal. Stat. 1913, ch. 323, § 3. For the first time a state residence requirement also appeared in the law: parents had to reside in the state for three years and to become citizens of the state. Cal. Stat. 1913, ch. 323, § 5.
561. Cal. Stat. 1921, ch. 890, §§ 1–4.

of current problems: "the child of a father who is incapacitated for gainful work by permanent physical disability, or is suffering from tuberculosis in such a stage that he cannot pursue a gainful occupation . . . ."[562]

Adjustment to the Social Security Act of 1935,[563] the next stage of significant development in California's aid-to-needy-children program, followed an eccentric course by comparison with the aid programs for the aged and the blind. The latter were integrated into the federal system fully and immediately with only token debate.[564] The process was made easy by the fact that those programs, newly established in 1929,[565] were built upon a mandatory state-county system and involved conditions of eligibility and standards of assistance contemplated by Congress when the federal act was adopted. Consequently, only minor administrative and program changes had to be made to conform with federal prescriptions. By comparison, accommodation of the aid-to-needy-children program to the federal act came slowly and grudgingly. It was not completely effected until 1949, fourteen years later, though minimum compliance, sufficient to start the flow of federal funds, was achieved in 1937.[566] Moreover, considerable modification had to be made in the state program.

Although a legislative and administrative foundation was laid early in the century for state supervision of county administration, for state operation through a single state agency, and for the machinery through which aggrieved applicants and recipients could take a direct appeal to the state from adverse county action, the full implementation of these notions, now set forth as federal requirements, in a sensitive political area and with respect to an aid program more controversial than that for the aged and the blind, could not be accomplished without difficulty. The fact that the same machinery had to be set up for the related aged and blind programs and in fact was in operation was a facilitating factor.[567] The lowering of the residence requirements from two years to one was also facilitated by the necessary reductions in the other programs.[568] Greater county resistance and continuing political activity was elic-

---

562. Cal. Stat. 1921, ch. 890, § 1.
563. 49 Stat. 627, ch. 531.
564. Cal. Stat. (Extra. Sess.) 1936, chs. 6–7.
565. Cal. Stat. 1929, chs. 529–30.
566. Cal. Stat. 1937, ch. 369.
567. Cal. Stat. 1937, ch. 369, pt. II, art. 4.
568. CAL. WELFARE & INST'NS CODE § 1525.

ited by state implementation of the 1939 amendment to the federal act stipulating selection of state and county welfare workers according to a merit system and authority in the state agency to fix minimum personnel standards both as to qualifications and compensation.[569]

The adjustments, however, made necessary by the federal requirements, which involved the greatest departure from past practices and had the greatest impact on the improvement and expansion of the program lay in other areas. County financial participation had to be shifted from a voluntary to a compulsory basis.[570] The standards of care were no longer left entirely to county discretion.[571] Finally, significant increases were made in the eligible groups of children. In 1939 the definition of a half orphan was broadened to include a child of a father who was continuously absent from the home for three years, during which time his whereabouts were unknown, and for whom a warrant had been issued on a charge of failure to provide.[572] In 1945 the father's continuous absence for three years was alone made sufficient.[573] In 1949 the federal formula was accepted outright, and the state constitutional language disappeared from the statutes.[574] Thereafter, eligible needy children were minors "under the age of 18 years . . . deprived of parental support or care by reason of the death, continued absence from the home, or physical or mental incapacity of a parent."[575] Death and incapacity clearly fitted two of the constitutional categories. Whether a child whose father is continuously absent for a short time is a half orphan or abandoned child within the meaning of article 4, section 22, of the constitution of California is not so obvious. This question has somehow never seriously been argued, let alone judicially decided. It appears to be one of those many constitutional issues settled by quiet acquiescence.

In 1963 pursuant to a change made in federal law, existing groups of eligible children were redefined, children of unemployed parents were made eligible, and the program was expanded to provide services as well as financial assistance to recipient families.

---

569. 53 Stat. 1360 (1939), 42 U.S.C. § 302(a)(5) (1958); CAL. WELFARE & INST'NS CODE § 119.5.
570. Cal. Stat. 1937, ch. 369, pt. II, art. 2.
571. CAL. WELFARE & INST'NS CODE § 1560.
572. Cal. Stat. 1939, ch. 1037, § 1.
573. Cal. Stat. 1945, ch. 1388, § 1.
574. Cal. Stat. 1949, ch. 889, § 1.
575. *Ibid.*

Aid, services, or both, shall be granted subject to the regulations of the state department, to families with related children under the age of 18 years, in need thereof because they have been deprived of parental support or care due to: (a) The death, physical or mental incapacity, or incarceration of a parent; or (b) The divorce, separation or desertion of his parent or parents and resultant continued absence of a parent from the home for these or other reasons; or (c) The unemployment of his parent or parents.[576]

An unemployed parent includes a natural, adoptive, or step-parent who: "Is not working but is available for and seeking employment or, as a result of unemployment, has been accepted for or is participating in a training project essential to future self-support" or who "is employed only part time according to standards set administratively by the State Department of Social Welfare consistently with federal law and regulations."[577]

## Public Support and Adoptions

In one circumstance under the California Civil Code of 1872 a parent might divest himself of his parental responsibilities of custody and support. That was when a new parent was found, and a legal transfer of parenthood effected. Formalized legal adoption was at that time a new development. The California statute of 1870,[578] superseded by the similar provisions in the Civil Code of 1872,[579] established a court-shared and court-approved process of adoption. Few qualifications were specified for adopting couples and not all of those tested their fitness directly or the suitability of their home. They had to be of "good moral character and standing in the community,"[580] over twenty-one years of age,[581] and fifteen years older than the minor being adopted.[582] A married woman was not permitted to adopt.[583] Parental consent to the adoption was the foundation of the availability of the child—consent of both natural parents in the case of a legitimate child, consent only of the mother in the case of an illegitimate child.[584] The consent of

---

576. Cal. Stat. 1963, ch. 510, § 1.7, CAL. WELFARE & INST'NS CODE § 1500.
577. Cal. Stat. 1963, ch. 510, § 1.11, CAL. WELFARE & INST'NS CODE § 1500.4.
578. Cal. Stat. 1869–1870, ch. CCCLXXXV.
579. Cal. Civ. Code of 1872, §§ 221–30, together with the 1870 provisions, were drawn from the Field Draft Civil Code, DRAFT N.Y. CIV. CODE §§ 107–16.
580. Cal. Stat. 1869–1870, ch. CCCLXXXV, § 1.
581. *Ibid.*
582. *Ibid.*; Cal. Civ. Code of 1872, § 222.
583. Cal. Stat. 1869–1870, ch. CCCLXXXV, § 1; Cal. Civ. Code of 1872, § 222.
584. Cal. Stat. 1869–1870, ch. CCCLXXV, § 3; Cal. Civ. Code of 1872, § 224.

the minor was necessary if he was over twelve years of age.[585] Based upon mixed notions of punishment for guilty parents or loss of rights to the child by unfit ones, the Civil Code obviated the necessity for parental consent in a series of situations: "from a father or mother deprived of civil rights, or adjudged guilty of adultery, or of cruelty, and for either cause divorced, or adjudged to be a habitual drunkard, or who has been judicially deprived of the custody of the child on account of cruelty or neglect."[586] The sections on adoption in the Civil Code of 1872 reveal the overall conception of the adoption program and its purposes. In a trenchant comment upon the adoption sections of the Field draft embodied in the 1872 California Civil Code, the New York Code Commissioners made plain that their primary interest was in defining, legalizing, and protecting the position of the adoptive parents.[587] Though the process of transferring the child depends on court action and though there is reference to the court's being "satisfied that the interest of the child will be promoted by the adoption,"[588] basically the child is treated as the subject of a transaction between the natural and adoptive parents. The underlying theory is that the parent-child relationship is similar to property ownership which can be transferred by contract. In 1893 the California Supreme Court said,

> The adoption of a child under . . . section [227] of the Civil Code . . . is not a judicial proceeding . . . although the sanction of a judicial officer is required for its consummation. The proceeding is essentially one of

---

585. Cal. Stat 1869–1870, ch. CCCLXXXV, § 3; Cal. Civ. Code of 1872, § 225.

586. Cal. Civ. Code of 1872, § 224.

587. "The total absence of any provision for the adoption of children is one of the most remarkable defects of our law. Thousands of children are actually, though not legally, adopted every year; yet there is no method by which the adopting parents can secure the children to themselves, except by a fictitious apprenticeship, a form which, when applied to children in the cradle, becomes absurd and repulsive. It is, indeed, so inappropriate in every case that it is rarely resorted to. The consequence is, almost invariably, that if the real parents of the child live to see it grow to an age of usefulness and intelligence they are certain to attempt to reclaim it, sometimes through the mere selfishness of natural affection, but more commonly from base and sordid motives. The chances of an adopting parent for the retention of the child upon which, perhaps, his whole heart is centered, are therefore in the inverse ratio to the degree of his benevolence in its selection, and of his care and affection in its training. Benevolence dictates a choice from among children whose parents are least able or willing to take care of them. To relieve a child from a cruel and heartless parent is a greater mercy than to take even an orphan. Yet these are the parents who are, of all others, most likely to reclaim the child as soon as any money can be made out of it. Affection will give the child such a training as will develop its beauty and intelligence to the highest degree. Yet every grace of the child is but a premium upon the extortion of its heartless parents. This is not mere theory. Facts within the knowledge of almost every one justify these statements. There are very many childless parents who would gladly adopt children, but for their well-founded fears that they could never hold them securely." Cal. Civ. Code § 221, *Legislation* (Deering, 1935).

588. Cal. Civ. Code of 1872, § 227.

contract between the parties whose consent is required. It is a contract of a very solemn nature, and for this reason the law has wisely thrown around its creation certain safeguards, by requiring, not only that it shall be entered into in the presence of a judge, but also that it shall receive his sanction, which is not to be given until he has satisfied himself . . . [of certain specified things].[589]

California's Civil Code[590] recognized this notion of contractual transfer of a property right in the requirement of an agreement by the adopting parent, which remains in our statutory law today.[591] It survives also in the basic premise of independent adoptions, that they are in the nature of a contract between the biological and the adoptive parents.[592]

One branch of adoption law, that which developed in connection with child-caring institutions, involved elements in addition to those featured in the Civil Code and, in any event, emphasized other considerations. The contract simile necessarily faded into the background. The consent of the natural parents clearly could not be the foundation of the arrangement in the case of full orphans. In the case of abandoned children the parents were unknown or had disappeared. In the case of half orphans the remaining parent often was a minor factor in planning for the child or might have completely surrendered its control to the asylum. In the case of illegitimate children all of the factors mentioned by Montesquieu would be in operation;[593] parental consent could not be a cornerstone of the arrangement.

Moreover, the dominant concern of the New York commissioners with the legal position of the adoptive couple was also absent. The asylums used the adoption machinery of the Civil Code, and benefits it conferred on the adoptive couple therefore accrued to the asylum. But these were not the main concern of the asylum

---

589. *In re* Johnson, 98 Cal. 531, 538, 33 Pac. 460, 461 (1893). In Estate of Sharon, 179 Cal. 447, 454, 177 Pac. 283, 286 (1918), this language was repeated with approval. See also Estate of McKeag, 141 Cal. 403, 74 Pac. 1039 (1903); *In re* Williams, 102 Cal. 70, 36 Pac. 407 (1894).

590. Cal. Civ. Code of 1872, § 227, as amended, Code Amendments 1873–1874, at 195.

591. CAL. CIV. CODE § 227.

592. CAL. CIV. CODE § 224.

593. "[T]hat the establishment of marriage in all civilized states is built on this natural obligation of the father to provide for his children; for that ascertains and makes known the person who is bound to fulfill this obligation; whereas, in promiscuous and illicit conjunctions, the father is unknown; and the mother finds a thousand obstacles in her way, shame, remorse, the constraint of her sex, and the rigour of laws, that stifle her inclinations to perform this duty; and, besides, she generally wants ability." Quoted in 1 BLACKSTONE, COMMENTARIES *447.

managers or of the public aid officials. The dominant factor was the additional element, that is, public support of the child. This was the precondition of asylum authority in the premises. Reduction in the public burden was the reason for providing the asylums with a role in adoptions. The laws dealing with asylums and adoptions say nothing about the suitability of the adoptive home, nothing about the adoptability of the child, nothing about whether the arrangements will be in the best interest of the child, nothing about accepting surrenders from the parent of a half orphan or from the mother of an illegitimate child only under conditions that provide such parent reasonable opportunity to make a firm and unpressured decision. They do, however, say much about the public cost of supporting children in the asylums; placing them for adoption was one method of reducing that cost.

When California enacted its pre-Code adoption statute in 1870,[594] it enacted two other statutes, apparently to be independently effective in the same field, both dealing with relinquishments to the asylums and one providing for a distinct system of adoption for certain asylum children. One provided that

> the surviving parent of any half orphan may surrender all control and authority over such child to the Managers of . . . any . . . asylum society . . . and such surrender, made in writing and acknowledged before a Notary Public or magistrate, shall vest in said Managers as full and complete authority over such half orphan child as they can legally exercise over orphan children.[595]

The other dealt with the relinquishment of illegitimate children to the San Francisco Lying-In Hospital and Foundling Asylum and with the power of the asylum over such children.[596] The statute declared that "Any child born out of wedlock and while the mother thereof shall be under the care" of the asylum may be given to the asylum by its mother.[597] "[C]onclusive proof of such gift" was "an entry made in a book of the corporation kept for that purpose, stating such gift, and signed by the mother of the child."[598] The trustees of the asylum were declared the guardians of every such child and also "of every foundling that shall come to the care of said asylum."[599] All such children, whether foundlings or ille-

---

594. Cal. Stat. 1869–1870, ch. CCCLXXXV.
595. Cal. Stat. 1869–1870, ch. CCXXIV, § 3.
596. Cal. Stat. 1869–1870, ch. CCXXXVII.
597. Cal. Stat. 1869–1870, ch. CCXXXVII, § 1.
598. *Ibid.*
599. Cal. Stat. 1869–1870, ch. CCXXXVII, § 2.

gitimates relinquished by the signature of the mother, might be given by the asylum "to such person as may be desirous of adopting the same." The "adopting" person was required to enter into an obligation to the State of California to raise the child as his own. Upon execution of the obligation, the "child shall become the child of the person . . . signing the same, and shall bear the name of such person, and shall be considered in law as the heir of such person . . . and shall inherit the estate of such person . . . in like manner as if born of the body of such person."[600] A more general statute in 1878, without mentioning parental consent, authorized the managers of orphan asylums to consent to the adoption of orphans or abandoned children who had been in the institution for the period of one year and who during that period had been supported wholly at the expense of the institution.[601]

In 1889 the California Supreme Court analyzed the relationship of this statute to Civil Code section 224, which itemizes the circumstances in which parental consent to adoption is necessary.[602] Section 224 said nothing about orphans or abandoned children, the two classes mentioned in the statute of 1878, and the court therefore held that the statute did not amend, repeal, or contradict the code provisions. It simply provided "for the adoption of a class of minor children, viz., those in orphan asylums, whose adoption is not provided for in the Civil Code."[603] The power to adopt having been created by statute and having been unknown to the common law, "the mode must be held to be the measure of the power."[604] A three-year-old orphan, who had been in the asylum for two years and who had been taken from it by an adoptive couple with the consent of some of the officers, could not be adopted without the consent of the managers, who by the statute were "authorized and empowered to consent to the adoption . . . in the same manner that parents are by law authorized to consent . . . ."[605]

From the date of the *Chambers*[606] case to 1927, when the whole institution-consent portion of Civil Code section 224 was re-

600. *Ibid.*
601. Cal. Stat. 1878, ch. DCXXVI, § 1. For a discussion of similar statutory provisions in other states, and cases construing them, see *In re* Kitchens, 115 Cal. App. 2d 254, 253 P.2d 690 (4th Dist. 1953); Estate of Hampton, 55 Cal. App. 2d 543, 131 P.2d 565 (4th Dist. 1942).
602. *Ex parte* Chambers, 80 Cal. 216, 22 Pac. 138 (1889).
603. *Id.* at 219, 22 Pac. at 139.
604. *Ibid.*
605. Cal. Stat. 1878, ch. DCXXVI.
606. *Ex parte* Chambers, 80 Cal. 216, 22 Pac. 138 (1889).

pealed,[607] a substantial, continually shifting, and confused body of
laws dealing with children in orphanages was added,[608] not as independent statutes or as changes in the act of 1878, but as amendments to Civil Code section 224, leaving the relationships of the various provisions in the greatest uncertainty.[609] The body of laws continued the authority of the asylums to consent to adoptions, redefined and varied from time to time the classes of children to which
the authority applied, devoted a great deal of attention to half orphans who had not been specifically mentioned in the act of 1878
but who constituted the major part of the population of the orphanages, and particularly emphasized the loss of parental power to consent by failure of the parent to provide reasonable support if able
to do so.

As of 1903, for example, the statutory law on the subject of
consents to adoptions was as follows: orphans, abandoned children, and the children of nonresident parents supported in an
asylum for more than one year could be adopted with the consent
of the managers; half orphans maintained in an asylum for more
than two years could be adopted with the consent of the managers
unless the parent had paid a reasonable sum toward maintenance
or, by inference, unless the parent was unable to pay toward maintenance;[610] a full orphan not in an asylum might be adopted without the consent of anyone; a child deserted by both parents or left
in the care of another for one year without any agreement or provision for its support could be adopted without the consent of
anyone.[611]

No less troublesome and vague than the treatment of the or-

607. Cal. Stat. 1927, ch. 691, § 1.
608. Cal. Stat. 1891, ch. XXXVII (consent of anyone unnecessary in adoption of abandoned child); Cal. Stat. 1893, ch. XCVI, § 1, deleting Cal. Stat. 1891, ch. XXXVII (half
orphans might be adopted "with the consent of the managers of such orphan's home,"
unless the parent has contributed support if able "so to do"); Cal. Stat. 1895, ch. XXXVI
(consent to adoption of abandoned child unnecessary); Cal. Stat. 1903, ch. CII, § 1 (abandoned child defined and adoption with consent of managers though two parents were living
if the child had been left "without any . . . provision for its support"); Cal. Stat. 1907,
ch. 268 (abandoned child may be adopted with consent of district attorney of county of
adoptive parents); Cal. Stat. 1911, ch. 450, § 1, repealing Cal. Stat. 1893, ch. XCVI, and
Cal. Stat. 1903, ch. CII (redefining abandonment); Cal. Stat. 1917, ch. 558 (increasing the
classes of children adoptable with the consent of the institution); Cal. Stat. 1921, ch. 229,
§ 1, slightly diminishing scope of Cal. Stat. 1917, ch. 558.
609. The statute of 1878 remained on the books until 1955 when it was repealed with
a number of acts classified as "obsolete." Cal. Stat. 1955, ch. 57, § 1. Compare the statement made in Adoption of McDonald, 43 Cal. 2d 447, 460, 274 P.2d 860, 867 (1954),
after reference to the statute of 1878 and the *Chambers* case, that "No such provision can
be found in the statutes of this state today." If the court had found the statute and had
treated it as in full force, an opposite result would have been necessary in the *McDonald*
case.
610. See *In re* Crutcher, 61 Cal. App. 481, 486, 215 Pac. 101, 103 (1923) (dictum).
611. *Ibid.*

phanage adoption-consent statute of 1878 were the relationships, effectiveness, and fate of the 1870 surrender statutes.[612] Were they superseded and nullified by the Civil Code, by the relinquishment statutes of 1911, 1913, and later? Did they remain in effect until 1937 when they were repealed in connection with the establishment of the Labor Code[613] and the Welfare and Institutions Code?[614] On its face the statute of 1870, authorizing a surviving parent to surrender his child to an orphanage, had a bearing on the orphanage adoption-consent statute of 1878. The 1870 statute gave asylum managers "as full and complete authority" over half orphans duly surrendered to them by the surviving parent as they could "legally exercise over orphan children."[615] By the statute of 1878, the managers could consent to the adoption of orphan children.[616] In the *Chambers* case there was no mention of this relationship between the statutes.[617]

---

612. Cal. Stat. 1869–1870, chs. CCXXXIV, CCXXXVII.
613. Cal. Stat. 1937, ch. 90, § 8100.
614. Cal. Stat. 1937, ch. 369, § 20000.
615. Cal. Stat. 1869–1870, ch. CCXXXIV, § 3.
616. Cal. Stat. 1878, ch. DCXXVI, § 1.
617. Unlike the orphanage adoption-consent statute, the two statutes of 1870 were passed before the adoption of the Civil Code. The Civil Code lays down principles of construction of prior acts; they are abrogated unless expressly continued regardless of whether they are consistent or inconsistent with the code. The only requisite is that they deal with a case "provided for by this code." CAL. CIV. CODE § 20. A strict application of these principles would appear to invalidate at least the adoption provisions applicable to the San Francisco Lying-In Hospital and Foundling Asylum. Those provisions, consummating an adoption by the mere informal gift of the child by the asylum to the adoptive parent and the execution of a written agreement by him, disregarded the judicial role which was an essential part of the Civil Code scheme. Thus it might be concluded that they were inconsistent with the provisions of the code and, in any event, were not expressly continued by it. It might also be argued that, since the provisions included relinquished illegitimates in addition to foundlings, they covered "cases provided for" by the code. Section 224 requires the consent of the mothers of illegitimate children "if living." However, the adoption provisions of the foundling asylum act were passed by the legislature at the same time as the regular adoption statute of 1870. Cal. Stat. 1869–1870, ch. CCCLXXXV. That statute embodied a plan very similar to the code plan and was incorporated in and superseded by it. If the foundling-asylum provisions were compatible with the adoption act of 1870, they were equally compatible with the code. The foundling-asylum provisions on adoptions—and even more clearly the provisions of both of the 1870 acts on relinquishment, a topic not mentioned by the code—might be treated as neither consistent nor inconsistent with the code provisions but simply rules in an area ungoverned by the code. This would support the ruling in the *Chambers* case that the children in orphan asylums were not "provided for" by the adoption provisions of the Civil Code. *Ex parte* Chambers, 80 Cal. 216, 219, 22 Pac. 138, 139 (1889).

By 1893 when amendments to the Civil Code dealt specifically with the adoption of groups of children in the orphan asylums, it was impossible to say that these children were cases "not provided for" by the code. The doctrine of the *Chambers* case became inapposite. Also inapposite was a refinement of the *Chambers* doctrine that, though some groups in the orphanages were now covered by the code, others were not, not having been specifically provided for. Of the two groups of asylum children covered by the act of 1870, foundlings were covered by the code amendments either under the general class of abandoned children in amendments beginning in 1891 or under the legal definition of foundlings—children left without provision for identification—incorporated in the amendments of 1911. The code amendments did not specifically deal with illegitimate children in orphan asylums.

Whatever inferences one may draw about the impact of the code amendments on the special adoption statute of 1870, they apparently were not drawn by the legislature. In a statute of 1903[618] that body clearly implied the present effectiveness of adoptions pursuant to the procedure provided in the special statute. The 1903 act established a system of licensing for "any maternity hospital or lying-in asylum where females may be received, cared for or treated during pregnancy, or during or after delivery; . . . or . . . any institution, boarding house, home or other place for the reception or care of children . . . ."[619] The licensed individuals and institutions were required to keep a register of the women and children cared for or born in the institution, the time of the reception and discharge of the children, the reasons therefor, "and also the name and age of every child who is given out, adopted, taken away, or indentured from such place, to or by any person, together with the name and residence of the person so adopting, taking away or indenturing such child . . . ."[620]

The 1911[621] and 1913[622] statutes providing for the state licensure of child-caring and child-placing institutions and the amendments to the Civil Code passed then[623] and later[624] appear to qualify the authority of orphanages and of the San Francisco Lying-In Hospital and Foundling Asylum to accept relinqishments under the acts of 1870.[625] The licensing statutes do not confer or specifically mention the authority of the licensed institutions to accept relinquishments; nor do they expressly repeal the earlier acts. They do, however, subject lying-in asylums, maternity hospitals, and child-placing institutions and individuals to licensing requirements, make it a penal offense to conduct such activities without a license, and allocate sweeping rulemaking power to the State Board of Charities and Corrections. The amendments[626] to Civil Code section 224 are more specifically in point, though there was no express repeal of the earlier statutes and though there are considerable differences in

---

618. Cal. Stat. 1903, ch. CCXXXIX.
619. Cal. Stat. 1903, ch. CCXXXIX, § 1.
620. Cal. Stat. 1903, ch. CCXXXIX, § 2.
621. Cal. Stat. 1911, ch. 569.
622. Cal. Stat. 1913, ch. 69.
623. Cal. Stat. 1911, ch. 450; Cal. Stat. 1913, ch. 92.
624. Cal. Stat. 1917, ch. 558; Cal. Stat. 1921, ch. 229; Cal. Stat. 1927, ch. 691.
625. Cal. Stat. 1869–1870, ch. CCXXXIV, § 3; ch. CCXXXVII, § 1.
626. Cal. Stat. 1911, ch. 450; Cal. Stat. 1913, ch. 92; Cal. Stat. 1917, ch. 558; Cal. Stat. 1921, ch. 229; Cal. Stat. 1927, ch. 691.

language.[627] These differences would perhaps sustain an argument for the continued effectiveness of the act of 1870 until its formal repeal in 1937. However, the substantially duplicatory coverage of the code amendments weighs against such a conclusion drawn from these relatively minor differences.

### Public Support and Apprenticing of Children

One historical method of both Anglo-American and Ibero-American law for providing support and education of children was the apprenticeship system. From the master's point of view this was also a system of labor.[628] The three elements of the arrangement—current support, occupational education which would enable the child to support himself in the future, and present labor of value to the master's enterprise—varied in their relative importance with the master, the child, the business, and the times. Parents might initiate the arrangement for training rather than support.[629] The statutes dealing with the poor and authorizing or directing the apprenticing of children viewed it primarily, though not exclusively, as a means to maintain the child.

California adopted a general indenture statute in 1858 authorizing children, with the consent of their parents, guardians, or certain public officials, to bind themselves out as clerks, apprentices, or servants in any profession, trade, or employment until age 21, if males, until 18, if females, or for any shorter period.[630] Under the indenture the master was obligated to teach the child to read and write and "the general rules of arithmetic"[631] or alternatively to

---

627. The amendments cover relinquishments "for the purpose of adoption"; *e.g.*, in Cal. Stat. 1913, ch. 92, the 1870 acts cover relinquishments of "all control and authority" over the child, Cal. Stat. 1869–1870, ch. CCXXXIV. The amendments cover relinquishments made by both parents; *e.g.*, in Cal. Stat. 1917, ch. 558, the acts of 1870 cover relinquishments by the surviving parent in the case of legitimate children, Cal. Stat. 1870, ch. CCXXXIV, or by the mother being cared for by the asylum in the case of illegitimate children, Cal. Stat. 1869–1870, ch. CCXXXVII. The amendments provide for relinquishments without indicating in whose hands the child will thereupon be placed; the acts of 1870 provide for relinquishments "to" the child-caring institutions, Cal. Stat. 1870, ch. CCXXXVII. However, a relinquishment acknowledged by the secretary of a child-placing society, permitted by the amendments after 1911, would presumably be a relinquishment to the society.
628. 43 Eliz. 1, c. 2 (1601); Recopilación de Leyes de los Reinos de las Indias, Book vii, Title iv (Spain 1680).
629. ABBOTT, THE CHILD AND THE STATE 187–255 (1938); SEYBOLT, APPRENTICESHIP AND APPRENTICESHIP EDUCATION IN COLONIAL NEW ENGLAND (1917).
630. Cal. Stat. 1858, ch. CLXXXII, §§ 1–4. Indians were expressly excluded from the application of this act since they were the subject of special indenture provisions. Cal. Stat. 1858, ch. CLXXXII, § 13. White children capable of becoming citizens of the state and coming from any other country, state, or territory might make an indenture to secure payment of passage money. Cal. Stat. 1858, ch. CLXXXII, § 11.
631. Cal. Stat. 1858, ch. CLXXXII, § 9.

send him to school three months a year. The master was not expressly required to teach the child his "profession, trade, or employment."[632] The indenture might be annulled for willful nonfulfillment by the master or for cruelty or maltreatment of the child without just cause or provocation.[633]

With some deletions, modifications, and additions these indenture provisions have remained in our law to the present time. When the Civil Code was adopted in 1872, they were incorporated.[634] A new general indenture statute was passed in 1876[635] and reenacted with minor changes in 1880.[636] These acts, among other differences from the earlier provisions, authorized the indenture of children only if they were age 14 or over, required "the consent of the minor, personally,"[637] dropped professional and added agricultural occupations to the list of employments for which the children might be indentured, detailed more fully the circumstances under which consent of the father, mother, and guardian were not necessary, forbade removal of apprentices from the state, omitted reference to immigrant children, and made the parties to the indenture liable to the master "for the breach of any covenant on their part . . . ."[638] In 1905 the acts of 1876 and 1880, with some modifications,[639] were codified in the Civil Code,[640] replacing the 1872 Civil Code sections which were then repealed.[641] In 1937 these Civil Code provisions were transferred to the new California Labor Code,[642] and in 1939

632. Cal. Stat. 1858, ch. CLXXXII, § 1.
633. Cal. Stat. 1858, ch. CLXXXII, §§ 9, 11, 14. Runaway apprentices could be returned to the master on court order or punished by jail sentence. Accomplices were guilty of a misdemeanor. Cal. Stat. 1858, ch. CLXXXII, §§ 16–17.
634. Cal. Civ. Code of 1872, §§ 264–76. Four provisions of the act of 1858 were not included in the 1872 Civil Code codification: § 13, exempting Indians; § 15, dealing with application for annulment; § 16, providing punishment for fleeing from service; § 17, providing for punishment of accomplices. The 1858 statute was not formally repealed until Cal. Stat. 1955, ch. 46, when the legislature repealed several hundred obsolete statutes.
635. Cal. Stat. 1875–1876, ch. DLIII.
636. Cal. Stat. 1880, ch. LXXXVII.
637. Cal. Stat. 1876, ch. DLIII, § 1.
638. Cal. Stat. 1875–1876, ch. DLIII, § 18.
639. Section 18 of the acts of 1876 and 1880, making the parties to an indenture of apprenticeship liable to the master for any breach thereof, was omitted from the codification. The code commissioners explained the reason as follows: "The theory of the statute is that the contract of apprenticeship is not made by the minor, but by his parent or guardian. If such parent or guardian is made personally liable on the contract, a parent will rarely, and the guardian almost never, enter into it. It seems sufficient that such parent or guardian be made answerable for the cost of the proceeding brought by the master to be released from the indenture, as provided for in section 274. The master on his part is not absolutely bound, because he may, if he wishes to remove from the state, or to quit his trade or business, apply to be released from his contract, and he may take like action whenever the apprentice is guilty of neglect, refusal to do his duty, or gross misbehavior." Cal. Civ. Code, at 73 (Sims ed. 1906).
640. Cal. Stat. 1905, ch. CDXVII, § 1.
641. Cal. Stat. 1905, ch. CDXVII.
642. Cal. Stat. 1937, ch. 90, CAL. LAB. CODE §§ 3070–91.

the indenture provisions of the Labor Code were repealed.[643] The Labor Code sections still in force were passed in 1939[644] and provide for a semipublic commission of industrial, union, and public members to set standards and generally to supervise industrial apprenticeship agreements. The commission has power to promulgate educational requirements and to limit the work hours apparently independently of the general wage and hour laws.

While California laws declaring that children might be "bound by covenant or indenture . . . to any mechanical trade or art, or the occupation of farming, as apprentices"[645] were general in their scope and application, many of their provisions, indeed, their dominant features, were oriented toward the problems of needy children deprived of parental support and care. They contained, as well, special clauses dealing with the apprenticing of children in orphan asylums and other institutions. If the child had parents, parental consent to the indenture might be dispensed with in circumstances creating or usually accompanying deprivation. The mother might consent to the indenture if the father had died, had become incompetent, had "willfully abandoned his family for one year without making suitable provision for their support," or had "become an habitual drunkard, vagrant"[646] or if the child were illegitimate. Subsequent marriage stripped the mother of her power to indenture her children whether legitimate or illegitimate; they could only be apprenticed with the approval of the county court.[647] Children having no parent or guardian competent to act could bind themselves with the consent of the county court. Facts of incapacity, desertion, drunkenness, and vagrancy were to be decided by a county-court jury before indenture.[648] The county court was authorized to bind out, without reference to whether the child had parents, any minor "who is poor, homeless, chargeable to the county, or an outcast, has no visible means of obtaining an honest livelihood . . . ."[649] Town officers were given a like authority in the case of any child "who, or whose parent or parents are, or shall be-

---

643. Cal. Stat. 1939, ch. 220, § 1.
644. Cal. Stat. 1939, ch. 220, § 2, CAL. LAB. CODE §§ 3070–90.
645. Cal. Stat. 1875–1876, ch. DLIII, § 1.
646. Cal. Stat. 1875–1876, ch. DLIII, § 2.
647. *Ibid.*
648. Cal. Stat. 1875–1876, ch. DLIII, § 6. Under the 1858 act these facts merely had to be "certified by a justice of the peace of the township or county, or sworn to by a credible witness . . . ." Cal. Stat. 1858, ch. CLXXXII, § 2.
649. Cal. Stat. 1875–1876, ch. DLIII, § 8. Under the 1858 act a child who was or might become chargeable to the county was to be bound out by the county supervisors. Cal. Stat. 1858, ch. CLXXXII, § 5.

come, chargeable to any such town or city."[650] By an act of 1862 the county supervisors were empowered to indenture "all children within their respective counties, who are destitute of parents or guardians, or means of support."[651] In 1905 children who were chargeable to the state were added to the list in the 1876 act of poor and homeless children, and a clause was introduced authorizing "any citizen" to initiate indenture proceedings for all such children.[652] Special responsibility was imposed upon the county courts to inquire into the treatment of these children and to "defend them from all cruelty, neglect, breach of contract, or misconduct on the part of their masters."[653] Masters were obligated to see that homeless and destitute apprentices were taught "to read and write, and the ground rules of arithmetic, the compound rules, and the ratio and proportion," were given "requisite instruction in the different branches of his trade or calling," and at the expiration of the term, were supplied with "two full new suits of clothes and the sum of fifty dollars, gold; the two new suits . . . to be worth at least sixty dollars, gold."[654] By separate statutes the power to bind out was also vested in the public and private institutions caring for dependent and delinquent children, in the boards of directors of the county infirmaries with respect to "all such indigent children as may belong" to them,[655] in the Board of Managers of the San Francisco Industrial School with respect to the inmates of that institution without restriction as to the conditions of the indenture except that it should inure to the general benefit and welfare of the child,[656] in the trustees of the State Reform School for inmates of that institution,[657] in the Board of Supervisors of the City and County of San Francisco with respect to any boy on the training ship in San Francisco Bay "to any merchant ship or vessel of the United States, for service thereon, upon such terms and conditions

650. Cal. Stat. 1858, ch. CLXXXII, § 6.
651. Cal. Stat. 1862, ch. CCXCI, § 1. The act of 1863 contained the same language. Cal. Stat. 1863, ch. LXVI, § 1.
652. Cal. Stat. 1905, ch. CDXVII, § 268.
653. Cal. Stat. 1875–1876, ch. DLIII, § 11.
654. Cal. Stat. 1875–1876, ch. DLIII, § 9.
655. Cal. Stat. 1860, ch. CCXLVII, § 21.
656. Cal. Stat. 1858, ch. CCIX, § 10. Cal. Stat. 1863–1864, ch. LXXVII, § 3, declared an apprentice who fled from his master a fugitive from the school.
657. Cal. Stat. 1860, ch. CCXXXIII, § 22. When the Reform School acts were repealed in 1868, inmates were to be sent under contract to the San Francisco Industrial School or the United States Apprentice Ship in San Francisco Harbor to be "cared for, maintained, apprenticed and governed . . . ." Cal. Stat. 1867–1868, ch. DXV, § 4(5). For the apprenticing provision in the act establishing the Preston School of Industry see Cal. Stat. 1889, ch. CIII, § 18.

as said Board shall prescribe, consistent with the original enlistment of said boys,"[658] in municipal councils with respect to children committed to their industrial schools,[659] and in private orphan asylums.[660]

The orphan asylum act of 1860 authorized orphans and half orphans "under the care, control, support and education" of the asylum to bind themselves, with the consent of the managers of the asylum, "to serve as a clerk, apprentice, or servant, in any profession, trade, or employment."[661] The board of managers of the asylum was to fix the amount of compensation, the time to be allowed for education during the period of indenture, or the profession, trade, or employment if the capacity of the infant so required. The consent of the parent of a half orphan was necessary if the parent resided in the state and was of legal capacity.[662] Under the amendatory act of 1870, if for a period of six months the parent or guardian neglected to pay for the board and education of the child as agreed with the asylum managers, the managers might at their discretion, "if deeming it for the welfare of such child" and if the child assented, bind him out without the consent of the parent. Assent of children under ten may be "assumed" by the asylum managers.[663] The special acts of 1862, 1863, and 1870 dealing with the San Francisco Ladies' Protection & Relief Society[664] and the San Francisco Lying-In Hospital and Foundling Asylum[665] authorized those institutions to bind out children without parental consent.

With so much legislative attention to the system for binding out children, one might suppose it to be a common method for securing their maintenance and education. Such, however, does not seem to have been the case. In fact, ample evidence exists that the formal process of indenture was seldom used either by parents or by child-caring institutions.[666]

---

658. Cal. Stat. 1875–1876, ch. LXXIX, § 3.

659. Cal. Stat. 1883, ch. XLIX, § 33; Cal. Stat. 1880, ch. CCXXXVIII, § 33.

660. The provisions were for the San Francisco Orphan Asylum Society or any other orphan asylum society in this state, Cal. Stat. 1860, ch. LXV; Cal. Stat. 1869–1870, ch. CCXXXIV, the San Francisco Ladies' Protection & Relief Society, Cal. Stat. 1862, ch. CCCXCI; Cal. Stat. 1863, ch. LXVI, and the San Francisco Lying-In Hospital and Foundling Asylum, Cal. Stat. 1869–1870, ch. CCXXXVII, § 1.

661. Cal. Stat. 1860, ch. LXV, § 1.

662. Cal. Stat. 1860, ch. LXV, §§ 2, 5.

663. Cal. Stat. 1869–1870, ch. CCXXXIV, §§ 1–2.

664. Cal. Stat. 1863, ch. LXVI; Cal. Stat. 1862, ch. CCXCI.

665. Cal. Stat. 1869–1870, ch. CCXXXVII.

666. Report on Labor, Stat. 1888, at 193; see tenBroek, *California's Welfare Law— Origins and Development*, 45 CALIF. L. REV. 241, 297 (1957).

Doubtless Grace Abbott's conclusion generally about apprenticing of poor children in the United States was as applicable to California as elsewhere:

> It was a cheap and easy way of providing what passed as care for these children, and as long as work at a very young age was considered necessary to prevent them from becoming paupers in later life, the system was approved and extended. Trade-training was not given or contemplated. Taken by farmers and housewives, not to give them a home or to train them for future work, but because they needed help and could not afford to pay farm hands or servants, the children were used for the most routine tasks so they learned little of farming and housekeeping. . . . If poor children were to pay for their care by the services they rendered the families to which they were apprenticed, they were certain to become overworked and undereducated little slaveys even when they were not treated unkindly. . . . Experience has shown that to rely upon free placement of dependent children under apprenticeship contracts means that many of them will become neglected children overworked by farmers and housewives and denied the education and opportunities for recreation needed by every child, and especially by children whose fathers and mothers cannot give them help and guidance during the adolescent period.[667]

## Public Support, Guardianship, and the Responsibility of Relatives

Guardianship and custody struggles fall into several classes based upon the interested parties: contests between the parents; contests between a parent and a legal stranger—a relative, a friend, or a person unknown to the parent; contests between third persons; contests between the state and a parent or another having charge of the child. As between the parents, when separated or divorced, neither has a claim of right, and the courts may with few restraints award custody as they deem proper. When the parents are not separated, the father had a primary right before 1913; since then the parents have been equally entitled to custody unless the child is illegitimate, in which case the mother alone is so entitled. In the second class of cases—struggles between parents and others— the applicable rule is that of dominant parental right, contained for many years in Code of Civil Procedure section 1751[668] and continued in judicial thinking,[669] modified by the requirement that

---

667. 1 Abbott, The Child and the State 192–93 (1938).
668. Cal. Code Civ. Proc. of 1872, § 1751, amended by Cal. Stat. 1891, ch. CXXIII, § 2, repealed by Cal. Stat. 1931, ch. 281, § 1700.
669. Stewart v. Stewart, 41 Cal. 2d 447, 260 P.2d 44 (1953); Roche v. Roche, 25 Cal. 2d 141, 152 P.2d 999 (1944); *Ex parte* Campbell, 130 Cal. 380, 62 Pac. 613 (1900); see text accompanying notes 370–94 *supra*.

the parent must be a fit and proper person, and influenced by the preference given the parent by Civil Code section 246[670] and Probate Code section 1407[671] unless the best interests of the child demand some other disposition.[672]

As to the third class—struggles between third persons or strangers—we have noted the provisions in Civil Code section 246 and Probate Code section 1407 that, of two persons equally entitled to custody in other respects, preference goes, after the parent, to one indicated by the wishes of a deceased parent, then to one in charge of the child's support funds, and finally, to a relative.[673] Suppose the third person does not fall into any of these categories? Could the court then freely dispose of the child as it saw fit, guided "by what appears to be for the best interests of the child in respect to its temporal, and its mental and moral welfare" and by the "intelligent preference" of the child itself?[674]

To which of these classes did the child-caring institution belong? Did it succeed to the legal position of the parents in the case of full orphans and abandoned children? If it was a third person, did it stand in a position different from that of other third persons with whom the child was left? Did the dominant parental-right rule apply to the surviving parent of half orphans or the parent or parents of abandoned children who turned up at the institution? In this area as in others many new rules were evolved and old ones modified. Among other things, the dominant parental right was less dominant when asserted against an orphanage than when asserted against relatives or other strangers.

Child-caring institutions obviously must have some legal standing with respect to the custody and control of the children in their charge. Such legal standing would be likely to be conferred by the legislature and/or the courts during a time when child-caring institutions were the principal method of caring for dependent children, when their managers were so influential as to secure large scale legislative appropriations for the operation of their establishments, and when they were able to sanctify themselves in a special

---

670. Cal. Civ. Code of 1872, § 246.
671. Cal. Prob. Code § 1407.
672. See text accompanying notes 353–69 *supra.*
673. A fifth preference was added in 1941: "If the child has already been declared to be a ward of the juvenile court, to the probation officer of said court." Cal. Stat. 1941, ch. 799, § 1. Cal. Stat. 1961, ch. 1616, § 11, added "or dependent child" following "ward."
674. Cal. Civ. Code of 1872, § 246, transferred to Prob. Code § 1406 by Cal. Stat. 1931, ch. 281, §§ 1406, 1700.

constitutional provision. Such legal standing would occur, however, in practice and by tacitly acknowledged authority, almost as a matter of necessity. Anybody who desired a child for whatever purpose could not be permitted simply to go to the asylum, select a child on sight, and remove it at will without identification, explanation, or claim of right. There would soon develop the institutional counterpart of the common-law right of possession or a presumptive right to custody in the institution which had the child, at least as against all comers who had no claim of right. The later-developed rule[675] that state aid was not available for a child for whom there had been an offer of a home at its worst required more formality than this. The offer had to be bona fide. There had to be a home. Implicitly, those making the offer had to be fit and proper persons, however low, uninspected, and unenforced the standards. So the institution would have to have the authority to protect its physical custody of the children living in the institution.

Suppose the managers voluntarily transferred physical custody to another and wished thereafter to regulate or terminate that custody. This became a fairly regular pattern of care by institutions,[676] greatly stimulated in later years by the state. Did the foster home acquire a right to custody, control, and disposition as against the institution? Were the institutions and the foster parents, or the persons with whom the children were placed by the institution, "two persons equally entitled to the custody in other respects,"[677] leaving the court free to make a decision in accordance with the best interests of the child, or did the institution have a preferred right, to be sustained unless the best interests of the child clearly required some other disposition? Would the competence or fitness of the institution as well as that of the person with whom the child was placed be a test of the right to custody or guardianship? Neither the legislature nor the courts ever developed a comprehensive statement on the rights of child-caring institutions to custody, control, or guardianship of the children in their care. Fragments of such an overall right, perhaps with implications larger than the area immediately covered, are seen in the statutes authorizing the institutions to indenture the children[678] and to consent to

675. Cal. Stat. 1913, ch. 323, § 5.
676. CAHN & BARY, WELFARE ACTIVITIES OF FEDERAL, STATE, AND LOCAL GOVERNMENTS IN CALIFORNIA, 1860–1934, at 22; [1916–1918] 8 CAL. STATE BD. OF CHARITIES AND CORRECTIONS BIENNIAL REP. 34.
677. Cal. Civ. Code of 1872, § 246 (now CAL. PROB. CODE § 1407).
678. Cal. Stat. 1869–1870, ch. CCXXXIV; Cal. Stat. 1869–1870, ch. CCXXXVII, § 2.

their adoption.[679]  The statute of 1870, permitting surviving parents of half orphans to surrender "all control and authority" over their children to the orphanages and giving the institution "as full and complete authority" over such children as they "can legally exercise" over orphans,[680] suggests that orphanage control and authority over orphans were quite complete and that surrender of a half orphan to the orphanage by the surviving parent terminated parental rights and vested comparable rights in the institution. The special statute of 1870 dealing with the San Francisco Lying-In Hospital and Foundling Asylum was more precise with respect to the institution's authority. The trustees were declared to be "the guardians" of the surrendered illegitimates and the foundlings in their care for a specified list of purposes: "To support, care for and educate" them; to bind them out as apprentices; "to give" them "to such persons as may be desirous of adopting" them.[681]  The right of custody required to discharge these functions was to all intents and purposes a general right of custody, comparable to that possessed by the parent himself. The authority, moreover, was legislatively vested. It was unnecessary under the statute for the trustees to proceed to court to secure letters of appointment as guardians. Hence, there would be no consideration of the best interests of any particular child and no judicial determination of the competence or fitness of the trustees of the asylum to be guardians.

In *Ex parte Chambers*,[682] the California Supreme Court affirmed and implemented, though it did not discuss and substantiate, a general right of custody on the part of orphanages, at least as against third persons. The asylum sued out a writ of habeas corpus to recover a child placed by it with a couple who had procured an adoption decree without the consent of the orphanage. The court held that the consent of the orphanage was prerequisite to the adoption under the statute of 1878.[683] It thus invalidated the adoption decree. But it also granted the writ, ordering the child restored to the asylum. There was no consideration by the court of the fitness of the institution, the qualifications of the adoptive couple with whom the child had been placed, or the best interests of

679. Cal. Stat. 1893, ch. XCVI, § 2; Cal. Stat. 1877–1878, ch. DCXXVI, § 1; Cal. Stat. 1869–1870, ch. CCXXXVII, § 2.
680. Cal. Stat. 1869–1870, ch. CCXXXIV, § 3.
681. Cal. Stat. 1869–1870, ch. CCXXXVII, § 2.
682. 80 Cal. 216, 22 Pac. 138 (1889).
683. See Cal. Stat. 1877–1878, ch. DCXXVI.

the child,[684] though the trial court had found that the adoptive couple were fit and proper persons and the welfare of the child would be promoted by the adoption. There was no consideration by the court of the sources or character of the right of the asylum. That right was not linked to the orphanage-adoption-consent statute or to any other statute. The court did refer to the fact that the orphanage was "a corporation duly organized under the laws of this state, and as such entitled to the care, custody, control, and management of orphans and abandoned children, and receives state aid for the support and maintenance of orphans under its care."[685] Whatever the basis of the *Chambers* decision, its authority cannot be doubted. Especially when the various special statutes on the topic are also considered, the decision stands for the proposition that the asylums had a general right of custody of the children left with them as against the claims of third persons. Whether the relinquishments under the two statutes of 1870[686] were irrevocable and foreclosed any future claims the parents might assert against the asylums for the custody of the child is not answered by the statutes or by the reported decisions of the courts. Presumably a revocation would not be effective to restore the rights of the natural parents against parents or masters who had received the children from the asylum by adoption or by indenture.

The principal statute [687] relative to the custody and guardianship rights of the child-caring institutions dealt, not with the relations of institutions to third persons, but with the relations of the asylums to the parent or parents. That statute curtailed the rights of the parent, defined those of the institution, and used criminal sanctions. Perhaps most strikingly of all, the statute vested guardianship rights in the institution, not primarily to enable it to conduct its business or to assure the protection of the best interests of the child, but to coerce the parents into contributing to the support of the child and thus to reduce the financial burden on the public for the child's support. The managers of the child-caring institutions saw little point in seeking support payments from the surviving parents of half orphans.[688] In their view, such parents were

---

684. 80 Cal. at 218, 22 Pac. at 139.
685. 80 Cal. at 216, 22 Pac. at 138.
686. Cal. Stat. 1869–1870, ch. CCXXXIV; Cal. Stat. 1869–1870, ch. CCXXXVII.
687. Cal. Stat. 1873–1874, ch. CXCIX.
688. 1880 STATE BD. OF EXAMINERS REP. 10, 1880 SEN. & ASS. J., app. II; FIFTEENTH AND SIXTEETNH [*sic*] ANNUAL REP., SAN FRANCISCO LADIES' PROTECTION & RELIEF SOCIETY, 1869–1870 SEN. & ASS. J., app. III, at 7, 13.

likely to be not only immersed in poverty but in other problems of their own. The state officials, however, viewed the matter differently.[689]

The support derived from "the children's relations," complained the state board of examiners,

> is very small, though at the time of the admission of the children to the asylums the parent or relations agree to pay a small sum monthly. After a few payments, in most cases, they cease altogether, and frequently neglect to pay anything. No suggestion has been offered by the management whereby those who are able and do not may be forced to contribute. It does not appear that the bounty of the state is or can be abused, except in this regard. However, if failure to contribute should cause the relative or guardian to lose control of the child, and the guardianship to be invested in the officers of the asylums, it might work a salutary change in this respect.[690]

Thus the proposed method of enforcement was not judicial compulsion or penal sanctions. It was rather to sever the right to the custody and control of the child and to vest it in the asylum. Increasing the support contributions of parents on behalf of children whom they had not abandoned but merely left with the asylums was, in this official view, one way of reducing public and private charitable expenditures. Preventing abandonment was another. Here the enforcement device of stripping the missing parent of his rights to his child appeared less promising. In addition, Penal Code section 271 defined abandonment as follows: "Every parent of any child under the age of six years . . . who deserts such child in any place whatever, with intent wholly to abandon it."[691] This covers only the starkest form of a series of acts, omissions, and attitudes taking many forms and involving many degrees. The state board of examiners urged rigid penal enforcement of the law against abandonment and the strengthening of that law.[692]

---

689. The subsidy legislation required detailed record keeping by the institution directed to the use of family resources and income. The institution records were to contain information about "the place where either parent or both died, nativity of the parents, where married . . . when they came to California, or Nevada, place of residence in California, and habits of sobriety." Cal. Stat. 1880, ch. XLIX, § 3. They were also to contain information about "the estate, if any, to which the child is heir, and the insurance, if any, on father's or mother's life . . . the amounts paid for the specific support" of the child. Cal. Stat. 1880, ch. XLIX, §§ 3(1), 3(4). The legislation further presumed contributions by some parents or relatives. Cal. Stat. 1880, ch. XLIX, §§ 3(4), 5(5). No state money was to be available for a child "for whose specific support there is paid to any such institution the sum of ten dollars or more per month." Cal. Stat. 1880, ch. XLIX, § 7(3).
690. 1881 STATE BD. OF EXAMINERS REP. 10, 1881 SEN. & ASS. J., app. II.
691. Cal. Pen. Code of 1872, § 271.
692. 1881 STATE BD. OF EXAMINERS REP. 9, 1881 SEN. & ASS. J., app. II.

The 1874 act embodied many of these elements.[693] Abandonment and failure to support were made penal offenses, thus in effect repeating Penal Code sections 270 and 271. Both resulted in loss of rights to the child. "Any parent who shall knowingly and willfully abandon, or who, having the ability so to do, shall fail, neglect, or refuse to maintain his or her minor child under the age of fourteen years, shall be deemed guilty of a misdemeanor . . . and shall forfeit the guardianship of such child."[694] It was also made a misdemeanor knowingly and falsely to represent a child to be an orphan when seeking his admission to an asylum.[695] A parent or a guardian who left a child in an asylum supported by charity for a year without notice to the managers that he was parent or guardian would "be deemed to have abandoned" and would "forever forfeit all right to the guardianship, care, custody and control of such child."[696] The managers were given "preferred right to the guardianship" of any such abandoned child, and the courts were directed to make the appointment upon application.[697] The managers were required to publicize in the newspapers the name, age, and sex "of each child received . . . as an orphan" and any other information likely to lead to the identification of the child by its "relations or friends."[698] The abandonment and support features of this measure, shorn of their penal sanction, eventually found their way in 1905 into the Civil Code[699] and in 1931 into the Probate Code.[700] With their penal sanctions in full force, they were embodied in 1905 in the Penal Code.[701]

The difference between ordinary abandonment and abandonment in orphanages in the provision's language as it was in the act of 1874 and as it is today in the Probate Code[702] is significant. Abandonment unconnected with an orphanage requires "knowingly or wilfully" to act or to fail to support. Leaving or permitting the child to remain in the asylum need only be done "knowingly." Intent must be found in the ordinary case of abandon-

---

693. Cal. Stat. 1874, ch. CXCIX, § 2.
694. *Ibid.*
695. *Ibid.*
696. Cal. Stat. 1874, ch. CXCIX, § 3.
697. Cal. Stat. 1874, ch. CXCIX, § 4.
698. Cal. Stat. 1874, ch. CXCIX, § 1.
699. Cal. Civ. Code § 246(4) (Sims ed. 1905).
700. CAL. PROB. CODE § 1409.
701. CAL. PEN. CODE § 271a, added by Cal. Stat. 1905, ch. DLXVIII, § 2 (misdemeanor), amended by Cal. Stat. 1909, ch. 190, § 2 (imprisonment up to one year or fine or both).
702. CAL. PROB. CODE § 1409.

ment.[703] No such requirement can be read into the language of the provision dealing with permitting a child to remain in an orphanage. By ordinary abandonment, the parent "forfeits" all rights to the guardianship of the child. By permitting the child to remain in the asylum under the conditions and for the time prescribed, a parent abandons and "forever forfeits" all rights to the guardianship of the child.[704] Presumably, in the case of an abandonment in an orphanage, the court could not reach the conclusion of *In the Matter of the Guardianship of Michels*[705] that a decree of abandonment only "strips the parent of the then present right to the guardianship"[706] but does not necessarily preclude future guardianship rights of the parent. The act of abandonment in an orphanage is completed within a year, and lack of notice of parental status is a governing element. Neither the length of time nor the notice of parental status plays a controlling role in ordinary abandonment. The key factor in the difference of requirements appears to be that also identified as a requirement in the case of an abandonment in an orphanage, namely, support during the specified time by charity, that is, by the public.[707]

As the twentieth century progressed, substantive changes in the responsibility-of-relatives provisions concerning children tended to make clear that the support obligation depended on parentage or merely on being a relative rather than on rights to custody, on a property interest in the child, or on a reciprocal relationship between the right to services and the obligation of support. Motivation for each change was the same, to minimize the financial burden on the public in supporting the poor. The instigating agencies were those in charge of public welfare programs.

---

703. *In re* Green, 192 Cal. 714, 221 Pac. 903 (1923); Estate of Akers, 184 Cal. 514, 194 Pac. 706 (1920); Estate of Moore, 179 Cal. 302, 176 Pac. 461 (1918); In the Matter of the Guardianship of Schwartz, 171 Cal. 633, 154 Pac. 304 (1915); In the Matter of the Guardianship of Snowball, 156 Cal. 240, 104 Pac. 444 (1909); 2 ARMSTRONG, CALIFORNIA FAMILY LAW 1006–14 (1953).
704. CAL. PROB. CODE § 1409; Cal. Stat. 1874, ch. CXCIX.
705. 170 Cal. 339, 149 Pac. 587 (1915).
706. *Id.* at 343, 149 Pac. at 589.
707. A statute of 1893 substantially qualified the guardianship rights forfeited to the managers of the asylum after one year of maintenance of the child. Cal. Stat. 1893, ch. CLXXII. The managers were to be appointed guardians "if there be no special reasons to the contrary in any particular case." One special reason to the contrary might be that the parent left the child in the asylum with "good cause therefor being shown." Another might be that the court found the managers unfit to be guardians, a matter into which the courts were told they were free to inquire. The managers could not be appointed guardians of a child over fourteen years of age without his consent. This statute did not repeal the act of 1874, nor was it in turn repealed in 1905 when the provisions of the act of 1874 were codified in the Civil Code; it remained on the books until 1931. Cal. Stat. 1931, ch. 281, § 1700.

Created in 1903, the State Board of Charities and Corrections[708] took up and intensified the campaign for enforcement of parental support obligations, long conducted by the board of examiners. Now, however, officialdom changed its mind about the wisdom and efficacy of its support enforcement device; permanent separation of children from parents was conceded to be an improper device.

> Many children are placed in the orphan asylum by the living parent [wrote the State Board of Charities] as a temporary home to tide over an emergency, and are taken out as soon as the emergency has passed. That this is by far the largest number is shown by the fact that the average stay of all children in the orphan asylum is less than two years. The asylum performs a good service for this class of people, who pay something towards the support of the children. We commend this practice as far better than the permanent separation of these children from their parents.[709]

The Board's recognition of a perversion of this practice and its proposed remedy has been frequently reiterated in the intervening half century with increasing emphasis in recent years:

> There is another class of parents, much smaller, who put their children into the orphan asylum to avoid the burden of their support, and then claim them at fourteen years of age, to be used for what they can get for their services . . . . In many of these cases, both parents are living, and then the asylum has to bear the full burden of the support, but probably in most of them, both the asylum and the state are imposed upon. There is no proper method of determining dependency, and it is easy, therefore, to get children into the orphan asylum and then abandon them. . . . We believe that if this Board were authorized to employ an agent, whose duty it would be to visit the orphan asylums, get the list of such dependent children, investigate the homes, and when the children had been abandoned by the parents in the orphan asylum to bring an action under the law for failure to support, that this evil could be easily remedied.[710]

Interpretative rules issued by the State Board of Control under the state statute providing aid to orphans, half orphans, and aban-

---

708. Cal. Stat. 1903, ch. CCCLXII.
709. [1910–1912] STATE BD. OF CHARITIES & CORRECTIONS, FIFTH BIENNIAL REP. 37 (1912).
710. 11 *id*. at 37–38. For a time, the State Board of Charities and Corrections had advocated that state aid should be granted only after a judicial determination of dependency. The court could at the same time, argued the board, sever parental relations if the child was abandoned or the home was unfit and, moreover, could enforce parental support obligations by direct order. [1904–1906] STATE BD. OF CHARITIES & CORRECTIONS, SECOND BIENNIAL REP. 15; [1906–1908] *id*., THIRD BIENNIAL REP. 169–70 (1909).

doned children, and a series of amendments to the statute itself dealt indirectly, but nevertheless drastically, with parental support by requiring a determination of dependency, as defined by state officials, and by authorizing allocation of partial support contributions among parents and other relatives. Previously state funds paid to institutions or to counties had not been contingent upon state-required determination of need. If the child was in an institution and the institution met size and record-keeping requirements, state money was automatically available. Institution managers set the terms and conditions, including parental ability and willingness to pay, for admission to the institution. The same was true of the counties; the supervisors were free to fix the conditions of eligibility, and they might or might not first determine that the child's parent or parents were unable to support it.[711] In 1907, as an incident to audit procedures, state agents began to review cases to determine, among other things, whether children receiving aid were needy. A considerable reduction in claims was reported as a result.[712] Rules published by the Board of Control were designed to standardize the need determination and to see that parental support was secured whenever possible.[713] In 1913 the legislature

---

711. Under the responsibility-of-relatives provision introduced into the Juvenile Court Act of 1905, Cal. Stat. 1905, ch. DCX, § 16, in any order providing for custody of a dependent or delinquent child, the judge was authorized to direct that the expense of maintaining the child be paid by the parent, parents, or guardian and to fix the amount. In the order, he was also to specify whether the parents were to exercise control over the child and how much. Disobedience of the order to pay or parental interference with the custody prescribed was, of course, contempt of court. *Ibid.* In 1909 this parental liability clause was linked with a county support provision. Cal. Stat. 1909, ch. 133, § 21. If the parent or guardian was found to be "unable to pay the whole expense," in the custody order the judge could direct that the remainder be met out of the county treasury.

712. 1909 State Bd. of Examiners Rep. 10.

713. Under them, aid was to be denied in all of the following circumstances: if sufficient showing was not made as to dependency; if it was evident to the Board of Control that a parent was able to pay $10 a month or more and was not doing so; if either or both parents died while residing in another state or country and documentary evidence of the death was not produced; if the child was brought to this state for the purpose of placing it in a state-aided institution; if the child was not "a bona fide resident of the state and fairly entitled to its protection and support"; if the child was abandoned but had not been abandoned "absolutely . . . for at least one year" and supported during that year by a state-aided institution; if the mother was dead or in a state institution and the father was not "physically disabled or otherwise absolutely unable to support such a child for some reason sufficient in the opinion of this board"; if the widow had more than $1000 assessed value real property or $500 in cash. If the father was committed to a state prison or insane asylum, the child was entitled to half orphan's aid. If both parents were so committed or one was dead and the other was committed, the child was entitled to full orphan's aid. The Board of Control proposed that parents in state hospitals and prisons be put on a wage basis so that they could support their families when possible. If a family of children were in an institution and some contribution was made for them, the contribution had to be so allocated as to render the maximum number of children ineligible. [1910–1912] State Bd. of Control Rep. 74–75 (1913); [1916–1918] State Bd. of Control, Children's Dep't Rep. 31, 52 (1919).

added its sanction to the system of state-created and -enforced
standards of need by granting to a mother denied county aid direct
appeal to the State Board of Control[714] and by authorizing the
Board to employ children's agents to review grants made by the
counties.[715] In 1921 the statute caught up with its administration
by specifying that orphans, half orphans, and abandoned and
foundling children must be "needy" to be eligible for state aid.[716]
This requirement remains in the law today.[717]

Other developments were stimulated by the usual need to conserve public funds. In response to a plea from the State Board of
Charities and Corrections which "earnestly recommended" it, not
on grounds of equal treatment and even-handed justice, but so
that the "reputed father" might be compelled "to support the
mother and the child, and relieve the county from any responsibility for the support,"[718] Civil Code section 196a was adopted in
1913, making the father as well as the mother of an illegitimate
child responsible for "support and education suitable to his circumstances." A civil suit to enforce this responsibility might be brought
by the mother or by a guardian,[719] and the court was given the
same power to compel performance that it had in a suit for divorce
by the wife.[720] As originally adopted, Penal Code section 270, supplying penal sanctions for support duties of relatives, had not applied to the father of illegitimate children, and Civil Code section

714. Cal. Stat. 1913, ch. 323, § 1.
715. Cal. Stat. 1913, ch. 323, § 3.
716. Cal. Stat. 1921, ch. 390, § 1.
717. CAL. WELFARE & INST'NS CODE § 1500. The degree to which these policies and
procedures were effective is largely left to speculation. The Board of Control, in its 1916–
1918 biennial report, asserted that by its review it was able "greatly" to reduce the institutional population. "In many cases," said the Board, "relatives and parents have been traced
and made to resume a responsibility toward their kin, sometimes by taking them into their
homes and at others by providing for them in foster homes or in the institution with
proper payment." Over one-third of the children who had been classed as dependent in
one institution intensively studied were found to have relatives fully able to support them.
[1916–1918] STATE BD. OF CONTROL, CHILDREN'S DEP'T REP. 17 (1919). The device by
which parental responsibility was enforced, however, was denial of state aid to the children.
Without a large staff to follow up closed cases, there were no means of knowing whether the
parental support thereafter supplied was adequate. The Board itself showed some un-
easiness on this topic by proposing in the same report that nonsupport cases be made a
county charge with the expectation that the counties would put into operation a law permitting them to employ offenders on the roads. *Id.* at 52. The Board of Control complained that in nonstate aid cases, beyond the jurisdiction of the Board, the institution
managers admitted children with very little investigation as to need and parental ability.
"Were the institution not so accessible and were there a diagnosis of the family need, fathers
and mothers might not come to rely on orphanages as an easy solution for their domestic
problems, and an inexpensive means of furnishing a home for their children." Institutions
by these practices are not only assisting in the shirking of family responsibility but "are
assisting in the disintegration of homes." *Id.* at 17, 18.
718. [1910–1912] STATE BD. OF CHARITIES & CORRECTIONS REP. 43 (1913).
719. CAL. CIV. CODE § 196a.
720. *Ibid.*

196a was held not to "change the application of that section in any way."[721] In 1915 the legislature returned to the task begun in 1913, amending section 270 to place the illegitimate child upon the same footing as the legitimate with respect to the parental obligation and the criminal offense. In 1921,[722] 1923,[723] and 1925[724] it recast the whole section, allocating primary criminal liability to the father for the support of legitimate and illegitimate children. The father's liability existed though the mother was entitled to custody and though the mother[725] or another person or organization "voluntarily or involuntarily" furnished the child's food, clothing, and shelter.[726] The mother was also subject to the section's criminal liability after the father's death or inability. In the 1950's the legislature added another use for section 270 by directing its use to enforce the support obligation of parents of children receiving public assistance.[727] Section 270 had begun its career as an enforcement tool for Civil Code-created obligations,[728] had moved through a middle pe-

---

721. *In re* Gambetta, 169 Cal. 100, 145 Pac. 1005 (1915).

722. Cal. Stat. 1921, ch. 911, § 1.

723. Cal. Stat. 1923, ch. 284, § 1.

724. Cal. Stat. 1925, ch. 325, § 1.

725. The addition of the mother at this place was made necessary by a judicial decision holding that she was not covered by the phrase "other persons" in the 1921 amendment declaring that "it shall be no defense" to an action against the father under Penal Code § 270 "that such child has been provided for by other persons." *In re* Kendrick, 60 Cal. App. 146, 212 Pac. 226 (1st Dist. 1922).

726. A new presumption was set up. The district attorney's case was made out if he showed that the father failed to provide his child with necessary food, clothing, and shelter. The burden of showing justification was shifted to the father. He had to show that he did not do so willfully or that he had lawful excuse.

727. Cal. Stat. 1951, ch. 709, as amended, CAL. WELFARE & INST'NS CODE §§ 1570–79.

728. People v. Green, 19 Cal. App. 109, 124 Pac. 871 (2d Dist. 1912), reviewed the relationship of Penal Code § 270 to the Civil Code sections on parental support and reaffirmed earlier California opinions. A 1905 amendment to Penal Code § 270 had removed the words making it dependent on the Civil Code sections—failure "to perform any duty imposed upon him by law" to furnish necessary food, etc. Read literally as amended, § 270 made it a criminal offense for "a parent" willfully to omit without lawful excuse "to furnish necessary food, clothing, shelter and medical attendance to his child." There was no differentiation among parents and no differentiation among children, legitimate or illegitimate. Notwithstanding, the district court of appeal reasserted the pre-1905 linkage and held the father of the illegitimate child without liability for support under Penal Code § 270. "Section 270 of the Penal Code seems to have been enacted," said the court, "with the purpose of furnishing a complement to those sections of the Civil Code which determine the obligations of parents to support and maintain their children. By the sections of the Civil Code it is determined what those obligations are, and by the section referred to of the Penal Code it is made a felony for a parent to fail to discharge his duties in those respects." *Id.* at 109, 124 Pac. at 872. California Civil Code § 196 imposed support obligations on the parent with custody. Civil Code § 200 gave the mother custody of the illegitimate child. "[S]he then has the whole burden of providing it with support and no duty in that regard rests upon the father." *Id.* at 109–10, 124 Pac. at 872. Once Civil Code § 196a was adopted, the California Supreme Court then immediately and unanimously repudiated the doctrine of the district court of appeal which it had earlier failed to reverse. *In re* Gambetta, 169 Cal. 100, 145 Pac. 1005 (1915). Penal Code § 270 now ceased to be a penal enforcement provision for the Civil Code-created obligations of support.

riod in which it defined its own crimes, and today has become an enforcement adjunct of duties specified in the Welfare and Institutions Code.

# 6

# Present Status and
# Constitutionality of
# the Family Law
# of the Poor

*Introduction*

It is no longer fashionable to speak of the poor law, let alone the law of the poor. The implications of these two forms of statement would appear to be quite different but they are not so in fact. Generally, the poor law is identified with a particular statute, containing presumably a limited set of provisions authorizing the granting of public aid to the destitute. Historically, that statute in England was 43 Elizabeth, chapter 2;[729] in California it was the Pauper Act of 1901,[730] locally enacting 43 Elizabeth, chapter 2, and the Indigent Act of 1933,[731] continuing it in force. The law of the poor, on the other hand, suggests a much wider scope: a body of laws governing the poor, regarded as a distinct class in society whose legal status is defined and whose lives are in many ways ruled by provisions and procedures which are not of general application. As shown earlier, however, 43 Elizabeth, chapter 2 was a whole series of acts collected into one, a comprehensive system or code of laws, authorizing the grant of public aid, it is true, but at the same time also subjecting the recipients to an array of public controls and special rules. These regulated their lives as to the time, manner, form, and recompense of labor, if any, movement and travel, place of abode and living arrangements, personal and civil rights, and family relationships. 43 Elizabeth, chapter 2 not only contained many such special legal provisions about the poor going far beyond the simple administration of aid, but it also

---

729. An Acte for the Reliefe of the Poore, 43 Eliz. 1, c. 2 (1601).
730. Cal. Stat. 1901, ch. CCX, at 636, repealed and reenacted by the Indigent Act of 1933, Cal. Stat. ch. 761, at 2005.
731. Cal. Stat. 1933, ch. 761, at 2005 (now Cal. WELFARE & INST'NS CODE §§ 2400–611, popularly known today as County Aid or General Relief).

was a seminal source of many others. It constituted in every important sense both a poor law and a law of the poor.

Labels and details have changed; the substance has not. California today has a law of the poor including a family law of the poor. This family law of the poor especially retains its ancient and essential character. In most respects, its present status is a reenactment of its past history. It remains today in basic matters what it has been from its beginnings in Elizabethan England, its transplantation and firm establishment into colonial and later constitutional America, and its development and adoption in California by a combined process of re-evolution and reception during and after local conditions that were in many ways quite unique.

The law of the poor today encompasses all those special rules and procedures dealing with or involved in the granting of welfare aids and services by the public to persons in need thereof and unable to secure them for themselves. It is not restricted to the relatively small group of undifferentiated indigents now covered by California's version of the Statute of Elizabeth.[732] It includes as well those numerous programs which cover differentiated categories of the total mass of the poor: the blind,[733] the disabled,[734] the aged,[735] families with dependent children,[736] the mentally ill and defective.[737] A good portion of the law of the poor is set forth in a comprehensive system or code of laws, the Welfare and Institutions Code, which for bulk, detail, and pervasiveness puts to shame as puny pamphlets the works of Coke, Bacon, and the other sixteenth and seventeenth century English ministers. Other parts of the law of the poor are to be found in various titles of the Federal Social Security Act,[738] in a number of other California codes, particularly the Penal

---

732. CAL. WELFARE & INST'NS CODE §§ 2400–611. As of December 1964 there were 42,400 persons receiving such aid. Cal. Dep't Social Welfare, Public Welfare in California, Table 1 (Statistical Series PA 3–63, Dec. 1964).

733. CAL. WELFARE & INST'NS CODE §§ 3000–473. As of December 1964 there were 12,215 blind persons receiving such aid. Cal. Dep't Social Welfare, Public Welfare in California, Table 1 (Statistical Series PA 3–63, Dec. 1964).

734. CAL. WELFARE & INST'NS CODE §§ 4000–192. As of December 1964 there were 55,232 persons receiving such aid. Cal. Dep't Social Welfare, Public Welfare in California, Table 1 (Statistical Series PA 3–63, Dec. 1964).

735. CAL. WELFARE & INST'NS CODE §§ 2000–386. As of December 1964 there were 270,678 persons receiving such aid. Cal. Dep't Social Welfare, Public Welfare in California, Table 1 (Statistical Series PA 3–63, Dec. 1964).

736. CAL. WELFARE & INST'NS CODE §§ 1500–79. As of December 1964 there were 125,600 families with 380,875 children and a total of 514,145 persons receiving such aid. Cal. Dep't Social Welfare, Public Welfare in California, Table 1 (Statistical Series PA 3–63, Dec. 1964).

737. CAL. WELFARE & INST'NS CODE §§ 5000–7511. As of June 1963 there were 37,998 persons in all state facilities including state-aided hospitals. CAL. ECONOMIC DEVELOPMENT AGENCY, CALIFORNIA STATISTICAL ABSTRACT 146 (1964).

738. Social Security Act, §§ 1–6, 49 Stat. 620 (1935), as amended, 42 U.S.C. §§ 301–06 (Supp. V, 1964) (Title I); §§ 301–03, 49 Stat. 626 (1935), as amended, 42 U.S.C. §§ 501–03 (1958), as amended, 42 U.S.C. § 501 (Supp. V, 1964) (Title III); §§ 401–06, 49 Stat. 627 (1935), as amended, 42 U.S.C. §§ 601–09 (Supp. V, 1964) (Title IV); §§ 511–15, 49 Stat. 631 (1935), as amended, 42 U.S.C. §§ 711–15 (1958), as amended, 42 U.S.C. §§ 711–14 (Supp. V, 1964) (Title

Code,[739] in the voluminous rules and regulations of the State Department of Social Welfare,[740] and in county ordinances, rules, and practices. However scattered and prolix its sources and provisions, the law of the poor is still very much the law of a distinct class.

That part of the law of the poor which deals with the relationships among members of a family or household is the family law of the poor. The welfare programs providing for the needs of families with minor children—the indigent aid program[741] and the program of aid to families with dependent children[742]—are prolific sources of this law; but regulations of the relationships of husband and wife and parent and adult children are also to be found in the so-called adult programs.[743] In California today, as in Tudor England and colonial America, the family law of the poor derives its substantive rules and characteristic features from the central concept of the poor law system: public provision for the care and support of the poor. Indeed, as an outgrowth or product of the assumption of the public responsibility for relieving the distress of poverty, it consists primarily, now as earlier, of concomitants of that assumption. These take the form of devices designed to minimize and regulate the fiscal expenditure by government. In addition, it consists of conditions attached to the grant of aid or services relating to the conduct, behavior, morals, and even the beliefs and attitudes of the eligible recipients.

The principal topics of family law are: (1) The relation of husband and wife—the methods of instituting and terminating the relationship, and the rights and duties of each toward the other; (2) the parent-minor child relationship—including the relationship between the parents with respect to the minor children; (3) other relatives—who are they, and what legal significance attaches to their relationship? With respect to each of these topics, there is a family law of the poor which in origin, administration, enforcement, content, and purpose is distinct from the family law of the rest of the community— the civil family law—though

V, pt. 2); § 521, 49 Stat. 633 (1935), as amended, 42 U.S.C. §§ 721–28 (Supp. V, 1964) (Title V, pt. 3); §§ 531–32, added by 77 Stat. 274 (1963), 42 U.S.C. §§ 729–29a (Supp. V, 1964); §§ 1001–06, 49 Stat. 645 (1935), as amended, 42 U.S.C. §§ 1201–06 (Supp. V, 1964) (Title X); §§ 1401–05, added by 64 Stat. 555 (1950), as amended, 42 U.S.C. §§ 1351–55 (Supp. V, 1964) (Title XIV); §§ 1601–05, added by 76 Stat. 197 (1962), 42 U.S.C. §§ 1381–85 (Supp. V, 1964) (Title XVI); §§ 1701–04, added by 77 Stat. 275 (1963), 42 U.S.C. §§ 1391–94 (Supp. V, 1964) (Title XVII).

739. *E.g.*, CAL. PEN. CODE §§ 270, 271, 278, 647.

740. These are contained in the following CAL. DEP'T OF SOCIAL WELFARE, MANUALS OF POLICIES AND PROCEDURES: OLD AGE SECURITY, AID TO THE BLIND, AID TO DISABLED, AID TO FAMILIES WITH DEPENDENT CHILDREN, ADOPTIONS IN CALIFORNIA, AGED INSTITUTIONS, BOARDING HOMES FOR CHILDREN AND AGED PERSONS, RESEARCH AND STATISTICS, FISCAL MANUAL [hereinafter cited respectively as OLD AGE SECURITY MANUAL, AID TO BLIND MANUAL, AID TO DISABLED MANUAL, AFDC MANUAL, ADOPTIONS MANUAL, AGED INSTITUTIONS MANUAL, BOARDING HOMES MANUAL, RESEARCH AND STATISTICS, FISCAL MANUAL].

741. CAL. WELFARE & INST'NS CODE §§ 2400–904.

742. CAL. WELFARE & INST'NS CODE §§ 1500–79.

743. *E.g.*, CAL. WELFARE & INST'NS CODE §§ 1508, 1511, 2160, 2181, 2224, 2500, 2576, 2881, 3011, 4011, 5077, 5151, 5260, 5265, 5402.5, 5404.

of course the two bodies of law overlap at points and have elements in common.

## Creating and Terminating the Marital Relation

In civil family law, the relation of husband and wife is entered by marriage, the required formalities being a license, solemnization, authentication, and the filing of a certificate of registry of marriage.[744] Thus, in California, under the Civil Code there is no common-law marriage initiated by openly living together as man and wife.[745] The relationship may be terminated by divorce[746] or annulment[747] or, in a modified form, by legal separation.[748] Undeniably, a poor person who is married or divorced according to the conditions of the Civil Code is nonetheless married or divorced because he is poor. Many families on relief are the products of wedlocks thus entered and perhaps thus brought to an end. At this point the two systems of family law coincide. But there are other methods by which the marital relation may be created or terminated in the family law of the poor.

Ceremonial marriage is often expensive and also may not be a part of the cultural mores of various minority groups. For many people at the lower end of the economic scale, divorce, the minimum cost of which in California is generally about 200 dollars is a luxury beyond their financial means.[749] When poor families break down, the husband simply leaves. Desertion has become known as "the poor man's divorce."[750] Thus, the civil relationship of marriage may often persist though it has in fact terminated. Other and less formal marital relationships may be entered during the legal continuance of the prior marriage.[751] In this context many concepts dependent upon the legality of the marriage relationship, such as bigamy, adultery, and in part legitimacy of offspring, are robbed of much of their traditional content.

---

744. CAL. CIV. CODE §§ 68–79a.
745. CAL. CIV. CODE § 79 allows unmarried adults who have been living together as man and wife to omit the license but not the solemnization requirement.
746. CAL. CIV. CODE §§ 90–108.
747. CAL. CIV. CODE §§ 82–89.
748. CAL. CIV. CODE §§ 136–37.
749. Legal aid societies generally have declined to assist in divorce cases on the ground that they do not want to encourage divorce and the breakup of families. *Transcript of Proceedings on Domestic Relations Before Assembly Committee on Judiciary* 82, 83 (Jan. 8–9, 1964) (statement of Harold Simmons, Deputy Director for Program Planning and Development, Cal. Dep't Social Welfare); *Hearings on Aid to Needy Children Program Before California Senate Fact Finding Committee on Health and Welfare* 108 (July 1, 1960) (C. Cohelan, Deputy District Attorney, Alameda County).
750. *Transcript of Proceedings on Domestic Relations, supra* note 749, at 71.
751. "The duration of these alliances is surprisingly long in view of the number of strikes against them. The statistics on such families known to AFDC show that 16% have been together eight or more years, nearly 30% more than five years, and almost half . . . at least three years. One of the unfortunate results of the illegal nature of these unions is that the offspring are labeled by many people as illegitimate regardless of the stability and duration of the relationship and despite the fact that under California law most of these children qualify as legitimate." *Id.* at 71–72.

The magnitude and character of these and related problems can be seen from analyses of the AFDC program produced by the State Department of Social Welfare.[752] Of a total of some 86,000 families receiving AFDC, some 77,000 were cases in which the father was absent from the home.[753] Of these,

4,210 were deceased;
4,184 were imprisoned;
693 were deported or excluded; and
68,355 were estranged by:

| | |
|---|---:|
| Divorce or annulment | 16,530 |
| Legal separation | 1,899 |
| Separation without court decree | 10,473 |
| Separation by desertion | 5,647 |
| Never married, never lived together | 25,721 |
| Never married, but lived together | 8,085[754] |

Of the total of 249,000 children receiving AFDC, 37.2 per cent, 85,000 were born to parents never married to each other.[755] Thus roughly 18,000 out of the 77,000 absent-father families consisted of families in which divorces, annulments, and legal separations according to the forms of civil law had occurred. In all of the other families some essential civil law step was missing: The parents were never married to each other; there was separation without a court decree; or there was desertion. The extent to which these caseload characteristics were the product of the preponderant percentage of recipient families coming from ethnic minorities can be seen from the following data.

By ethnic background the largest group of families with children who in other states would be described as the offspring of a common-law relationship is of Mexican derivation.[756] Almost two out of three Mexi-

---

752. *Id.* at 288; Clayton, *The ANC Program Yesterday and Today*, in Cal. Dep't Social Welfare, The Status of the Aid to Needy Children Program, pt. 1 (1960); Cal. Dep't Social Welfare, Characteristics of Recipients of Aid to Needy Children (Research Series Rep. No. 20, July 1962).

753. *Ibid.* At the time of the 1962 study, to be eligible a child had to be deprived of parental support or care by reason of the death, continued absence from the home, or physical or mental disability of a parent. Continued absence from the home was defined as an absence exceeding three months. Cal. Stat. 1951, ch. 1699, § 1, at 3910 (formerly Cal. Welfare & Inst'ns Code § 1500 (1961) ). Since that time children of unemployed parents have been made eligible. Cal. Welfare & Inst'ns Code § 1500 (c), added by Cal. Stat. 1963, ch. 510, § 1.7, at 1374. Thus the percentage of absent parent cases will decline but there is no reason to suppose that the total number will do anything but increase.

754. Cal. Dep't Social Welfare, Characteristics of Recipients of Aid to Needy Children (Research Series Rep. No. 20, July 1962). The bases of deprivation other than absence of the father were: absence or incapacity of the mother, 1,309; incapacity of the father, 7,659.

755. *Ibid.*

756. *Ibid.* In the total 1962 AFDC caseload the following represents the distribution of ethnic groups:

| | | |
|---|---:|---:|
| White other than Mexican | 35,422 | 41.0% |
| Mexican | 19,739 | 22.8% |
| Negro | 28,775 | 33.3% |
| Indian | 1,258 | 1.5% |
| Other | 770 | 0.9% |
| Unknown | 435 | 0.5% |

can families, 64.5 per cent, in which the parents were never married to each other meet this description. Common-law marriage is an accepted custom among many Mexican families at the lower socio-economic level and is a legally recognized form of marriage in Mexico.

The "now or formerly married" and the "never married" to the mother are approaching equality in size in the total caseload. There are striking differences in the proportionate sizes of the groups of voluntarily absent fathers based on their ethnic backgrounds—68 per cent of the white fathers are voluntarily absent, 71 per cent of the Mexican fathers, and 89 per cent of the Negro fathers. (Not voluntarily absent fathers are those who are dead, deported, excluded, or imprisoned.) In addition, half of the white fathers who were estranged were divorced or legally separated, in contrast to two out of five, 19.1 per cent, of the Mexican fathers and one out of seven, 14.3 per cent, of the Negro fathers. Stated in terms of whether the parents of the children were ever married to each other, the opposite side of the picture is exposed: while only one out of four white fathers, 25.1 per cent, was never married to the mother, the proportion increased to just under six out of ten Mexican fathers, 57.4 per cent, and to more than six out of ten Negro fathers, 62.3 per cent.[757]

Though the principal aim of the Social Welfare Department and the Legislature of California was not to cope with these social problems, they have created a distinctive type of common-law marriage to be applied exclusively in the law of the poor. The "adult male assuming the role of spouse" has been known to the Welfare and Institutions Code since 1961,[758] but before that he appeared for many years in the regulations of the department.[759] The de facto status was thus given legal recognition and carried with it the legal obligation of support of the children which the woman brings to the union. "The adult male person" is assimilated to the stepfather, established as such by ceremonial marriage, on whom the liability for the support of the stepchildren had earlier been imposed in the law of the poor.[760] Indeed, the "adult male person" is simply incorporated in the stepfather liability section in the Welfare and Institutions Code, and his liability along with that of the

---

757. Cal. Dep't Social Welfare, Facts About Fathers in the Aid to Needy Children Program at 17 (Research Series Rep. No. 11, Jan. 1959).

758. CAL. WELFARE & INST'NS CODE § 1508, amended by Cal. Stat. 1961, ch. 2105, § 1, at 4369.

759. AFDC MANUAL, Reg. §§ C–155, C–212.36 (1954); Cal. Social Welfare Bd., Minutes Feb. 26, 1954, at iii, 6. In People v. Rozell, 212 Cal. App. 2d 875, 28 Cal. Rep. 478 (3d Dist. 1963), the court rejected appellant's contention that the statute was *ex post facto* as applied because the same rule had been in effect by way of regulation at the time in question. "We do not believe that this court should construe the amendment as indicating an intention to change the law, but that it should be construed as a clarification of the law." *Id.* at 878, 28 Cal. Rep. at 480.

760. CAL. WELFARE & INST'NS CODE § 1508, added by Cal. Stat. 1951, ch. 1349, § 1, at 3256.

stepfather is extended to "his wife's children" and limited to her "community property interest in his income."[761]

In effect, thus, in California, while there are no common-law husbands under the Civil Code, there are common-law stepfathers under the Welfare and Institutions Code; and by illicit cohabitation with a man, the mother of needy children, under the law of the poor, acquires a community property interest in his income. The motivation for this innovation was the one omnipresent in the poor law: to cut down the public cost of maintaining the poor. No such legal obligation of support is imposed either on the adult male or the stepfather if, without their support, the "wife's children" would not be "needy children eligible for aid" under the AFDC program.[762] The Welfare and Institutions Code section attaches the liability to the relationship which the adult male assumes as spouse to the mother, not the relationship which he assumes as parent to the children. For welfare purposes, the latter relationship is the significant one in programs dealing with aid to families with dependent children. The one relationship, however, spills over to the other: being a spouse to a mother of children is assumed to involve parental relations with her children. The State Department of Social Welfare has provided guides[763] and established regulations[764] on this principle,[765] and has in addition expanded the statutory liability to include responsibility for the support of the wife. The adult male has the same responsibility as the stepfather not only for the needy children but for the mother as well. He is considered to have assumed the role of spouse if:

  a. He is in or around the home and is maintaining an intimate relationship with the mother, or is the father of one or more of the children, and
  b. He has assumed substantial financial responsibility for the ongoing expenses of the ANC family, and/or
  c. He has represented himself to the community in such a way as to appear in the relationship of husband and/or father.[766]

The existence of items *a* plus *b* and/or *c* creates a rebuttable presumption that the adult male has assumed the role of spouse.[767]

The man assuming the role of spouse in the family law of the poor represents a quite different concept from the de facto or putative spouse

---

761. Cal. Welfare & Inst'ns Code § 1508.
762. *Ibid.*
763. AFDC Manual, Handbook § C–155.
764. AFDC Manual, Reg. § C–155.
765. See People v. Rozell, 212 Cal. App. 2d 875, 878, 28 Cal. Rep. 478, 480 (3d Dist. 1963): "Appellant contends also that section 1508 is vague and uncertain and therefore unconstitutional. We do not agree. 'To assume the role of spouse' is not a vague and uncertain term. It means to live with a person of the opposite sex as a husband . . . though there has been no marriage."
766. AFDC Manual, Reg. § C–155.
767. *Ibid.*

in civil family law. The essential basis of the latter is "a *bona fide* belief on the part of the 'wife' in the existence of a valid marriage."[768] Good faith is indispensable. When an "innocent" woman has lived with a man as his wife, with the requisite belief, the courts have applied equitable principles in order not to defeat the putative wife's expectations.[769] This judicial sympathy, unaided by statute, has been based largely on the fact that the

> de facto wife attempted to meet the requisites of a valid marriage, and the marriage proved invalid only because of some essential fact of which she was unaware, such as the earlier undissolved marriage of one of the parties . . . a consanguineous relation between the parties . . . or the failure to meet the requirements of solemnization. . . .[770]

Upon termination of the relation the courts have looked to the annulment and divorce statutes as analogous standards to determine division of the property acquired during the putative relationship[771] or to probate law in cases where the relationship is terminated by death.[772] In the absence of community property, especially where one party has procured the invalid marriage by fraud or caused its interruption by misconduct, the innocent spouse has been awarded the reasonable value of her services less support received by her during the relationship,[773] and payment has been secured by the typical alimony device of a lien despite the fact that the nonexistence of a marriage precludes any right to alimony in the strict sense.[774] Thus, the difference between the putative spouse and the man assuming the role of spouse in many ways symbolizes the difference between the two systems of family law. While the putative spouse concept deals primarily with the claim of the woman with regard to property acquired during the putative marriage, alternative remedies extend to recovery of the value of services contributed by her to the relationship. The concept of the man assuming the role of spouse deals with a current obligation of the man to provide support for the woman and her children. In a manner of speaking, the one deals with sharing wealth; the other, with spreading poverty.

---

768. Flanagan v. Capital Nat'l Bank, 213 Cal. 664, 666, 3 P.2d 307, 308 (1931).
769. See Schneider v. Schneider, 183 Cal. 335, 339–40, 191 Pac. 533, 535 (1920); Turknette v. Turknette, 100 Cal. App. 2d 271, 274, 223 P.2d 495, 498 (1st Dist. 1950); 1 ARMSTRONG, CALIFORNIA FAMILY LAW 856–61 (1953).
770. Vallera v. Vallera, 21 Cal. 2d 681, 684, 134 P.2d 761, 762 (1943).
771. See Turknette v. Turknette, 100 Cal. App. 2d 271, 274, 223 P.2d 495, 498 (1st Dist. 1950).
772. See Feig v. Bank of America Nat'l Trust & Sav. Ass'n, 5 Cal. 2d 266, 273, 54 P.2d 3, 6–7 (1936); Kunakoff v. Woods, 166 Cal. App. 2d 59, 67–68, 332 P.2d 773, 778 (2d Dist. 1958); Union Bank & Trust Co. v. Gordon, 116 Cal. App. 2d 681, 689–90, 254 P.2d 644, 649–50 (2d Dist. 1953); Estate of Krone, 83 Cal. App. 2d 766, 769, 189 P.2d 741, 743 (2d Dist. 1948).
773. See Sanguinetti v. Sanguinetti, 9 Cal. 2d 95, 100, 69 P.2d 845, 847 (1937); Lazzarevich v. Lazzarevich, 88 Cal. App. 2d 708, 723, 200 P.2d 49, 58 (2d Dist. 1948).
774. See Sanguinetti v. Sanguinetti, 9 Cal. 95, 102, 69 P.2d 845, 848 (1937).

## Support and Property Relations of Husband and Wife

### In civil family law.

Writers upon civil family law and code sections providing for it commonly refer to marriage as a civil status or as a personal relationship.[775] And so it is in many ways. But it is a civil status or personal relationship with important juristic and historic foundations in contract. Blackstone's statement, "Our law considers marriage in no other light than as a civil contract," [776] was toned down a little and embodied in California's first statute upon the subject: "Marriage is considered in law as a civil contract."[777] Even today, when the Civil Code defines marriage as "a personal relation,"[778] the qualification is added, "arising out of a civil contract, to which the consent of the parties capable of making that contract is necessary."[779] The personal relations features have come to prevail over the contract foundations.[780] Though the consent of the parties is necessary to enter the marriage relation, the terms and condition of that relation, the rights and responsibilities of the spouses, for the most part are fixed by the law and may not be changed by the parties whatever their agreement.[781] The license and solemnization requirements,[782] too, do not sound in ordinary contract. Yet in some respects the aura of contract still clings to the relation and this is particularly true about matters which are the concern of this study. Rules about community and separate property strongly influence the personal relation, and in the context of these rules and those concerning the mutual obligation of support which are linked to property, the personal relation is not inaptly described as a sort of partnership. This is true concerning both the prescriptions laid down in the Civil Code and the freedom left the parties to make their own arrangements. Property acquired by the labor or skill of either partner during the continuance of the partnership belongs to both of them,[783] and their interest in it is "present, existing and equal" though it is "under the management and control of the hus-

---

775. See, *e.g.*, 1 Armstrong, California Family Law 1–2 (1953) (marriage is personal relationship arising out of civil contract); 1 Bishop, Marriage and Divorce § 3 (4th ed. 1864) (civil contract is source of marriage); 1 Blackstone, Commentaries *433.
776. *Ibid.*
777. Cal. Stat. 1850, ch. 140, § 1, at 424.
778. Cal. Civ. Code § 55.
779. *Ibid.*
780. In Clevenger v. Clevenger, 189 Cal. App. 2d 658, 665 n.l, 11 Cal. Rep. 707, 710 n.l (1st Dist. 1961), Justice Tobriner characterized recent "trends in the field of family law . . . " as involving "the acceptance of a relationship, and the *status* that flows from such relationship, rather than volitional agreement or contract."
781. See Cal. Civ. Code § 159.
782. Cal. Civ. Code § 55.
783. Cal. Civ. Code § 164.

band"[784] except as to the earnings of the wife.[785] Each partner, however, may have property in which the other has no interest[786] and may enter into separate transactions "respecting property" just as if he were not married.[787] Indeed, the partners may enter such transactions with each other subject only to the special duties arising from the confidential relationship between them.[788] Contracts about property are explicitly excepted from the general pronouncement, "A husband and wife cannot, by any contract with each other, alter their legal relations . . . ."[789]

According to the Civil Code, the obligations of mutual respect, fidelity, and support which the marital partners assume are matters about which they "contract towards each other."[790] The terms of the "contract" about support, however, are also established by the Civil Code. The obligations are mutual but not identical, those of the husband being the more comprehensive and also penally enforceable.[791] Thus the husband must support the wife if he has "sufficient ability . . . or . . . is able to earn the means" to do so "unless by her misconduct he was justified in abandoning her."[792] The wife must support the husband "when he has not deserted her, . . . and he is unable, from infirmity, to support himself."[793] In addition, the inter-spousal support obligation is stated in terms of a civil remedy for the third-person creditor who has met the need. Good faith suppliers to the wife of "articles necessary for her support" can "recover the reasonable value thereof from the husband."[794] The earnings of the wife and some of her separate property are liable for the payment of debts contracted by the husband or by the wife for the necessaries of life furnished to them or either of them while they are living together.[795] In contrast, property of the wife held by her at the time of the marriage or acquired afterward by devise, succession, or gift (other than by gift from husband), is not so liable.[796] In the civil family law, what constitutes the items and standards of support is determined by the judges with the slight qualification that the legislature has said that the husband's penal obligation extends to supplying the wife with necessary food, clothing, shelter, and medical attention.[797]

---

784. CAL. CIV. CODE § 161a.
785. See CAL. CIV. CODE § 171c.
786. See CAL. CIV. CODE §§ 157, 162, 163, 163.5.
787. See CAL. CIV. CODE § 158.
788. *Ibid.*
789. CAL. CIV. CODE § 159.
790. CAL. CIV. CODE § 155.
791. CAL. CIV. CODE § 155; CAL. PEN. CODE § 270a.
792. CAL. PEN. CODE § 270a.
793. CAL. CIV. CODE § 176.
794. CAL. CIV. CODE § 174.
795. CAL. CIV. CODE § 168.
796. CAL. CIV. CODE § 171.
797. CAL. PEN. CODE § 270a.

*In the family law of the poor.*

As it emerges from the California Welfare and Institutions Code in implementive administrative material, the family law of the poor reflects a different conception of the marital rights and duties relating to property and support. Husband and wife are not seen as semi-independent partners, standing in a contractual relationship to each other, and maintaining distinct interests in community income and property and unshared interests in separate income and property; they are viewed rather as a single, integrated entity, having a single, undivided, and unseparated interest in a common pool of family resources derived from the income and property of both spouses. Withdrawals from the common pool might, indeed must, be made by both to meet the costs of living. The family law of the poor, by contrast with the civil family law, puts greater emphasis upon the community, less upon the individuals; greater emphasis upon meeting the needs of both spouses for support, less upon their individual rights to separate property and income. In general, whatever either spouse possesses is made available for the support of the other. Only after the family resources, whether for other purposes they are called community or separate, are utilized and have proved insufficient, can the public be called upon to intervene and supply aid to either of the spouses. In the family law of the poor, the unitary theory of marriage is not a proposition about the moral, sociological, or psychological integrity of the union; nor is it the positing of a goal aimed at the strengthening of family life. It is a device for minimizing the public cost of supporting the poor by tapping what would otherwise be the separate property or income of one spouse for the support of the other.

In carrying out this principle the categories in the family law of the poor in respect to the support and property relationships of the spouses are often quite different from those in civil family law. Distinctions are drawn between earning and nonearning, recipient and nonrecipient, eligible and ineligible spouses, but none between husband and wife. There is no reason to be concerned in the Welfare and Institutions Code about which of the spouses has the right to manage community property, who is the head of the family, and the rights of third-party creditors to recover for necessaries supplied, and no mention of such matters is to be found there. The civil family law provision imposing less liability upon the wife for the support of the husband than upon the husband for the support of the wife also cuts across the governing principle of the poor law and is rejected by the Welfare and Institutions Code. For poor law purposes, whether property is real or personal, community or separate, is less important than whether it is utilized for needs that the public

[624]

would otherwise have to meet. Except as real property may be used to provide shelter or as personal property consists of consumption items, needs are met through the use of income. Thus, the family law of the poor distinguishes between dwellings and other property;[798] treats alike property used as a dwelling or retained to secure a dwelling whether, as in the case of a house, it is real property, or, as in the case of a trailer or houseboat, it is personal property, or, as in the case of the proceeds from the sale of property held for the purchase of a home or furnishings, it is cash assets;[799] requires other real property held by the recipient or in combination with his spouse to be used to produce income reasonably consistent with its value, the income in turn being devoted to the support of the recipient;[800] limits the amount of other property, personal and real, an eligible recipient may own to a small reserve to meet contingencies;[801] takes into account the separate and community property of a recipient's spouse when determining his eligibility for aid and the amount of his grant;[802] provides different rules for personal property and income,[803] defines income restrictively, treats earned income differently from unearned income and earnings resulting from present participation in the labor market differently from the product of past earnings, and, in general, provides for the apportionment of income,[804] community and separate, between the spouses in ways enabling them to meet their need.

Carried to rigorous extremes, the principle of sharing income and property of the spouses would defeat the very object sought to be achieved in the conservation of public resources. The absence of incentive to productive activity might operate to discourage employment and thus would actually increase the public burden. To offset this effect part of the earnings of the spouse are exempted from the requirement of sharing. The Welfare and Institutions Code was recently amended to provide that the net earnings of a recipient's spouse up to 200 dollars a

798. See Cal. Welfare & Inst'ns Code § 454; Old Age Security Manual, Reg. § A-132.05; Aid to Blind Manual, Reg. § B-132.05.

799. See Cal. Welfare & Inst'ns Code § 454; Old Age Security Manual, Reg. § A-132.05; Aid to Blind Manual, Reg. § B-132.05.

800. Cal. Welfare & Inst'ns Code §§ 453, 455; Old Age Security Manual, Reg. § A-132.10; Aid to Blind Manual, Reg. § B-132.10; Aid to Disabled Manual, Reg. § D-132.10.

801. See Cal. Welfare & Inst'ns Code §§ 453, 456, 1521; Old Age Security Manual, Reg. § A-132.10; Aid to Blind Manual, Reg. § B-132.10; AFDC Manual, Reg. § C-132.10; Aid to Disabled Manual, Reg. § D-132.10.

802. See Cal. Welfare & Inst'ns Code §§ 455, 456; Old Age Security Manual, Reg. § A-135.05; Aid to Blind Manual, Reg. § B-135.05; Aid to Disabled Manual, Reg. § D-135.05.

803. See Cal. Welfare & Inst'ns Code §§ 442, 448.5, 454–58; Old Age Security Manual, Reg. §§ A-135.10, A-135.30, A-136, A-211.02; Aid to Blind Manual, Reg. §§ B-135.10, B-135.30, B-136, B-211.02; Aid to Disabled Manual, Reg. §§ D-135.10, D-135.30, D-136, D-211.02.

804. Cal. Welfare & Inst'ns Code §§ 2020.05, 3084.3; Old Age Security Manual, Reg. §§ A-212.10, A-212.30, A-212.50; Aid to Blind Manual, Reg. § B-212.50.

month "shall not be considered community property in computing how much of such earnings should be allocated to the applicant as income to him."[805] Thus is it hoped to encourage the spouse "to retain or seek employment in order to be self-supporting, taxpaying, and to avoid becoming a recipient of public aid . . . ."[806] This device is also applied to the recipient. Eighty-five dollars a month of the earnings of a blind aid recipient, plus fifty per cent of all earnings above that amount,[807] and 1,500 dollars a year plus one-half of all income above that amount, from whatever source derived, of a potentially self-supporting blind recipient,[808] are not considered either in determining eligibility or the amount of the grant. The earnings in the one case and the income in the other are not in any part allocable to the spouse, even though they would otherwise constitute community income. Above these exempted sums, only so much of the recipient's community earnings may be allocated to the spouse as are necessary to meet the spouse's need, though that be far less than half. Blind aid recipients may retain additional earnings for a period not exceeding one year when they are necessary to carry out an approved plan for self-support.[809] The exempt earnings principle, introduced into the blind aid program in California in 1937[810] and into the Federal Social Security Act in 1950,[811] has only recently been added by virtue of federal amendments, though on a greatly reduced scale, to the federal-state programs for the aged[812] and aid to families with dependent children.[813] Since 1963 the exempt earnings principle has been enacted in

---

805. CAL. WELFARE & INST'NS CODE § 460, added by Cal. Stat. 1963, ch. 1800, § 1, at 3629.
806. *Ibid.*
807. CAL. WELFARE & INST'NS CODE § 443 (formerly Cal. Welfare & Inst'ns Code § 3084.3 (1963)); AID TO BLIND MANUAL, Reg. § B–212.10.
808. See CAL. WELFARE & INST'NS CODE § 3472; AID TO BLIND MANUAL, Reg. § B–212.20.
809. AID TO BLIND MANUAL, Reg. §§ B–212.10, B–313.
810. See Cal. Stat. 1937, ch. 369, § 3084, at 1105, adding CAL. WELFARE & INST'NS CODE § 3084.
811. 64 Stat. 553 (1950) provided "that the State agency shall, in determining need, take into consideration any other income and resources of an individual claiming aid to the blind; except that in making such determination, the State agency shall disregard the first $50 per month of earned income" and now provides, 76 Stat. 206 (1962), 42 U.S.C. § 1202(a)(8) (Supp. V, 1964), "that the State agency shall, in determining need, take into consideration any other income and resources of the individual claiming aid to the blind, as well as any expenses reasonably attributable to the earning of any such income; except that, in making such determination, the State agency shall disregard (A) the first $85 per month of earned income, plus one-half of earned income in excess of $85 per month, and (B) for a period not in excess of twelve months, such additional amounts of other income and resources, in the case of an individual who has a plan for achieving self-support approved by the state agency, as may be necessary for the fulfillment of such plan."
812. See Social Security Act, § 2, as amended, 76 Stat. 207 (1962), 42 U.S.C. § 302 (Supp. V, 1964) (allowing the state to exempt the first $10 plus one-half of any additional net earned income up to $50); CAL. WELFARE & INST'NS CODE § 2020.05; OLD AGE SECURITY MANUAL, Reg. § A–212.10 (exempting the first $10 plus one-half of any additional net earned income up to $40).
813. Social Security Act § 402(a)(7), as amended, 76 Stat. 188 (1962), 42 U.S.C. § 602(a) (7) (Supp. V, 1964), permitting a state using federal funds for aid to families with dependent children to exempt any or all income when determining need, subject to limitations prescribed by the Secretary of the Treasury.

[626]

unqualified form in California for all federally aided public assistance programs.[814]

## Other Relatives

### In civil family law.

Relatives other than spouses, parents, and minor children appear in the Probate, Civil, and Penal Codes in various guises. They step into line as lineal heirs,[815] collateral kindred,[816] or next of kin[817] to claim property descending by intestate succession. They are found as a single group, without distinctions among them, low in the order of priorities of persons to be awarded custody or guardianship of children.[818] A "relative within the third degree" of a child may institute a civil action, as may the child itself or the board of supervisors of the county, to bring abuse of parental authority to judicial cognizance.[819] One may use "any necessary force . . . to protect from wrongful injury" the person or property of "other relative, or member of one's family,"[820] just as he may protect, on the one hand, himself, wife, husband, parent, or, on the other hand, his ward, servant, master, or guest.[821] Ancestors and descendants of every degree, brothers and sisters of the half as well as the whole blood, uncles and nieces, aunts and nephews are in the class of persons who may commit incestuous marriages which are declared to be void from the very beginning.[822]

Relationship beyond the immediate family of husband, wife, mother, father, and minor children, is an amorphous legal concept. Its juristic foundations are obscure. The character of the concept and its foundations can only be inferred from the disparate provisions just summarized. Primarily, the legal concept would appear to be erected on the foundation of a biological concept, namely, that relatives are persons of the

814. CAL. WELFARE & INST'NS CODE § 443, added by Cal. Stat. 1963, ch. 510, § 1, at 1372, provides: "In determining the income of the recipient, the following requirements shall be observed: (a) To the extent permitted by federal law, earned income of a recipient of aid under any public assistance program for which federal funds are available shall not be considered income or resources of the recipient, and shall not be deducted from the amount of aid to which the recipient would otherwise be entitled. . . . "

The purpose of the provision is formulated as follows: "In order that recipients of public assistance may become self-supporting and productive members of their communities it is essential that they be permitted to earn money without a proportionate deduction in their aid grants. It is the intention of the Legislature to promote this objective to the extent possible within the limitations imposed by federal law, and the State Social Welfare Board, in implementing public assistance laws, is directed to do so in the light of this objective."

815. CAL. PROB. CODE § 252.
816. CAL. PROB. CODE § 253.
817. CAL. PROB. CODE § 226.
818. CAL. PROB. CODE § 1407.
819. CAL. CIV. CODE § 203.
820. CAL. CIV. CODE § 50.
821. *Ibid.*
822. CAL. CIV. CODE § 59.

blood, *i.e.*, having a common blood. This idea is now recognized as a misconception and must be replaced by the concept of common genes. The extent to which even this theory accurately represents the groupings of the natural world is not here a matter of importance. We are concerned with whether these groupings should be given social and legal significance and the extent to which they have been. As the foregoing summary shows, the legal categories do not coincide even roughly with the natural categories, supposed or actual. For some purposes, relatives outside the immediate family are at one and the same time placed on the same footing both as members of the immediate family and with such outsiders as wards, servants, guests, and members of the county board of supervisors. Moreover, among such relatives, those occupying a given blood or genetic relationship are treated differently by the law for different purposes. The line of such relatives is much shorter for purposes of incest than for purposes of inheritance. Nor is the group limited to those having some blood or genetic relationship. Entrance into it may be secured by adoption, applicable to adults as well as to minors, or by relatives of those who marry into the family. For most purposes, however, relatives outside the immediate family are distinguished from those inside: they do not share the significance of the marital relation, described by the United States Supreme Court as "the foundation of the family and of society, without which there would be neither civilization nor progress."[823] Nor are they intricately entangled with community and separate property notions as are husband and wife. Nor do such relatives approach the relationship of parent and minor child with its extensive list of rights and responsibilities having to do with supervision, custody, rearing, education, control, and management.

The outside relatives are similar to each other in that they possess a right of inheritance and are under a special ban as to marriage. In a loose way also they have some rights to protection, physical and judicial, but in this respect they are not different from groups of outsiders. Whatever the legal concept or juristic theory which sustains the class of other relatives, some, though not all of them, have another distinguishing characteristic: they are placed under a legal responsibility for providing financial support to their destitute kinsmen.

The civil family law provisions imposing duties of support upon relatives are embodied in two code sections, the one in the Civil Code and the other in the Penal Code. The Penal Code section is not simply a criminal enforcement sanction for the Civil Code obligation. Civil Code section 206 provides: "It is the duty of the father, the mother, and the children of any poor person who is unable to maintain himself by work,

---

823. Maynard v. Hill, 125 U.S. 190, 211 (1888).

to maintain such person to the extent of their ability. The promise of an adult child to pay for necessaries previously furnished to such parent is binding." Penal Code section 270c states: "Except as provided in Section 206.5 of the Civil Code, every adult child who, having the ability so to do, fails to provide necessary food, clothing, shelter, or medical attendance for an indigent parent is guilty of a misdemeanor."

Thus the penal sanction applies only to adult children; the civil obligation extends to parents as well as to children whether adult or not. The items of support are listed in the Penal Code: "necessary food, clothing, shelter or medical attendance"; the Civil Code leaves the obligation more general. The penal duty of the adult child runs to an "indigent parent," without reference to the reason for the indigency; the civil obligation runs to a "poor person who is unable to maintain himself by work," thus focusing on one cause of poverty but at the same time not distinguishing between individual and social factors resulting in inability to gain support by work. Ability to pay is the measure of the liability in both penal and civil codes, and neither mentions support in cash. Presumably aid in kind, supplying the necessaries themselves, would satisfy the obligation.[824]

*In the family law of the poor.*

The most striking aspect of today's poor law provisions respecting responsible relatives is their diversity, the comparison of the programs in which they have remained relatively static and those in which great change has occurred in recent years, the extent to which they have been abolished, their legislative fluidity, and the rising crescendo of constitutional clamor about them.

*Responsibility of relatives in county indigent aid and aid for the mentally irresponsible.*—Even in the programs in which responsible relatives provisions are most static—indigent aid and care of the mentally irresponsible—the circle of those liable has been constricted and the rigors of enforcement abated. Liability is no longer imposed on grandparents, grandchildren, brothers, and sisters. There is now common agreement and legislative prescription that those liable shall not be pushed to the point of rendering them eligible for public assistance.[825] With these

---

824. CAL. CIV. CODE § 206 has been held to be enforceable by any appropriate judicial proceeding though no method of enforcement is specified in the statute. Paxton v. Paxton, 150 Cal. 667, 89 Pac. 1083 (1907). The section gives an incapacitated adult child the right to obtain a support order against her father. Tuller v. Superior Court, 215 Cal. 352, 10 P.2d 43 (1932) (dictum). The obligation imposed by the section is individual and several rather than joint. Garcia v. Superior Court, 45 Cal. App. 2d 31, 113 P.2d 470 (4th Dist. 1941). The statute does not authorize an indigent parent, already being supported by one child, to bring suit to force the other children to bear their share. Duffy v. Yordi, 149 Cal. 140, 84 Pac. 838 (1906). Finally, the statute does not require that a mother be "absolutely destitute" in order to obtain support. Janes v. Edwards, 4 Cal. App. 2d 611, 41 P.2d 370 (2d Dist. 1935).
825. CAL. WELFARE & INST'NS CODE § 6655.

qualifications, however, the responsible relatives provisions in these programs have changed over the years only in detail.[826]

In the indigent aid program, both the liability of responsible relatives and the discretion of the board of supervisors are comprehensive. All aid rendered by the county is made "a charge against the spouse, parent and adult child of the recipient . . . and the county . . . shall be entitled to reimbursement therefor."[827] The board of supervisors "shall determine" if the relatives currently have ability to contribute to the support of the recipient or had such ability at the time aid was granted.[828] If in their "opinion" the ability exists and existed, they must request the district attorney to proceed against any or all of the relatives.[829] The legal officer "shall maintain an action . . . to recover . . . aid rendered and to secure an order requiring the payment of any sums which may become due in the future."[830] At this point judicial enforcement takes over. There are here no distinctions as to community and separate property of the spouses, no prescription as to order of liability or distribution of burden among those pecuniarily able, not the slightest suggestion of any standards for determining financial ability to support.

In the programs for the mentally irresponsible, responsible relatives provisions are numerous and varied. They differ with each program, the subgroup of the larger class of irresponsibles, and the proceeding, care, confinement, or treatment involved. There are separate provisions in the chapters and articles dealing with: The mentally ill and insane;[831] the mentally disordered;[832] the feeble-minded and other incompetents

---

826. The California Supreme Court in County of Los Angeles v. Frisbie, 19 Cal. 2d 634, 643, 122 2d 526, 531 (1942), relied upon a forty-year course of conduct by county officials as a long-continued contemporary and practical construction of the indigent aid provision appearing in the Welfare and Institutions Code. In Department of Mental Hygiene v. McGilvery, 50 Cal. 2d 742, 329 P.2d 689 (1958), it held that the relatives responsibility provisions for the mentally irresponsible were to be construed as continuations of the earlier provisions rather than as new enactments.

827. CAL. WELFARE & INST'NS CODE § 2576.

828. *Ibid.* The character and date of commencement of such liability begin at the time aid is in fact rendered, not when the board of supervisors makes a finding regarding the relatives' ability to pay. See County of Los Angeles v. Read, 193 Cal. App. 2d 748, 753, 14 Cal. Rep. 628, 631 (2d Dist. 1961). The board of supervisors is presumed to have made a finding of the relatives' ability to pay if it authorizes suit to recover. Thus the courts are tending toward the position that liability is unconditional. But in Turnboo v. County of Santa Clara, 144 Cal. App. 2d 728, 301 P.2d 992 (1st Dist. 1956), the court held that liability was not unconditional but dependent upon the relatives' ability to pay both at the time aid was rendered and at the time the supervisors instituted their action to reimburse the county. In the absence of evidence of the former, the court held liability was not established. On the other hand, the California Supreme Court interpreted CAL. WELFARE & INST'NS CODE § 2576 to mean that the liability of the named relatives is absolute. It construed the later provisions of § 2576 as relating only to the collectibility of the obligation and as conditioning county proceedings for that purpose on the ability of the relative to pay. Department of Mental Hygiene v. McGilvery, 50 Cal. 2d 742, 758, 329 P.2d 689, 697 (1958) (dictum).

829. CAL. WELFARE & INST'NS CODE § 2576. Turnboo v. County of Santa Clara, 144 Cal. App. 2d 728, 732, 301 P.2d 992, 995 (1st Dist. 1956).

830. CAL. WELFARE & INST'NS CODE § 2576.

831. CAL. WELFARE & INST'NS CODE §§ 5048, 5151.

832. CAL. WELFARE & INST'NS CODE § 5077.

not insane;[833] epileptics;[834] narcotic drug addicts;[835] dipsomaniacs, inebriates, and habit-forming drug addicts;[836] sexual psychopaths;[837] mentally abnormal sex offenders.[838] In one or another of the various provisions, the county indigent aid sections are incorporated by reference;[839] liability is imposed on relatives "in the order named";[840] those responsible are identified as "parent, guardian, or other person charged with the support";[841] the judge at the time of the proceeding is authorized to fix "the reasonable cost"[842] or any sum he "deems proper"[843] or "just."[844]

The most important of these provisions concern the relatives of mentally ill persons and inebriates in state institutions. The husband, wife, father, mother, or children are declared to be liable for care, support, and maintenance. The liability, the state supreme court has held, is not only joint and several, as the code clearly says,[845] but absolute and unconditional, as to which the code is not so clear.[846] Moreover, not only is the liability of the relatives joint and several but the liability of the patient's estate is not prior and independent. Accordingly, the administrative officials are at liberty to select among the relatives at will and to seek recovery from a relative before or without tapping or exhausting the resources of the patient. The Department of Mental Hygiene is directed to investigate and discover whether there are responsible relatives, to ascertain their financial condition, and "to determine" whether they are "in fact" able to pay the charges.[847] The task of making the collection is assigned to the Department, which is empowered to "take such action as is necessary" for that purpose.[848]

The county program for indigent aid and state programs for mental irresponsibles are those which also contain rigorous and detailed provisions dealing with the obligation of the recipient to pay for his own care.

---

833. CAL. WELFARE & INST'NS CODE §§ 5260, 5265.
834. CAL. WELFARE & INST'NS CODE § 5302.
835. CAL. WELFARE & INST'NS CODE § 5356.
836. CAL. WELFARE & INST'NS CODE §§ 5402.5, 5404.
837. CAL. WELFARE & INST'NS CODE § 5516.
838. CAL. WELFARE & INST'NS CODE § 5606.
839. CAL. WELFARE & INST'NS CODE § 5265.
840. CAL. WELFARE & INST'NS CODE § 5077.
841. CAL. WELFARE & INST'NS CODE § 5260.
842. CAL. WELFARE & INST'NS CODE §§ 5402.5, 5404.
843. CAL. WELFARE & INST'NS CODE § 5260.
844. CAL. WELFARE & INST'NS CODE § 5356.
845. CAL. WELFARE & INST'NS CODE § 6650.
846. See Department of Mental Hygiene v. McGilvery, 50 Cal. 2d 742, 756, 329 P.2d 689, 696 (1958). The alternative possibility, as the dissent points out, *id.* at 762, 329 P.2d at 700, is to read the code sections imposing liability and those making collection depend on ability to pay together, thus in effect making the liability conditional on ability to pay.
847. CAL. WELFARE & INST'NS CODE § 6653.
848. CAL. WELFARE & INST'NS CODE § 6652. The director of the department may reduce, cancel, or remit the amount to be paid by the relatives on satisfactory proof that they are unable to pay. CAL. WELFARE & INST'NS CODE § 6651. The rate of care is to be fixed by the director at the average per capita cost of maintaining patients in all state hospitals. *Ibid.*

In the indigent aid program, the county board of supervisors is authorized to "establish its own policies with reference to the amount of property, if any, a person shall be permitted to have while receiving public assistance." So far as it is possible the indigent "shall be required to apply his own property to his support."[849] This general authorization is reinforced by an extensive array of the specific means by which the supervisors may insure the application of the indigent's resources to his own support. These include liens on his property,[850] transfer of property to the county and its management by the board of supervisors,[851] and recovery from the estate of the recipient should he acquire property after public moneys have been expended for his support.[852] While recent amendments have qualified the county's discretion in a number of more or less minor ways,[853] that discretion remains basically intact. Similar self-support provisions in the state programs for the mentally irresponsible are more understandable since mental irresponsibility, unlike indigence, does not necessarily presuppose poverty (though it may be likely soon to result in it), and often supervision of the person involving his protection and that of society are such that property and income limits may not be imposed as conditions of eligibility.[854]

---

849. CAL. WELFARE & INST'NS CODE § 2600.
850. CAL. WELFARE & INST'NS CODE § 2601.
851. *Ibid.*
852. CAL. WELFARE & INST'NS CODE § 2603. In County of Los Angeles v. First Security Nat'l Bank, 84 Cal. App. 2d 575, 578, 191 P.2d 78, 80–81 (2d Dist. 1948) (relying on County of Alameda v. Janssen, 16 Cal. 2d 276, 283, 106 P.2d 11, 15 (1940) ), the court uttered some much quoted language on the statutory origin of the duty of repayment: "It was the rule at common law that in the absence of fraud in procuring relief a recipient of charity from the state was under no obligation to repay the governmental agency disbursing such charity; nor was the estate of such pauper under obligation to make reimbursement, notwithstanding that the indigent at the time the charities were furnished owned property. . . . Prior to the effective date of section 2603 the common-law rule prevailed so generally that in the absence of a special statute no liability rested upon a recipient of public charity to reimburse the state and county for aid legitimately obtained."
853. Although the county still retains large discretion as to the content of policies established under CAL. WELFARE & INST'NS CODE § 2600, it is no longer free simply to decide each case individually without establishing any policies at all. The county is required by CAL. WELFARE & INST'NS CODE § 200.1 to "adopt standards of aid and care for the indigent and dependent poor . . . ." "Standards of aid" include retention of resources for the use of the recipient. Though this provision was adopted in 1957, compare the 1961 decision, County of Los Angeles v. Read, 193 Cal. App. 2d 748, 752, 14 Cal. Rep. 628, 631 (2d Dist. 1961), where the court said that no allegation was necessary that the county had established such policies.
The recipient is allowed to retain at a minimum small specified amounts of cash, personal effects, household furniture, burial trust funds, insurance policies, and an interment plot. CAL. WELFARE & INST'NS CODE § 2611. The county may not deny medical care to persons eligible under the medical assistance to the aged program, take a lien upon such person's property, or require him to apply his property to his support. CAL. WELFARE & INST'NS CODE § 2600.5. It may not enforce a lien against the home of a recipient of indigent aid during his lifetime or that of his spouse, during the minority of his children if they reside in the home, or during the lifetime of any dependent adult child residing in the home who, because of mental and physical disability, is incapable of self-support. CAL. WELFARE & INST'NS CODE § 2601.5. It may not charge any interest or carrying charge in connection with any debt incurred for county hospital care, and may not take a lien against the property of a relative, except for a parent of a minor or a spouse.
854. The emphasis in the code provisions and in administrative policy on collecting from the estate of the patient and the responsible relatives permits minimizing the hardship on living persons and at the same time maximizing recovery by the state when such hardships are no longer at issue. The contest is then between the state and the heirs, and whatever the foundation of the claim of the state, that of the heirs is usually only one of windfall. The pursuit of estates accounts for the large

*Responsibility of relatives in other adult programs.*—Striking contrasts are revealed when one compares the county indigent aid program and the state mentally irresponsible program with the federal-state-county adult categorical aid programs. There are also striking differences between and among these categorical aid programs. In the program for the aged, administrative discretion has practically vanished in determining what relatives have ability to pay, in selecting the relatives to be charged, and in establishing the standard of assistance to the recipient which bears upon the exactions from the relatives. Only adult children are liable for support.[855] Maximum liability of the adult child for both parents is the same as for one, and accordingly full support of one parent discharges the adult child from liability for the other.[856] Before the liability of the adult child begins at all, he is entitled to support himself, his dependent spouse, and his minor children.[857] Most important of all, the support obligation is not declared in general terms. It is set forth in the code in precise detail in the form of a table specifying the amount of monthly payments for which the responsible relative is liable in relation to his monthly net income and the number of persons dependent on it.[858] The eligibility of the applicant or recipient for old age assistance is not conditioned upon the financially liable relative discharging his obligation. If the relative actually makes the contribution, the state reduces its grant accordingly. If he does not, the state must make the full payment and thereafter may seek to recover from the adult child.[859] The California Welfare and Institutions Code also speci-

---

amount of litigation as to the responsibility of relatives in the mentally irresponsible programs by comparison with other public aid programs. The executors are not as responsive to administrative pressures as the relative himself. Unlike the relative, they act much more under the advice of counsel and are under obligations to make only legally required payments out of the estate. They do not have the same reasons for not committing the estate to lawsuits that operate upon persons when managing their own affairs. They are also less likely to translate their resistance into resentment, expressed at the polls and in hostile political actions, though political action by the mentally irresponsible themselves is prevented by their condition and their relatives have shown no organized tendency in this direction.

855. See Cal. Welfare & Inst'ns Code §§ 2181, 2224; Old Age Security Manual, Reg. § A–152.

Cal. Welfare & Inst'ns Code § 2160(d), providing that eligible persons may not be "receiving adequate support from a husband or wife, or child," is largely anachronistic, does not in any event impose liability on the named relatives, and does not modify §§ 2181 and 2224. A person is not eligible for aid if he is receiving "adequate support" from anyone, relatives or nonrelatives and quite regardless of any obligation to supply the support.

856. Old Age Security Manual, Reg. § A–152.

857. Old Age Security Manual, Reg. § A–153.3.

858. Cal. Welfare & Inst'ns Code § 2181. For example, a single person with a net monthly income of $400, a married person with two children and a net monthly income of $1,000, or a married person with four children and a net monthly income of $1,150 is not liable for any contribution. A single person with a net monthly income of $600 is liable for $20 a month; a married person with three children and a net monthly income of $1,150 is liable for $10. These amounts are the maximum liability. To avoid both "undue hardship upon the adult child" and "administrative time and effort . . . on nonproductive investigative activities," the liability may be reduced in particular cases pursuant to regulation by the State Department of Social Welfare. *Ibid.*; Old Age Security Manual, Reg. § A–153.3.

859. Cal. Welfare & Inst'ns Code §§ 2160(d), 2224; Old Age Security Manual, Reg. § A–153.5.

fies the needs of the recipient and the standards at which they are to be met, thus limiting the relative's liability within the tabular maximums, as well as determining the amount of the public grant.[860]

Responsibility of relatives provisions in the blind programs[861] evolved in conjunction with those of the aged and at most stages of their development were closely similar to them.[862] The provisions in the disabled program, however, were quite different. They appeared in that program when it was created in 1957[863] in the form of two sections, one drawn from the aged[864] and the other from the blind programs,[865] but without the related provisions in those programs which gave these sections much of their meaning. The disabled provisions thus presupposed liability rather than created it, directed the board of supervisors to request the district attorney or other civil legal officer to proceed against the pecuniarily able spouse, parent, or adult child in the order named, indicated that the courts would make findings as to ability to pay without providing any standards to guide the courts in the performance of the task, and made the receipt of aid independent of any recovery.[866] These provisions remained in this shape until 1961. In that year, the legislature abolished responsibility of relatives altogether in the blind[867] and disabled programs.[868] In doing so, the legislature was not content simply to repeal the Welfare and Institutions Code sections dealing with relatives' liability. It went further, positively to forbid such liability,[869] extend the prohibition to some forms of county aid,[870] mark out the relationship of this action to Civil and Penal Code sections,[871] proscribe

---

860. Cal. Welfare & Inst'ns Code §§ 2020, 2020.002; Old Age Security Manual, Reg. §§ A–200, A–208. The needs are divided into basic and special, and the amounts which may be budgeted to meet them are set forth partly in the code and partly in the regulations.
861. Cal. Welfare & Inst'ns Code §§ 3000–93 (federal-state-county aid to the blind); Cal. Welfare & Inst'ns Code §§ 3400–75 (state-county aid to the potentially self-supporting blind).
862. *Compare* Cal. Stat. 1955, ch. 892, § 1, at 1519, *and* Cal. Stat. 1957, ch. 571, § 4, at 1665, *with* Cal. Welfare & Inst'ns Code § 2181 *and* Cal. Welfare & Inst'ns Code § 2224.
863. Cal. Stat. 1957, ch. 2411, § 2, at 4156, adding Cal. Welfare & Inst'ns Code § 4160 and Cal. Welfare & Inst'ns Code § 4189 (1961), repealed, Cal. Stat. 1961, ch. 1998, § 1, at 4210.
864. Cal. Welfare & Inst'ns Code § 4160(e), copied from Cal. Welfare & Inst'ns Code § 2160(f).
865. Cal. Welfare & Inst'ns Code § 4189 (1961), copied from Cal. Welfare & Inst'ns Code §§ 3088, 3474 (1961).
866. Cal. Welfare & Inst'ns Code § 4160(f) (1961); see tenBroek, *Welfare in the 1957 Legislature*, 46 Calif. L. Rev. 331, 332–44 (1958).
867. Cal. Stat. 1961, ch. 1999, § 3, at 4211, adding Cal. Welfare & Inst'ns Code § 3011.
868. Cal. Stat. 1961, ch. 1998, § 2, at 4211, adding Cal. Welfare & Inst'ns Code § 4011.
869. "No relative shall be held legally liable to support or to contribute to the support of any applicant for or recipient of aid" under these programs. Cal. Welfare & Inst'ns Code §§ 3011, 4011.
870. "No relative shall be held liable to defray in whole or in part the cost of any medical care or hospital care or other service rendered . . . pursuant to any provision of this code" to an applicant for or recipient of blind or disabled aid. *Ibid.*
871. "Notwithstanding the provisions of Section 206 of the Civil Code, or Section 270c of the Penal Code, or any other provisions of this code no demand shall be made upon any relative to support or contribute toward the support of any applicant for or recipient" of blind or disabled aid. *Ibid.*

administrative pressure on relatives to make contributions in the absence of their legal liability,[872] and, on the whole, to uproot the institution in all of its parts, implications, and manifestations. At the same time, in the aged program, the legislature made changes in the responsible relatives provisions which fell just short of abolition by altering the figures in the liability table[873] to exempt roughly ninety-seven per cent of the relatives obligated to make payments.

### Wall of separation.

Thus, in the phase of family law which deals with the legal liability of relatives to contribute support, as in other phases, California today maintains a wall of separation between political and civil family law, though this is the phase in which the wall has most frequently been attacked and occasionally, for a short time, breached. A confusion of the two systems of family law in this respect was rendered particularly likely in California because of the origin of Civil Code section 206, the principal provision in civil family law. It will be recalled that the provision was copied verbatim from the Field Draft Civil Code and that Field derived it from New York's poor law. Field's intention, as he made explicit at the time, was to make the poor law principle "a ground of legal liability independent" of the poor law provisions.[874] The language employed by him to do this not only was incorporated into our Civil Code in 1872, but it remains in that code today and in precisely the same form. The forces which separate the two family law systems, however, aided by the peculiarities of our welfare history, have prevailed over this clause which Field intended to make common to both.

On one side of the wall, that of the poor law, there has been continual legislative activity affecting the various programs in different ways. The blind aid responsibility of relatives provisions, after forty-five years of progressive legislative changes specifically designed to limit the liability, withdraw administrative discretion, and free the aid recipient from its consequences, have now been abolished altogether. Over a somewhat shorter history, the responsibility of relatives provisions in the aged laws have followed a similar legislative course but have not yet been fully extirpated. The provisions for the disabled, introduced into the Welfare and Institutions Code in truncated form but administratively put into force in ways comparable to the other two adult aid programs, were legislatively eradicated after four years of existence. In the indigent aid

872. County employees are forbidden to "threaten" relatives "with any legal action" or "penalty whatsoever." *Ibid.*
873. Cal. Welfare & Inst'ns Code §§ 2181, 2224.
874. N.Y. Code Comm'rs, Draft Civil Code § 97, note (Final Report 1865).

law, relatively little change has occurred since the adoption of the program in 1901,[875] though there has been some legislative elaboration and such change as has occurred has moved in the direction of limiting arbitrary discretion in the boards of supervisors and providing minimum protection to the relatives and recipients. This is also the story of the programs for the mentally irresponsible, though the history is far longer and the administrators are state officials. On the other side of the wall, that of civil family law, legislative activity has been very slight. This is the province of judges and their interpretation has remained quite static.

Though generally the legislature and the courts have deliberately built and assiduously maintained the wall, both have from time to time permitted or created some fissures in it. In 1955, the legislature amended Civil Code section 206 to provide for a judicial proceeding to relieve an adult child of responsibility for the support of a parent who had abandoned him when he was a child.[876] The judgment relieves the child from responsibility both under Civil Code section 206 and under the aid programs, a prior application to the board of supervisors for such relief being required if the parent is a recipient under any of those programs.[877] In 1955 the legislature adopted the Uniform Civil Liability for Support Act.[878] The act is in the Civil Code but purports in part to integrate the liability provisions in civil and political family law. Under it the person entitled to support may enforce his right against a relative, and if the county furnishes support to the person, it is subrogated to his right to secure reimbursement and assure continuing support.[879] However, the factors to be considered in determining the amount due for support—such as the relative wealth, income, standard of living and situation of the parties, and the ability of each to earn—cut across those used in welfare programs and are traditional with civil family law.[880] Furthermore, the subrogation section is loosely drawn, apparently conferring on the county the right of recovery only with respect to aid paid under the indigent program, and subjecting the county's right "to any limitation otherwise imposed by the law of this State,"[881] including presumably the limitation imposed by the Welfare and Institutions Code on the county

---

875. *Compare* Cal. Stat. 1901, ch. CCX, §§ 6–7, at 638, *with* CAL. WELFARE & INST'NS CODE §§ 2576–77.

876. Cal. Stat. 1955, ch. 613, § 1, at 1103, adding CAL. CIV. CODE § 206.5.

877. CAL. CIV. CODE § 206.7. In County of Alameda v. Clifford, 187 Cal. App. 2d 714, 722, 10 Cal. Rep. 144, 150 (1st Dist. 1960), the district court of appeal used some careless language tending to suggest that the responsible relative provisions in the aid programs are implementive of the statutory liability embodied in Civil Code § 206.

878. Cal. Stat. 1955, ch. 835, § 1, at 1451, adding CAL. CIV. CODE §§ 241–54.

879. CAL. CIV. CODE § 248.

880. See CAL. CIV. CODE § 246; County of Contra Costa v. Lasky, 43 Cal. 2d 506, 275 P.2d 452 (1954); Woolams v. Woolams, 115 Cal. App. 2d 1, 251 P.2d 392 (1st Dist. 1952); In the Matter of Kendrick, 60 Cal. App. 146, 212 Pac. 226 (1st Dist. 1922).

881. CAL. CIV. CODE § 248.

right of reimbursement from responsible relatives. The counties, accordingly, have not made any particular effort to utilize the link thus established between political and civil family law.[882] These instances of legislatively created breaches in the wall of separation between the two family law systems must be viewed in light of the general legislative separation effected by placing them in different codes with distinct provisions, by constantly changing the ones in the Welfare and Institutions Code while leaving those in the Civil Code untouched, and by allocating their administration to different departments.

As the legislature has occasionally faltered in its maintenance of the wall of separation so have the courts. There are holdings and dicta in the cases based upon these general propositions: That the responsibility of relatives, especially adult children, to support their destitute kinsmen is "pre-existent and independent"; that it is founded upon a moral obligation given legal sanction in Civil Code section 206; that Civil Code section 206 was adopted long before relatives responsibility provisions were generally established in the state's welfare programs, and particularly, long before the adult categorical aid programs were created; and that relatives responsibility provisions in the categorical aid programs merely create a county right to reimbursement and establish the procedure for enforcement of the right.[883] The absence in the categorical aid programs of any clear and affirmative statement imposing upon relatives the duty to contribute lent additional credence to this view. The view, however, could not withstand the test of a somewhat longer span of history, the character of the provisions of the Welfare and Institutions Code and their differences with those in the Civil Code, and the basic separation of the two systems of family law. Thus, the California Supreme Court has closed the breach, reinforced the wall, and reasserted the judiciary as its keeper.[884] The system of provisions in the Welfare and Institutions Code specifying the circumstances under which relatives are liable for support and the methods of county recovery from the rela-

---

882. For a discussion of the relationship between the Uniform Civil Liability for Support Act and other support sections of the Civil Code see CALIFORNIA STATE BAR COMM. FOR THE CONTINUING EDUCATION OF THE BAR, REVIEW OF SELECTED 1955 CODE LEGISLATION 15–22 (1955).

883. See Department of Mental Hygiene v. McGilvery, 50 Cal. 2d 742, 755–56, 329 P.2d 689, 695–96 (1958); County of Los Angeles v. Lane, 113 Cal. App. 2d 476, 479, 248 P.2d 479, 481 (2d Dist. 1952); Kelley v. State Bd. of Social Welfare, 82 Cal. App. 2d 627, 632, 186 P.2d 429, 432 (2d Dist. 1947); Garcia v. Superior Court, 45 Cal. App. 2d 31, 33, 113 P.2d 470, 471 (4th Dist. 1941); County of Los Angeles v. Hurlbut, 44 Cal. App. 2d 88, 100, 111 P.2d 963, 969 (2d Dist. 1941); State Comm'n in Lunacy v. Eldridge, 7 Cal. App. 298, 305–06, 94 Pac. 597, 600 (3d Dist. 1908).

884. See County of San Bernardino v. Simmons, 46 Cal. 2d 394, 296 P.2d 329 (1956); County of Contra Costa v. Lasky, 43 Cal. 2d 506, 275 P.2d 452 (1954); County of Los Angeles v. La Fuente, 20 Cal. 2d 870, 129 P.2d 378 (1942), *cert. denied*, 317 U.S. 689 (1943). See also County of San Bernardino v. Johnson, 141 Cal. App. 2d 616, 297 P.2d 21 (4th Dist. 1956); Kelley v. State Bd. of Social Welfare, 82 Cal. App. 2d 627, 186 P.2d 429 (2d Dist. 1947); County of Lake v. Forbes, 42 Cal. App. 2d 744, 109 P.2d 972 (3d Dist. 1941).

tives, said the court, covers the subject completely.[885] Moreover, there is nothing in Civil Code section 206 suggesting that the responsible relatives are liable to any public agency which may supply assistance. Indeed, although the section mentions liability to third persons, such liability is confined to those who have supplied necessaries and to whom the adult child has made a promise to pay. Accordingly, the counties may not recover derivatively under Civil Code section 206 and cannot be subrogated to the rights of poor persons against their relatives under that section.[886] The court also emphasized the differences in the scope of coverage between the Welfare and Institutions Code and Civil Code section 206. Being in "need" under the Welfare and Institutions Code "manifestly . . . is not the same as being 'poor' and 'unable to maintain himself by work'" under Civil Code section 206. Eligible "needy" persons under the Welfare and Institutions Code may have considerable income and property and may be able to maintain themselves by work. Payment of aid, therefore, cannot be regarded as the performance of a duty to support a poor person unable to maintain himself by work, and on this account too the theory of subrogation is inappropriate.[887]

## The Kirchner Case—A Landmark Decision in the Law of the Poor

The responsibility of relatives provisions in the mentally irresponsible program, after a full century of existence in California in which they were legislatively changed in detail from time to time and eventually greatly elaborated, and in which they had been unsuccessfully attacked on constitutional grounds,[888] were declared unconstitutional by the California Supreme Court in *Department of Mental Hygiene v. Kirchner*.[889] The Department of Mental Hygiene brought suit under section 6650 of the California Welfare and Institutions Code against the estate of the daughter to recover the cost of the mother's maintenance in a state hospital. The court held that the burden of maintaining a state institution (the mental hospital) and providing adequate care for its inmates (decedent's mother) could not be transferred to relatives (decedent) without selecting them for the imposition of a species of taxation in violation of the equal protection clause.[890] The importance of this decision cannot

885. County of San Bernardino v. Simmons, 46 Cal. 2d 394, 398, 296 P.2d 329, 331 (1956).
886. *Id*. at 399, 296 P.2d at 332.
887. *Id*. at 400, 296 P.2d at 332.
888. Department of Mental Hygiene v. McGilvery, 50 Cal. 2d 742, 329 P.2d 689 (1958); Estate of Yturburru, 134 Cal. 567, 66 Pac. 729 (1901); State Comm'n in Lunacy v. Eldridge, 7 Cal. App. 298, 94 Pac. 597 (3d Dist. 1908).
889. 60 Cal. 2d 716, 36 Cal. Rep. 488, 388 P.2d 720 (1964), *vacated*, 33 U.S.L. Week 4245 (U.S. March 8, 1965) (No. 111).
890. Reasoning that the court had failed to indicate whether it relied on the federal or the state equal protection clauses, the Supreme Court vacated and remanded for determination of that issue. 33 U.S.L. Week 4245 (U.S. March 8, 1965) (No. 111). On April 2, 1965, the California court held it had relied on the state ground. S.F. Chronicle, April 3, 1965, p. 4, cols. 5–6.

be overestimated; nor can the holding be confined to the relatives of the mentally irresponsible. The principle enunciated applies with equal force to the relatives of other public aid recipients. If the public assumes responsibility when mentally ill individuals are given care in state hospitals, it equally assumes responsibility when needy individuals are given public support in their own homes. That much was determined by the first revolution in welfare as long ago as 1601. Once the public has assumed the responsibility, the cost must be derived from publicly apportioned taxation. It cannot be shifted to private persons—not to relatives, nor friends, nor other arbitrarily selected persons in the community who happen to have the money.

The central reasoning of the court[891] in the *Kirchner* case is expressed in three summary passages: First, the enactment and administration of laws providing for treatment of persons in appropriate state institutions is a proper state function. Being so, the costs should be borne by the state.[892] Second, "A statute obviously violates the equal protection clause if it selects one particular class of persons for a species of taxation and no rational basis supports such classification. . . . Such a concept for the state's taking of a free man's property manifestly denies him equal protection of the law."[893] Third, the cost of a proper state function conducted for the public benefit "cannot be arbitrarily charged to one class in the society."[894] Imposing liability for the cost on the relatives of recipients does arbitrarily charge it to one class in society and violates the basic constitutional guarantee of the equal protection of the law.[895]

The court makes a number of points having at best an unexplained bearing on the rationality of the basis of the classification, heart of the equal protection problem: The social revolution of the past half-century has brought expanded recognition of the *parens patriae* principle and other social responsibilities; the administrative agency selected the rela-

891. We need not here concern ourselves with any of the incidental or auxiliary issues which have encumbered the discussion of this case, important though some of them are for jurisdictional purposes: Whether the court was relying on the federal equal protection clause or on the state constitution; whether the principle of the *Hawley* case, Department of Mental Hygiene v. Hawley, 59 Cal. 2d 247, 28 Cal. Rep. 718, 379 P.2d 22 (1963), involving an insane person charged with crime, was dispositive of this case as the court said; whether the three cases cited by the court as ruling out a distinction based on family relationships really did so and were apposite; whether the court's statement is correct that no case can be found "which squarely faced, considered, discussed and sustained such statutes in the light of the basic question as to equal protection of the law," 60 Cal.2d at 720–21, 36 Cal. Rep. at 491, 388 P.2d at 723; whether the court should have called for a discussion of the equal protection issue before deciding the case on that ground. For discussions of the *Kirchner* case see 49 CORNELL L.Q. 516 (1964); 77 HARV. L. REV. 1523 (1964); 16 HASTINGS L.J. 129 (1964); 39 N.Y.U.L. REV. 858 (1964); 40 N.D.L. REV. 202 (1964).
892. Subject, according to the court, "to reasonable exceptions against the inmate or his estate." 60 Cal. 2d at 719–20, 36 Cal. Rep. at 490, 388 P.2d at 722 (quoting Department of Mental Hygiene v. Hawley, 59 Cal. 2d 247, 255–56, 28 Cal. Rep. 718, 723–24, 379 P.2d 22, 27–28 (1963)).
893. *Id.* at 722–23, 36 Cal. Rep. at 492, 388 P.2d at 724.
894. *Id.* at 720, 36 Cal. Rep. at 490, 388 P.2d at 722.
895. *Id.* at 717, 36 Cal. Rep. at 488, 388 P.2d at 720.

tive to be held liable from a class of persons designated by the legislature; the state could not reduce the patient's estate below a minimum necessary for self-support but might so reduce the estate of the relative; the liability of the relative is absolute but he is not given "any right of control over, or to recoup from, the assets of the patient."[896] The developing sense of social responsibility certainly has a bearing upon the character and extent of welfare programs including those dealing with persons with mental problems. Though many believe that this evolution points to the abolition of responsible relatives provisions, the court does not suggest that this is so or point out how. The administrative discretion argument is suggestive of separation of powers and due process rather than equal protection issues. The difference in treatment of the resources of patient and relative raises an equal protection problem but not one that necessarily calls for the elimination of any responsibility on the relative. Allowing the relative control over the patient and recoupment from his estate, a novel proposal indeed, would itself raise serious constitutional and social issues; but, in any event, the absence of such provision only remotely bears upon the rationality of the major classification. So, while these comments are appropriate in an opinion upon this topic, their relevance to the central problem is not self-evident and the court does nothing to supply the deficiency. The court's conclusion on the central problem is thus apocalyptic, unargued, and unexplained, leaving the conclusion to stand on its intrinsic merits and the reader to his own analysis.

Does a statute which is part of a welfare law and which imposes the financial burden of support and care upon the recipient's spouse, parents, and children select persons who stand in a reasonable relationship to the purpose (to be defined in a moment), and include all who are similarly situated? This is the problem of the "rational basis" for the classification mentioned by the court. What is there about relatives which puts them in a special relation to this purpose? Are all relatives similarly situated with respect to this purpose and do they stand in a different relationship to it from all other persons? If the class is reasonably related to the purpose and not over- or under-inclusive, is the classifying trait one which is not constitutionally forbidden such as race or nationality?

Of the explanations of the special relationship of relatives to the purpose—relatives receive a special benefit from the welfare program; the responsibility of relatives provisions merely attach "legal significance to the natural bonds of consanguinity"[897] and enforce a moral obligation; it has been accepted historically and traditionally; the welfare provision merely enforces by positive legislation a long-standing common-law duty

---

896. *Id.* at 722, 36 Cal. Rep. at 492, 388 P.2d at 724.
897. Beach v. Government of D.C., 320 F.2d 790, 793 (D.C. Cir. 1963).

—some are quickly eliminated and others will not stand the test of close scrutiny.

The purpose of responsibility of relatives provisions, it might be said, is to keep public welfare costs at a minimum. This statement can be accurately understood, however, only as a qualification upon a larger and more affirmative purpose of which it is a part, the purpose of maintaining the poor and caring for them in their poverty. The method of minimizing cost to the public under these provisions is by imposing the burden upon relatives and providing enforcement machinery. Responsibility of relatives provisions are, therefore, a publicly created and enforced method of raising money to achieve a public purpose—caring for the poor. When seen in the context of the law of the poor of which they are a part, which accounts for their existence and which gives them their meaning, therefore, the purpose of responsibility of relatives provisions must be formulated somewhat as follows: Publicly to assume the financial and administrative responsibility of relieving the distress of poverty for the public benefit with funds supplied largely from general taxation; but also, when available, to exact these funds from relatives of the recipient in order to minimize costs.

The purpose of public welfare is a public good, not a private benefit. This is necessary and implicit. It is also explicit: "The purpose of this Code," declares section 19 of California's Welfare and Institutions Code, "is to provide for protection, care, and assistance to the people of the state in need thereof, and to promote the welfare and happiness of all of the people of the state by providing appropriate public assistance and services to all of its needy and distressed." The Federal Social Security Act declares itself to be an act "to provide for the general welfare,"[898] and "to promote the well-being of the nation."[899] Thus it is clear that these statutes were not intended to serve only the particular interests of the beneficiary groups which are to be served by these programs. The interests of the general public, the well-being of the nation itself, the welfare and happiness of all of the people are basic purposes which these programs of public assistance are designed to further and protect.

The public purpose and the public benefit would exist whatever the causes of poverty, whether personal or impersonal, characterological or a product of the general system. In many cases, need is demonstrably economic and its cause is lack of employment. The close statistical correlation between rising unemployment and rising AFDC rolls is no accident. Moreover, the fundamental economic need seldom exists in isolation for the families who comprise the bulk of the caseload. It exists

---

898. Preamble, ch. 531, 49 Stat. 620 (1935).
899. Declaration of Purpose, ch. 836, 70 Stat. 846 (1956).

in an atmosphere of racial prejudice and discrimination, of shifting industrial demands and obsolescence of traditional skills. The economics
of distress are intricately bound up with social and psychological factors
in the environment. Accordingly, the principal cause of dependency is
not individual, but social, a need for protection arising from the com-
plexities of modern society and the imperfections of a rapidly advancing
economy. Since a major cause of poverty is social, over which the individual has no control, relief is a proper charge against the total economy.

In the light of the public purpose of welfare legislation and in the
context of the social and economic causes of dependency, it is virtually
irrelevant to say that the relatives of persons receiving assistance are spe-
cially benefited. All members of the public benefit equally and the total
economy must bear the cost of its imperfections. Welfare, like education,
or the provision of police and fire protection, is a basic public function
benefiting all who live in the community. Questions as to who derives
special benefits—the mentally gifted from education, the person who is
protected against criminal assault by the police, the person whose home
is saved from the flames by the firemen, the recipient of welfare grants
and services, let alone his relatives—are irrelevant. Similarly situated
persons are persons who stand in the same relation to the valid purpose
of a law, not persons who stand to gain more or less from the implementation of such purpose.

The bonds of consanguinity and moral duty arguments are but a form
of the special benefit argument and must stand or fall with it. There
are, however, additional complications. The bonds of consanguinity are
roughly the same for all close relatives. Is a classification under-inclusive
which does not cover the grandparents, grandchildren, and siblings along
with parents and children? Moreover, within the circle of persons made
liable consanguinity is not the only basis. Spouses are made responsible
but are not consanguineal, indeed may not be under the incest law.
Blackstone, among others, thought that nature made a relevant implan-
tation in the father's breast. But he relied principally upon the act of
begetting as implying a voluntary assumption of liability for all who
"descend from his loins."[900] Presumably, there is the same consanguinity, though perhaps not the same bond, between child and father as between father and child, but the voluntary assumption inference cannot
operate in reverse. Perhaps the natural duty and moral responsibility do
not coincide, unless reciprocity is implied in the law, whatever the fact.
The consanguineal tie and whatever natural and moral duty relatives

---

900. 1 Blackstone, Commentaries *448.

and friends may have with respect to welfare recipients do not, in any event, place the relatives in a special relation to the welfare purpose; but, if they did, there would still remain many unresolved classification problems within the group of relatives made responsible.

It has been asserted that tradition establishes the rational basis of classification.[901] Tradition is not evidence of rationality but only of practice. In the age of *Brown v. Board of Educ.*,[902] *Griffin v. Illinois*,[903] *Gideon v. Wainwright*,[904] *Baker v. Carr*,[905] and *Reynolds v. Sims*,[906] neither tradition nor charges of judicial legislation dispose of constitutionality. Mr. Justice Holmes's statement that a certain statute was the outcome of a thousand years of history was used more to explain than to justify the measure, which he would have sustained on other and nonhistorical grounds.[907] Mr. Justice Cardozo's equally apt phrase—"not lightly vacated is the verdict of the quiescent years"—was not a declaration that the verdict could not and should not be vacated; "the quiescent years" only provided "the setting" and "the method of approach," not the constitutional answer.[908] Three and a half centuries of uncritical quiescence add no virtue to this particular tradition, bearing as it does the names of despots like Henry VIII and Elizabeth I, and the character of an age of autocracy and aristocracy in which labor and the poor were a separate and degraded class, politically unenfranchised, economically subjugated, and unknown to the benefits of the Constitution. A few remarkable methods of raising money for governmental purposes had long been forbidden by Magna Carta, and a few others such as forced loans and compulsory contributions were soon afterwards forbidden by the Petition of Right. These, however, were not guarantees to the poor. Parliament had entered the field but there were not then, as there are now, constitutional standards for taxation requiring uniformity, due process, and equal protection. It is by these standards that the rationality of this classification must now be measured—and measured in the light of the fact that only recently in this nation are the poor becoming known to the protections of the Constitution.

The short answer to the long-standing common-law duty argument is that there has been no such duty. Responsibility of relatives, as shown

---

901. Brief for Petitioner Before U.S. Sup. Ct., p. 9, Department of Mental Hygiene v. Kirchner, 33 U.S.L. Week 4245 (U.S. March 8, 1965) (No. 111).

902. 347 U.S. 483 (1954).

903. 351 U.S. 12 (1956).

904. 372 U.S. 335 (1963).

905. 369 U.S. 186 (1962).

906. 377 U.S. 533 (1964).

907. Hoeper v. Tax Comm'n, 284 U.S. 206, 219 (1931).

908. Coler v. Corn Exch. Bank, 250 N.Y. 136, 141–42, 164 N.E. 882, 884 (1928), *aff'd*, 280 U.S. 218 (1930).

earlier in this work,[909] was a product of the poor law statutes, confined for centuries to the law of the poor. It emerged in the common-law system of civil family law in England and New York about the middle of the nineteenth century, deriving some poor law support from the Field Draft Civil Code. In California, a wall of separation has been maintained between civil and political family law both generally and as to responsibility of relatives. Imposition of liability is not the enforcement of a common-law duty; it is the enactment of a poor law command.

The rational basis of the overall classification—the family law of the poor—and the source of its distinction from the family law of the rest of the community, is that the families who are its subjects are poor. It is this basic fact, the poverty of the class of persons entitled to assistance under the state's welfare laws, which underlies the further and altogether dependent classification of certain relatives of such persons as responsible. One classification based on poverty is thus built upon another, and the whole system is accordingly doubly invidious. In this age of a renewed quest for equality and a national rediscovery of the human and moral elements in the Constitution, should not poverty as a classifying trait be declared inherently discriminatory and outlawed because of its very nature, and "the mere fact of being without funds" be held "constitutionally an irrelevance like race, creed or color" as Mr. Justice Jackson said[910] and as *Griffin*[911] and *Gideon*[912] imply?

Finally, quite untenable distinctions are drawn among relatives of recipients based on the factor of eligibility for aid. For constitutional purposes what difference does it make to the relatives' liability whether the recipient is poor and eligible because he is blind rather than indigent, sick rather than senile, handicapped physically rather than mentally? In what sense do the relatives stand in a different relation to welfare purposes dependent on the cause of the recipient's poverty? The answers must surely be in no sense. In the *McGilvery* case,[913] the California Supreme Court sustained relatives responsibility provisions in the mentally irresponsible program against a charge of unconstitutional discrimination among relatives of the various categories of aid recipients. Unsound as that decision may have been on the narrow issue presented, the court confined the discussion to conditional or absolute liability as the only difference among the groups of relatives and concluded that all the relatives were unconditionally liable. It did not consider the existence of liability

909. tenBroek, *California's Dual System of Family Law: Its Origin, Development, and Present Status*, 16 Stan. L. Rev. 257, 283–85, 287–91, 294–96, 298–306 (1964).
910. Edwards v. California, 314 U.S. 160, 184–85 (1941).
911. Griffin v. Illinois, 351 U.S. 12 (1956).
912. Gideon v. Wainwright, 372 U.S. 335 (1963).
913. Department of Mental Hygiene v. McGilvery, 50 Cal. 2d 742, 329 P.2d 689 (1958).

in some programs and nonexistence in others. By way of dictum, however, the court suggested that a constitutional distinction could be drawn on the basis of the governmental source of the funds utilized in the welfare programs.[914] In the indigent aid program the cost is entirely on the county; in the aid to the mentally irresponsible programs it is entirely on the state; and in the AFDC, aged, blind, and disabled programs the cost is shared by the county, state, and federal governments. Although the governmental source of funds may have a bearing on the willingness of the legislature to abolish relatives responsibility programs, it has nothing whatever to do with the relation of relatives' responsibility to the welfare purpose, which is the same in all of these programs. That more or less local money is at stake does not change the character of that relationship or create it where it is absent.

The reason for the differences as to responsibility of relatives between county aid and aid to the mentally irresponsible, on the one hand, and the aged, blind, and disabled programs, on the other, is practical and political rather than doctrinal and constitutional. The aged and blind, and recently the disabled, have been able to organize and bring concerted pressure to bear upon the legislature. The mentally irresponsible and the undifferentiated and different groups of recipients of indigent aid have not found this possible. The establishment of the categorical aid programs for the aged, blind, and disabled, by withdrawing relatively homogeneous groups from the indigent aid program and treating them thereafter as distinct groups for purposes of welfare legislation and adding the financial resources of the state and nation to those of the county, both was a consequence of the ability of these groups to organize and act and, at the same time stimulated and facilitated such organizations. While not articulated in the *Kirchner* opinion,[915] this state of facts and events is not without significance in interpreting the result. Relatives responsibility provisions were eliminated in the blind and disabled programs and drastically reduced in the aged by group activity and political action. This was the method. The motive was that long maintained by a large body of social work opinion that liability of relatives creates and increases family dissension and controversy, weakens and destroys family ties at the very time and in the very circumstances when they are most needed, imposes an undue burden upon the poor (for such the relatives

---

914. The purpose of relatives responsibility provisions "is to minimize the cost to the state and its agencies . . . ." *Id.* at 755, 329 P.2d at 695. Therefore, the court argued, the purpose can be effectuated most completely when only state and local funds are involved. When federal funds carry part of the burden "there is not as urgent a necessity that the local government recover the funds expended in such programs in order that its costs be minimized and that the purpose of the recovery provisions be realized." *Id.* at 756–57, 329 P.2d at 696.

915. Department of Mental Hygiene v. Kirchner, 60 Cal. 2d 716, 36 Cal. Rep. 488, 388 P.2d 720 (1964), *vacated*, 33 U.S.L. Week 4245 (U.S. March 8, 1965) (No. 111).

almost always are), and is therefore socially undesirable, financially unproductive, and administratively unfeasible.[916] Broadly speaking, the same social policy reasons exist for taking the same action in connection with the other programs even though the means of political action are not so readily available or are nonexistent. Where the forces moving the political branches of government are absent, and where evenhanded justice and principles of equal treatment imperatively call for fulfillment, the court intervened to apply and enforce the Constitution. This is the state supreme court counterpart of the active and positive role of the United States Supreme Court in civil rights and state legislative reapportionment. The *Kirchner* court left its normal domain of civil family law and creatively entered the arena of political family law. This the court does upon occasion when great constitutional principles require or some obvious injustice must be corrected. So with the legislature—it enters the field of civil family law at long intervals and upon some great occasion of overall review to consolidate gains made by the judiciary or, more likely, to pull judicial action up to date.

## Parents and Minor Children

### In civil family law.

In an earlier part of this work, I have discussed the Civil Code provisions and related judicial interpretations dealing with parental custody and control of minor children.[917] Included in the term "custody" and standing in a reciprocal relationship to each other are, on the one hand, the right to control, services, and earnings, and, on the other hand, the duty of support and suitable education. When the family is broken and the parents are contending against each other for custody, the courts place emphasis on the best interests of the child and give relatively little weight to the wishes of the parents.[918] If the contest is between a parent

---

916. See 1 ABBOTT, PUBLIC ASSISTANCE 164, 167–68, 175, 258–82 (1940); BOND, OUR NEEDY AGED 315–20 (1954); GREENFIELD, ADMINISTRATION OF OLD AGE SECURITY IN CALIFORNIA 31, 32, 46 (1950); SHORR, FILIAL RESPONSIBILITY IN THE MODERN AMERICAN FAMILY 31, 33, 36 (1960); WILENSKY & LEBEAUX, INDUSTRIAL SOCIETY AND SOCIAL WELFARE 78, 178 (1958); Abbott, *Abolish the Pauper Laws*, 8 SOCIAL SERVICE REV. 1, 9, 15 (1934); Beard, *Are the Aged Ex-Family?*, 27 SOCIAL FORCES 275–78 (1949); Goldstein, *Case-Work Services in the Aid to Dependent Children Program: A Study in Cook County*, 18 SOCIAL SERVICE REV. 478, 486 (1944); Hart, *The Responsibility of Relatives Under the State Old Age Assistance Laws*, 15 SOCIAL SERVICE REV. 24, 26, 29, 46 (1941); Hart, *Administration in Old Age Assistance*, 15 SOCIAL SERVICE REV. 285, 298–300 (1941); Hitrovo, *Responsibility of Relatives in the Old Age Assistance Program in Pennsylvania*, 18 SOCIAL SERVICE REV. 67, 69, 72–75 (1944); Hollingshead, *Class Differences in Family Stability*, 272 Annals 39, 45 (Nov. 1950), in SOCIAL PERSPECTIVES ON BEHAVIOR 45, 50, 51 (Stein & Cloward 1958); Wickenden, *The Needs of Older People*, 1953 AM. PUBLIC WELFARE A. 70, 71.

917. tenBroek, *California's Dual System of Family Law: Its Origin, Develeopment, and Present Status*, 16 STAN. L. REV. 900, 915–27 (1964).

918. *Id.* at 916–19; see Munson v. Munson, 27 Cal. 2d 659, 666, 166 P.2d 268, 272 (1946); Taber v. Taber, 209 Cal. 755, 756–57, 290 Pac. 36, 37 (1930). And see CAL. CIV. CODE §§ 138, 199, 214.

and a stranger, including relatives, the governing principle, according
to the California Supreme Court, is paramount parental rights supported by a presumption of parental fitness.[919]

A handful of sections in the Civil Code deals specifically with the obligation of support. The primary responsibility for support of a legitimate
child rests upon the father.[920] If for any reason the father is unable to
provide adequate support, the mother is then obliged to assist the father
in the discharge of the duty to the extent of her ability.[921] When the
child is illegitimate, the responsibilities of the father and mother are
more nearly equal;[922] Civil Code section 196 does not distinguish between primary or secondary duties of support. If the normal family
situation is disrupted the primary, equal, or subordinate responsibilities
of the father and mother may all be shifted.[923] "When determining the
amount due for support," the court is directed to "consider all relevant
factors" including: The standard of living, the situation, the relative
wealth, the ability to earn, the age of the parties, and the need of the
child.[924] Few standards or guides are laid down for determining need.
Support, maintenance, and education[925] are mentioned in the Civil Code,
sometimes qualified by "suitable to his circumstances."[926] But the items
of support are not given nor are specific standards by which they are to

919. Stewart v. Stewart, 41 Cal. 2d 447, 260 P.2d 44 (1953); Roche v. Roche, 25 Cal. 2d 141,
152 P.2d 999 (1944); Stever v. Stever, 6 Cal. 2d 166, 56 P.2d 1229 (1936); *In re* Campbell, 130
Cal. 380, 62 Pac. 613 (1900). See CAL. CIV. CODE §§ 197, 200; CAL. PROB. CODE § 1407; tenBroek,
*supra* note 917, at 919–27.
920. Fox v. Industrial Acc. Comm'n, 194 Cal. 173, 178, 228 Pac. 38, 39–40 (1924); Newell v.
Newell, 146 Cal. App. 2d 166, 178, 303 P.2d 839, 847 (2d Dist.), *appeal dismissed*, 46 Cal. 2d
861, 299 P.2d 849 (1956); Metson v. Metson, 56 Cal. App. 2d 328, 132 P.2d 513 (1st Dist. 1942);
Blain v. Williams, 86 Cal. App. 676, 680, 261 Pac. 539, 541 (2d Dist. 1927); see CAL. CIV. CODE
§ 196. The stepfather is expressly declared not to be liable. CAL. CIV. CODE § 209; Spellens v.
Spellens, 49 Cal. 2d 210, 223, 317 P.2d 613, 620–21 (1957) (dictum).
921. Luis v. Cavin, 88 Cal. App. 2d 107, 118, 198 P.2d 563, 571 (3d Dist. 1948); see *In re*
Cattalini, 72 Cal. App. 2d 662, 670, 165 P.2d 250, 256 (3d Dist. 1946); White v. White, 71 Cal.
App. 2d 390, 163 P.2d 89 (2d Dist. 1945). The *Cattalini* case holds that primary civil liability rests
upon the mother if she has lawful custody and there is no support order against the father. CAL.
CIV. CODE §§ 242–43 impose liability upon the father and mother for support of children if they
are "in need." However, the duty imposed by these sections is explicitly made subject to CAL. CIV.
CODE § 196, which contains no such qualification in the obligation of support. Kruly v. Superior
Court, 216 Cal. App. 2d 589, 593, 31 Cal. Rep. 122, 125 (2d Dist. 1963) (dictum).
922. See CAL. CIV. CODE § 196a; Reed v. Hayward, 23 Cal. 2d 336, 340, 144 P.2d 561, 563
(1943); Kilcrease v. Kilcrease, 132 Cal. App. 2d 869, 283 P.2d 300 (1st Dist. 1955); Kemppainen
v. Hester, 113 Cal. App. 2d 472, 248 P.2d 103 (2d Dist. 1952); Myers v. Harrington, 70 Cal. App.
680, 683–84, 234 Pac. 412, 413 (3d Dist. 1925); Demartini v. Marini, 45 Cal. App. 418, 187 Pac.
985 (1st Dist. 1920); Guay v. Superior Court, 147 Cal. App. 2d 764, 769, 305 P.2d 990, 993 (2d
Dist. 1957) (dictum).
923. See, *e.g.*, CAL. CIV. CODE §§ 137, 137.1, 139, 199. And see Pacific Gold Dredging Co.
v. Industrial Acc. Comm'n, 184 Cal. 462, 194 Pac. 1 (1920); Lewis v. Lewis, 174 Cal. 336, 163
Pac. 42 (1917); Goto v. Goto, 187 Cal. App. 2d 603, 10 Cal. Rep. 20 (2d Dist. 1960); Dickens v.
Dickens, 82 Cal. App. 2d 717, 187 P.2d 91 (2d Dist. 1947); Bernard v. Bernard, 79 Cal. App. 2d
353, 179 P.2d 625 (3d Dist. 1947); Adoption of Kelly, 47 Cal. App. 2d 577, 118 P.2d 479 (1st
Dist. 1941); tenBroek, *supra* note 917, at 916–19 and cases there cited.
924. CAL. CIV. CODE § 246.
925. CAL. CIV. CODE §§ 137.1, 137.2, 139.
926. CAL. CIV. CODE §§ 196, 196a.

be met. The mode of enforcement is by civil action and continuing judicial control.[927]

Parental obligations are also imposed by section 270 of the Penal Code. Section 270 provides criminal sanctions for some obligations similar to those imposed by the Civil Code and for others which are not. Under both the Civil Code and the Penal Code, the father's liability is primary; the mothers', secondary.[928] Inability to give adequate support—whether arising from death, mental or physical infirmity, or lack of funds—does not explicitly excuse the father from liability under either code section.[929] Under Penal Code section 270 the mother's obligation arises if the father "is dead or for any other reason whatsoever fails to furnish" support; under Civil Code section 196 it arises if the father is not "able" to give adequate support. Unlike Civil Code section 196, Penal Code section 270 puts legitimate and illegitimate children upon the same footing.[930] Unlike Civil Code section 196a, which equally obligates the father and the mother to support illegitimate children, Penal Code section 270 imposes primary responsibility upon the father. Under Penal Code section 270, the father's obligation continues regardless of its civil reallocation, that is, "regardless of any decree made in any divorce action relative to alimony or to the support of the child,"[931] any order giving the mother lawful custody of the child[932] or the support of the child supplied voluntarily or involuntarily by any other person or organization.[933] Under the Penal Code the character and extent of the liability in any given case is left to the court; under the Civil Code, "when determining the amount due for support," the court is required to give consideration to seven specified factors among others.[934] Under both codes, the courts have wide discretion as to the needs of the child for which the parent will be held responsible and the standard of care, though a list of items to which the child is entitled is provided and includes "necessary clothing, food, shelter, or medical attendance or other remedial care."[935]

---

927. CAL. CIV. CODE § 137.1; see Dimon v. Dimon, 40 Cal. 2d 516, 524, 254 P.2d 528, 532 (1953); Paxton v. Paxton, 150 Cal. 667, 89 Pac. 1083 (1907); Ackerman v. Superior Court, 221 Cal. App. 2d 94, 34 Cal. Rep. 182 (2d Dist. 1963).

928. CAL. CIV. CODE § 196.

929. In Department of Mental Hygiene v. McGilvery, 50 Cal. 2d 742, 756, 329 P.2d 689, 696 (1958), the obligation of a parent to support a minor child under the Civil Code was declared to be absolute. *But cf.* CAL. CIV. CODE § 246. Insufficiency of funds has been held a defense against criminal prosecution. People v. Caseri, 129 Cal. App. 88, 18 P.2d 389 (3d Dist. 1933); People v. Wallach, 62 Cal. App. 385, 217 Pac. 81 (1st Dist. 1923); 2 ARMSTRONG, CALIFORNIA FAMILY LAW 1143 (1953).

930. Dimon v. Dimon, 40 Cal. 2d 516, 523, 254 P.2d 528, 531 (1953) (by implication); see *In re* Clarke, 149 Cal. App. 2d 802, 309 P.2d 142 (2d Dist. 1957).

931. See Dixon v. Dixon, 216 Cal. 440, 14 P.2d 497 (1932); Bernard v. Bernard, 79 Cal. App. 2d 353, 179 P.2d 625 (3d Dist. 1947).

932. People v. Champion, 30 Cal. App. 463, 158 Pac. 501 (2d Dist. 1916).

933. People v. Frazier, 87 Cal. App. 65, 261 Pac. 1071 (2d Dist. 1927); People v. Curry, 69 Cal. App. 501, 231 Pac. 358 (3d Dist. 1924).

934. CAL. CIV. CODE § 246.

935. CAL. PEN. CODE § 270.

*In the family law of the poor.*

In the family law of the poor, the nature of custody, the rights of the parents, and the obligation of support are quite different from civil family law. The elements of custody—control, services, earnings, rearing, support, and education—linked and interdependent in civil family law, possess no necessary relationship in the family law of the poor. Most social workers think these elements are to be separately considered and evaluated individually. In the family law of the poor, parental right necessarily plays a smaller role. Courts do not operate welfare institutions. They presuppose a family or a situation in which someone has the child in hand or wants to secure its custody. Under these presuppositions, dominant parental right gives the courts a rule for assigning the custody of the child to one or another of contending parties. Once the assignment is made, "the supremacy of the mother and father in their own home in regard to the control of their children is generally recognized."[936] Underlying this is the theory of Blackstone, Kent, and Mr. Chief Justice Traynor of the California Supreme Court that the natural impulses of parents to support and care for children in the proper way can be relied upon.

The situation in the family of the poor is otherwise. In the first half-century of California's history, when the emphasis was on child-caring institutions, the child was separated from both parents, care was provided in the institution and custody was in the managers. In the next sixty years when the child has been left in the family, there has generally been only one parent in the home, usually the mother, whose parental right as head of the household has not stood on the same ancient footing as that of the father. Though the child is in the custody of the parent, custody and parental right are separated from support which is being supplied by the public. Parental right is diminished by the more or less continuing contact and active interest of social workers and other officials. To some extent, this curtails the exclusiveness of parental control, leaving the parent less free to determine the place of abode and the manner and standard of living. It also leaves the parent less free to live his or her private life. Because of the presence of the social worker, however occasional, questions of fitness are more likely to arise with regard to the management of the household and budget, the suitability of the home for the rearing of the children, issues of morality, extra-marital relations, drinking, and the like.

Not only in the separation of the right to custody and the duty to support but in all of its main features, the support obligation of parents

---

936. Odell v. Lutz, 78 Cal. App. 2d 104, 106, 177 P.2d 628, 629 (2d Dist. 1947).

for minor children differs in the two systems of family law. These differences may be summarized as follows: In the Welfare and Institutions Code the obligation is formulated in terms quite distinct from those in the Civil Code and is made the same for both parents. In the Welfare and Institutions Code, in addition to parents, natural and adoptive, stepfathers are made liable as are otherwise unrelated adult males assuming the role of spouse to the mother. In the family law of the poor, ability to support, the items of need of the children to be met, and the standards at which they are to be met are all legislatively and administratively established and are quite different from those selected by the code and the courts in civil family law. Administration and enforcement of the obligation in the family law of the poor is first of all assigned to welfare administrators including the county board of supervisors and is thereafter backed up by a system in which the district attorney and penal enforcement machinery loom large.

### The support obligation of parents to minor children.

In the family law of the poor, parental liability for support of minor children is stated in terms of the purpose of the program, the conditions of eligibility of the children for assistance from the public, rules about the amount and utilization of property and income, and the duties imposed on welfare officials and workers to investigate and determine parental ability to pay. These terms are intended to be applicable uniformly to all, unconditioned by such factors as those mentioned in Civil Code section 246 and Civil Code section 196 dealing with the relative wealth, standards of living, and situations of the parents and children. They are without distinction as to whether the parent is father or mother or as to the primary or secondary character of the parental duty. Under the Federal Social Security Act to which the state program is tied, federal grants to states are made available

> for the purpose of encouraging the care of dependent children in their own homes or in the homes of relatives by enabling each State to furnish financial assistance and rehabilitation and other services, as far as practicable under the conditions in such State, to needy dependent children and the parents or relatives with whom they are living.[937]

Elsewhere the federal act refers to those to be aided as "needy families with children"[938] or "families with dependent children."[939] Under the

---

937. Social Security Act, § 401, as amended, 70 Stat. 848 (1956), as amended, 42 U.S.C. § 601 (Supp. V, 1964).
938. Social Security Act § 402(a), 49 Stat. 627 (1935), as amended, 42 U.S.C. § 602(a) (Supp. V, 1964).
939. Social Security Act § 402(a)(4), 49 Stat. 627 (1935), as amended, 42 U.S.C. § 602(a) (4) (Supp. V, 1964).

California law children are eligible for a public grant or for publicly supplied services if they are "in need thereof."[940] The need must arise because the children are deprived of parental support or care.[941] Accordingly, though need is not defined in financial terms alone—deprivation of parental care is something more than the absence of purchaseable necessities—need arising from the lack of the monetary wherewithall to maintain life at defined minimum standards is a basic condition of eligibility; and in determining that need, state and federal law require that welfare administrators "shall take into consideration any other income and resources of any child or relative claiming aid . . . ."[942] Whether the parents are living together or apart, children are ineligible for assistance if they or their parents either individually or collectively own more than a specified amount of real[943] and/or personal property.[944] Since the object of these provisions is not only to establish conditions of eligibility, but to require the devotion of all possible family resources to the purposes of support, real property within the specified limits, if not occupied as

---

940. CAL. WELFARE & INST'NS CODE §§ 19, 1500.

941. CAL. WELFARE & INST'NS CODE § 1500. According to the statute, the deprivation in turn must be due to: "(a) The death, physical or mental incapacity, or incarceration of a parent; or (b) The divorce, separation or desertion of his parent or parents and resultant continued absence of a parent from the home for these or other reasons; or (c) The unemployment of his parent or parents." Thus the major sources of deprivation are covered, but not all.

942. Social Security Act, § 402(a)(7), as amended, 76 Stat. 188 (1962), 42 U.S.C. § 602(a) (7) (Supp. V, 1964); see CAL. WELFARE & INST'NS CODE §§ 1500, 1511; AFDC MANUAL, Handbook §§ C–012(4), C–210, C–212.25. The needs of the child are defined to include the needs of relatives with whom the child is living. CAL. WELFARE & INST'NS CODE § 1501.5.

From the requirement that other income and resources be considered, the federal act excepts "all or any portion of the earned or other income to be set aside for future identifiable needs of a dependent child . . . ." Social Security Act, § 402(a)(7), as amended, 76 Stat. 188 (1962), 42 U.S.C. § 602(a)(7) (Supp. V, 1964). This exception is governed by "limitations prescribed by the Secretary." *Ibid.* Pursuant to this authority, federal policy permits the conservation "of all or any portion of the family's earned or other income for future identifiable needs of the child," U.S. BUREAU OF PUBLIC ASSISTANCE, HANDBOOK OF PUBLIC ASSISTANCE ADMINISTRATION § 3140(2), provided that the amount conserved "shall be reasonable . . . to the purpose for which it is being held." *Id.* § 3131(4). In taking advantage of this provision, California permits conservation of income for future education plans. However, the county welfare department must agree to and supervise devotion of savings to this purpose in each case. AFDC MANUAL, Reg. §§ C–212.36, C–212.55(3).

943. CAL. WELFARE & INST'NS CODE § 1520. The maximum allowable amount in combined assessed value as assessed by the county assessor, less all encumbrances of record thereon, is $5,000. See AFDC MANUAL, Reg. §§ C–132.10, C–132.70. The following are excluded when considering the real property limits: "1. Real property held in trust if the child or parent does not have control of the trust of which he is the beneficiary. 2. The separate and community share of real property of a parent who has surrendered full custody of his child pursuant to a court order. 3. The separate and community share of real property of a parent who has relinquished his child for adoption and the relinquishment has been signed. 4. The separate and community share of real property of the father of a child who is not married to the mother and the parents are not maintaining a home together. Exception: If the father has legitimatized the child under Section 230 of the Civil Code, his property is included whether or not the parents are maintaining a home together. 5. The separate and community share of real property of a stepfather." AFDC MANUAL, Reg. § C–132.50.

944. CAL. WELFARE & INST'NS CODE § 1521. The allowable total combined value of children and parent's personal property under the statute is $600. See AFDC MANUAL, Reg. §§ C–135.08, C–135.10. This does not include the value of "clothing, furniture, household equipment including musical instruments and other recreational items, food stuffs, fuel, personal effects and personal jewelry." CAL. WELFARE & INST'NS CODE § 1521.2. For other exclusions see AFDC MANUAL, Reg. § C–135.30.

a home, must be utilized "to provide for the needs of the child or his parent, or both,"[945] and personal property held by an absent parent and for one reason or another not available for the support of the child is not to be considered in determining eligibility.[946] And, because including the value of tools and equipment used by a parent in a rehabilitation plan would be self-defeating as to both the financial and welfare objectives of the program, their value is to be disregarded in determining eligibility.[947]

In many ways limits on income are more important than limits on property. The child is eligible for assistance only if the family income is insufficient to meet its needs and the amount of assistance is determined by the gap between income and needs.[948] Accordingly, the Welfare and Institutions Code and welfare administrators define income for these purposes,[949] identify the family members whose income will be considered,[950] prescribe the permissible deductions from the gross to reach the net,[951] and generally provide for the treatment of income.[952] Involved in this process is the establishment of rather complete directions as to the uses of income, so defined and circumscribed, for family support when the income is insufficient to meet all of the needs of the family and the child is eligible for aid. Many distinctions are drawn with respect to the family—such as those dealing with the so-called family budget unit;[953] the presence in or absence from the home of the parents,[954] and needy and non-needy relatives and caretakers;[955] and the regularity,[956] casualness,[957] and disposal of income[958]—which have relevance only to families receiving public assistance. In these provisions is found much of the actual meaning and precise nature of parental liability for the support

---

945. CAL. WELFARE & INST'NS CODE § 1520. Such utilization occurs when "it is making a reasonable contribution toward current needs, when a plan for its use supports a conclusion that it will so contribute in the immediate future, or when it is sold for an amount consistent with its current market value, and the plan and terms of sale are consistent with the requirement of reasonable contribution toward current needs." AFDC MANUAL, Reg. § C–133.10. See *id.* § C–133.40.

946. CAL. WELFARE & INST'NS CODE § 1521.3; AFDC MANUAL, Reg. § C–135.08.

947. CAL. WELFARE & INST'NS CODE § 1523.5; AFDC MANUAL, Handbook § C–130.30.

948. See CAL. WELFARE & INST'NS CODE §§ 1500, 1511; AFDC MANUAL, Reg. §§ C–221.01, C–221.02, Handbook § C–210.

949. CAL. WELFARE & INST'NS CODE §§ 1508, 1511.1, 1563; AFDC MANUAL, Reg. § C–211.

950. CAL. WELFARE & INST'NS CODE §§ 1508, 1552.46, 1571; AFDC MANUAL, Reg. § C–212.30.

951. AFDC MANUAL, Reg. §§ C–212.35, C–212.36, C–212.40.

952. AFDC MANUAL, Reg. §§ C–212.31, C–212.55, C–212.70.

953. "Include[d] in the Family Budget Unit, if living in the home [are]: 1. Each eligible child, including the unborn child; 2. Each needy ineligible child under 21, including the unborn child and other children of the stepfather or man assuming the role of spouse; 3. Each natural parent; 4. The stepfather or man assuming the role of spouse; 5. The needy adult relative who acts as caretaker." AFDC MANUAL, Reg. § C–201.10.

954. CAL. WELFARE & INST'NS CODE §§ 1500, 1508, 1564; AFDC MANUAL, Reg. §§ C–132.50, C–135.08, C–135.30, C–212.55.

955. See AFDC MANUAL, Reg. §§ C–201.10 exception 5, C–212.31.

956. AFDC MANUAL, Reg. §§ C–211, C–212.10.

957. *Ibid.*

958. CAL. WELFARE & INST'NS CODE § 1552.2.

of minor children in the family law of the poor. These provisions are augmented by a specific directive to county welfare workers to determine the ability of absent parents to contribute to the support of their aided children,[959] and to the State Department of Social Welfare to "establish a scale of suggested minimum contributions to assist counties and courts in determining the amount that a parent should be expected to pay toward the support of his child under this chapter."[960] The scale must include consideration of gross income, authorize an expense deduction for determining net income, designate other available resources to be considered, specify the circumstances which should be considered in reducing liability on the basis of hardship. The scale is to be distributed to courts, district attorneys, and county welfare departments for their optional use.[961] Finally, another provision of the Welfare and Institutions Code authorizes county recovery of family resources not discovered, assessed, and distributed as before indicated.[962] The county may bring suit to recover the assistance paid if, during the continuance of aid, it determines "that the parent of a recipient has been gainfully employed or has had sufficient assets to enable him to reasonably assist the recipient during the period . . . ."[963] This provision is not a general declaration of parental liability in the family law of the poor. The emphasis is on a county investigation and determination of resources of the family not earlier revealed pursuant to the family's reporting duty[964] or the county's investigating duty[965] and which would have affected either eligibility for or the amount of the grant.

Just as the basic provisions of parental liability in the family law of the poor are different from those in civil family law, so are the provisions dealing with the needs of the children and the measure of their accommodation which at one and the same time determine the amount of the public grant and the parental liability. The items of need are carefully specified: Safe, healthful housing; minimum clothing for health and decency; low cost, adequate food; utilities; essential household furniture and equipment; essential medical, dental, or other remedial care not available through a public facility.[966] Other items are included in special circumstances when verified as needed: Special diets upon the recommendation of a physician, transportation, laundry, housekeeping service,

---

959. See CAL. WELFARE & INST'NS CODE § 1564; AFDC MANUAL, Reg. § C–156.30.
960. CAL. WELFARE & INST'NS CODE § 1552.45.
961. *Ibid.*
962. CAL. WELFARE & INST'NS CODE § 1506.5.
963. *Ibid.*
964. See CAL. WELFARE & INST'NS CODE §§ 104.2(b), 1577.
965. CAL. WELFARE & INST'NS CODE §§ 449.2, 1550.6; AFDC MANUAL, Reg. § C–012.40.
966. CAL. WELFARE & INST'NS CODE § 1511.5; AFDC MANUAL, Reg. §§ C–202–03, C–205.

and telephone; and utilities in excess of the basic minimum need.[967] These items of need are to met in accordance with "minimum basic standards of adequate care" which the State Department of Social Welfare is explicitly directed to determine and to distribute to the counties which are bound by them.[968]

### Liability of stepfathers and men in the home.

In recent times, while relatives responsibility was being drastically diminished in the aged program[969] and abolished in the blind[970] and disabled programs[971] and while the long-standing common-law and civil code provision exempting a man from a duty to support the children of his wife by a former husband was being steadfastly maintained,[972] in the aid to families with dependent children program there has been a striking enlargement of the circle of persons held liable for child support to include stepparents[973] and otherwise unrelated adult males living in the relation of spouse to the mother.[974] The liability of the stepparent and unrelated adult male is not absolute even in the sense conceived in the *McGilvery* case.[975] Under Welfare and Institutions Code section 1508 they are "bound to support, if able to do so . . . ." No reference is made in this provision to the source or character of the limiting inability, and presumably its origin—whether physical infirmity, general hard times, technological unemployment, or personal inadequacy—is immaterial. Section 1508 places a ceiling upon the obligation; it is not to exceed "the wife's community property interest in his income," an interest which the mother has whether she is ceremonially established as the wife or is only the other half of the unrelated adult male assuming the role of spouse to her. The stepfather or unrelated adult male's ability is to be determined administratively by the county under regulations set forth by the State Department of Social Welfare. The discretion thus vested by section 1508 is only slightly qualified. The amount of the public grant to the children is to be computed "after consideration is given to the income" of the stepfather or adult male. The county's determination of whether the stepfather or adult male is "able to support the child either

---

967. CAL. WELFARE & INST'NS CODE § 1511.5(h); AFDC MANUAL, Reg. §§ C–202–03, C–205.

968. CAL. WELFARE & INST'NS CODE § 1511.5.

969. *Compare* Cal. Stat. 1950, 1st Ex. Sess., ch. 22, § 1, at 463, *with* CAL. WELFARE & INST'NS CODE § 2181.

970. CAL. WELFARE & INST'NS CODE § 3011.

971. CAL. WELFARE & INST'NS CODE § 4011.

972. CAL. CIV. CODE § 209.

973. *Compare* Cal. Stat. 1951, ch. 1349, § 1, at 3256, *with* CAL. WELFARE & INST'NS CODE § 1508.

974. *Ibid.*

975. Department of Mental Hygiene v. McGilvery, 50 Cal. 2d 742, 755–56, 329 P.2d 689, 698 (1958).

wholly or in part" is to be based upon "a standard which takes into account the . . . income and expenses" of the stepfather or adult male. Judging by the language, "expenses" include those connected with gaining the income, alimony payments to an earlier wife, support payments to children by previous relationships, perhaps even indebtedness incurred before the present relationship or certain kinds of indebtedness incurred since. How such expenses are to be taken into account, whether at full value, part value, or no value, is to be established by regulation, though the origin and language of the code provision plainly suggests a better standard for stepfathers and adult males than for natural fathers. Over the years, the regulations have given less and less account to the expenses of the stepfather and adult male, thus bringing them closer to the standards applicable to the natural parents, until differences relate primarily to medical expenses.[976]

The claim that the imposition of liability for support on the unrelated male assuming the role of spouse unconstitutionally deprives him of property without due process of law was denied but not squarely met by the district court of appeal in the *Rozell* case.[977] Ignoring the clause of Welfare and Institutions Code section 1508 that imposed the duty, and expressing doubts whether the constitutional issue could properly be raised, the court said that the section does not deprive the man of his property at all. It merely provides that his income shall be taken into consideration in determining the amount of the grant.

> The purpose . . . is to administer the program fairly and to safeguard public funds. It is a reasonable device to determine the needs of a child. It is based on the assumption that a man assuming the role of spouse will contribute to the support of the mother and her children. It takes nothing from him. It merely requires that his income be considered.[978]

The court relied on expressions in the California Supreme Court case that upheld the administrative regulations regarding the unrelated adult

---

976. Deduction from the income of natural parents is allowed for court-ordered support of a spouse or child not living in the home only for three months if the parent requests court review of the order and thereafter only if the court so orders. AFDC MANUAL, Reg. § C–212.36(A). Deduction is made from the income of a stepparent, or a man assuming the role of spouse, in the amount of: "1. The support payments actually to be made to or for dependents living elsewhere and alimony payments to his ex-wife in the amount of the court order; 2. The cost of medical care of the stepfather . . . and other persons in the Family Budget Unit for whom there is no federal eligibility as child or caretaker." AFDC MANUAL, Reg. § C–212.36(B).

Unlike the natural parents, the stepfather or unrelated adult male living in the home may be excluded from the family budget unit if his property, when combined with that of persons in the unit, exceeds the allowable limit. AFDC MANUAL, Reg. § C–201.10, exception (4).

By the regulation put into effect in December 1953, shortly after the stepfather provision assumed its present form, the stepfather was allowed an automatic 10% deduction from his net income plus the amount of contributions actually made for the support of his dependents living out of the home. CAL. DEP'T SOCIAL WELFARE, MANUAL OF POLICIES AND PROCEDURES, AID TO NEEDY CHILDREN, Reg. §§ C–356, C–364(B) (1954).

977. People v. Rozell, 212 Cal. App. 2d 875, 28 Cal. Rep. 478 (3d Dist. 1963).

978. *Id.* at 878, 28 Cal. Rep. at 481.

male before the Welfare and Institutions Code section had been enacted, a case in which the supreme court explicitly asserted that the regulations did not impose a duty of support.[979]

In the *Coley* case,[980] decided after *Kirchner*,[981] the constitutional issue was again bypassed. The *Kirchner* case was distinguished. The county sought restitution from an AFDC mother for a portion of the aid granted. The alleged overpayment was due to the presence of a man in the home assuming the role of spouse and having income which had not been taken into account in fixing the amount of the grant. The court found no attempt to hold the man liable, since suit was against the mother; thus it was "unnecessary to discuss"[982] whether the mother had any community property interest in his income. In *Kirchner*, the court argued, liability of relatives had been held "an invalid class discrimination in violation of a constitutional guarantee."[983] No such issue was involved here. "In the case before us . . . aid to needy children not being a right, but based on need, we are concerned only with the reimbursement of funds illegally obtained by the mother . . . and not for a direct contribution based on her own resources."[984] But if aid is based on need and need depends on the mother's resources, then whether she has any community property interest in the man's income is very material in determining whether the funds were illegally obtained. Accordingly, the basic issue becomes whether, as the court concludes, the liability of the unrelated male for support and the rule measuring the child's need by his income may be dissociated.

That this may be done is a doctrine traceable to the *Shirley* case,[985] which sustained the rule in the absence of liability. The reasoning in *Shirley*, however, is not unmixed. On the one hand, it treats the rule as "a practical solution of the difficulty"[986] experienced by welfare workers in ascertaining the amount actually contributed by the unrelated male. On the other, it assumes that the unrelated male and the stepfather are in the same situation at least with respect to the financial resources made available to the child and "the safeguarding of public funds";[987]

---

979. People v. Shirley, 55 Cal. 2d 521, 525–26, 11 Cal. Rep. 537, 539, 360 P.2d 33, 35 (1961).
980. County of Kern v. Coley, 229 Adv. Cal. App. 216, 225, 40 Cal. Rep. 53, 58 (5th Dist. 1964).
981. Department of Mental Hygiene v. Kirchner, 60 Cal. 2d 716, 36 Cal. Rep. 488, 388 P.2d 720 (1964), *vacated*, 33 U.S.L. Week 4245 (U.S. March 8, 1965) (No. 111). See text accompanying notes 888–916 *supra*.
982. 229 Adv. Cal. App. at 222, 40 Cal. Rep. at 56.
983. *Id*. at 225, 40 Cal. Rep. at 58.
984. *Ibid.*
985. People v. Shirley, 55 Cal. 2d 521, 11 Cal. Rep. 537, 360 P.2d 33 (1961).
986. 55 Cal. 2d at 525, 11 Cal. Rep. at 539, 360 P.2d at 35.
987. *Ibid.*

that "it is unlikely that the financial need of a child will vary substantially depending upon the legality of relationship"; and that "it is reasonable to infer that a man assuming the role of spouse will contribute to the support of the mother and her needy child."[988] Whether "the legality of the relationship," without more, has a sufficient psychological impact upon the stepfather to affect substantially the child's financial need may be set aside as an unanswered question of fact since something is added to "the legality of the relationship." The ceremonial stepfather is under a legal obligation to support the child.[989] The doctrine of the *Shirley* case ignores the fact that the rule measuring the child's need by the man's income originated in connection with legal liability to support. It was first applied to the income of natural parents living in the home, persons under the legal obligation; and the legislative imposition of legal liability on the stepfather living in the home antedated the application of the rule to him.

The truth is that the rule was adopted not so much as a measure of contributions actually being made as it was as a means of seeing to it that contributions were made. The rule was designed primarily as an enforcement device to compel the parent or stepparent to discharge a legal duty of support. In the same way, the child is denied public assistance if the mother refuses to cooperate with law enforcement officers,[990] or to accept vocational rehabilitation,[991] or to engage in reasonable employment.[992] The theory of the state is that if the public aid to the child is withdrawn or diminished in accordance with the man's income, he will devote that income to the child instead of to himself or others. Thus, the rule is not only associated historically with the liability, but is intended as "a practical solution of the difficulty" experienced by social workers and others of enforcing the liability. When applied to the unrelated man in the home, the rule carried its context and purpose with it, a conclusion equally established by the sequence of legal events, the undisguised but underlying motive, and the debates of the state social welfare board at the time the rule was adopted.[993] Indeed, that the rule presupposed and implied the obligation, and was intended to put the unrelated male in this respect upon the same footing as the stepfather, the court itself finally made clear in the *Shirley* case: to invalidate the rule, the court said, "would place a premium upon an illegal relationship and operate as a deterrent to marriage of the mother and the man assum-

---

988. *Ibid.*
989. Cal. Welfare & Inst'ns Code § 1508.
990. Cal. Welfare & Inst'ns Code § 1572.
991. Cal. Welfare & Inst'ns Code § 1523.5.
992. Cal. Welfare & Inst'ns Code § 1523.6.
993. Cal. Social Welfare Bd., Minutes at iii, 6, Feb. 1954.

ing the role of spouse,"[994] a remark utterly irrelevant if the question were the extent to which the unrelated male relieved the need of the child. Unless the unrelated male escaped the obligation imposed upon the stepfather, there would be no "premium upon an illegal relationship," whether or not it operated as a deterrent to marriage.

The court in the *Coley* case[995] presumed that the man-in-the-home statute was designed to meet Mr. Justice Peters's dissent in *Shirley*. Mr. Justice Peters, it is true, spoke of the "usurpation of legislative power by an administrative board"[996] in issuing the regulation; but he also challenged as "obviously unsound" the "reasonable" inference by which the majority justified the rule, and he stressed the fact that the unrelated male was under no legal obligation to support the child.[997] Consistent with the court's presumption of the legislative purpose, the statute both declared the liability and embodied the rule.[998] It is thus only if the court can sunder what history, purpose, and the statute have joined, that the *Shirley*, *Rozell*, and *Coley* rhetoric can be treated as other than an evasion of the real legal and constitutional problem and that the *Kirchner* holding as to the unconstitutionality of the responsibility of relatives can be set aside as irrelevant.[999]

---

994. 55 Cal. 2d at 525, 11 Cal. Rep. at 539, 360 P.2d at 35.

995. County of Kern v. Coley, 229 Adv. Cal. App. 216, 222, 40 Cal. Rep. 53, 56 (5th Dist. 1964).

996. 55 Cal. 2d at 527, 11 Cal. Rep. at 540, 360 P.2d at 36.

997. *Id.* at 527, 529, 11 Cal. Rep. at 540, 541–42, 360 P.2d at 36, 37–38. "The effect of the majority opinion," said Mr. Justice Peters, "is to hold that the Board of Social Welfare, by a regulation adopted by it, can determine that a needy child, who is otherwise entitled to state aid, can be deprived of a certain portion of that minimum aid which the Legislature has determined to be necessary to support him . . . solely because his mother is engaged in an extramarital relationship with a man who has no legal obligation to support the child, and who may, in fact, legally refuse to do so." *Id.* at 527, 11 Cal. Rep. at 540, 360 P.2d at 36. "[T]he reason why the Legislature provided that a stepfather's income may be used in computing the amount of aid granted to the child is that Section 1508 carefully makes the stepfather legally obligated to support his stepchildren up to an amount representing his wife's community property interest in his income. The support of the child, the paramount concern of the statute, is thus assured. The child is given as a substitute for aid, the legal right to enforce his right to support from a stepfather." *Id.* at 529, 11 Cal. Rep. at 541–42, 360 P.2d at 37–38.

998. CAL. WELFARE & INST'NS CODE § 1508.

999. The ground taken in the *Shirley* opinion that "it is reasonable to infer that a man assuming the role of spouse will contribute to the support of the mother and her needy child," People v. Shirley, 55 Cal. 2d 521, 529, 11 Cal. Rep. 537, 542, 360 P.2d 33, 38 (1961), requires investigation before acceptance, if it is not "obviously unsound" as Mr. Justice Peters says. Instances are numerous in which the unrelated male not only contributes nothing to the support of the mother and her children but draws on their resources to meet his own necessity or pleasure. In its report on Operation Weekend conducted in July 1962, the Kern County Welfare Department says, for example, "We have learned that the tenth of the month when ANC warrants are received, is known as 'Mother's Day' in some parts of the community, and it is common knowledge that the boy friend is there to receive his spending money or, as we have discovered in a few cases, the amount to make his car payment." The legislature thought this enough of a problem to declare that "Any person other than a needy child, as defined in Section 1500, who willfully and knowingly receives or uses any part of an aid grant paid pursuant to this chapter for a purpose other than support of the needy children and the caretaker involved is guilty of a misdemeanor." CAL. WELFARE & INST'NS CODE § 1575. It may be admitted that the unrelated male with income is more likely to contribute than the one without.

It should be noted too that the deterrent effect upon marriage of the "premium upon an illegal relationship" must be counterbalanced by the deterrent effect on stable common-law unions providing a two-parent home for the child by the withdrawal of the premium.

## Law Enforcement Officers

### Relations with welfare departments.

In 1952, Noleo (notice to law enforcement officers) went into effect under the Social Security Act,[1000] thus imposing a new requirement on the states and giving national legal expression to a very old welfare motive. Noleo is the requirement that "prompt notice" be given "to appropriate law enforcement officials" that aid has been granted for "a child who has been deserted or abandoned by a parent." Before the emergence of this federal mandate a standard method of recovering aid payments from responsible relatives had been for the county supervisors to turn the matter over to the district attorney or other law enforcement officer who was either required or permitted by law to bring suit.[1001] In addition to recovery provisions of this sort in the aid laws, Penal Code section 270 for many years had been an independent source of penal enforcement authority for support obligation. However, the role of the district attorney and other law enforcement officers had been fairly minor: the boards of supervisors exercised a free discretion in selecting the cases to be referred; Penal Code section 270 was not expressly linked to the welfare program; and the political and financial potential of the systematic use of criminal sanctions was not fully realized. Today, all of this is changed. Federal and state laws require the county supervisors and welfare departments to maintain active relations with the district attorney, precisely prescribing the character of the relationship, the circumstances in which each must act and the action to be taken, and generally providing for a major role for the district attorney in the AFDC program.[1002] Furthermore, Penal Code section 270 is now specifically made a penal enforcement adjunct of the AFDC program.[1003] The fiscal and political potential of a greatly augmented role for the district attorney is being fully exploited.[1004]

---

1000. Social Security Act § 402(a)(10), as amended, 64 Stat. 550 (1950), as amended, 42 U.S.C. § 602(a)(10) (Supp. V, 1964).

1001. Cal. Stat. 1901, ch. CCX, § 6, at 637; Cal. Stat. 1933, ch. 761, § 3, at 2006; CAL. WELFARE & INST'NS CODE § 2576. In 1950 the Aid to Needy Children Law assigned law enforcement officials no role in connection with enforcing the support obligation of absent parents. They did have a role in connection with the presumptive death of a parent. CAL.WELFARE & INST'NS CODE §§ 1570–74 (1957), repealed by Cal. Stat. 1957, ch. 609, § 1, at 1819.

1002. Social Security Act § 402(a)(10), as amended, 64 Stat. 550 (1950), as amended, 42 U.S.C. § 602(a)(10) (Supp. V, 1964); CAL. WELFARE & INST'NS CODE §§ 1571–79.

1003. CAL. WELFARE & INST'NS CODE § 1570.

1004. See *Hearings Before the Senate Fact Finding Committee on Labor & Welfare*, Cal. Legislature, July 1, 1960, at 64. "The Adult Probation Department's 'Family Division' cash collections for 1949–1950 [before enactment of CAL. WELFARE & INST'NS CODE § 1552.4] totaled $92,-171.95; their collections for 1963–1964 amounted to $798,429.00, of which $478,320.00 were made for cases originating in this office through arrests, voluntary probation, and uniform reciprocal support action.

"In addition to the above, it is estimated our ANC Investigators saved the taxpayers another $150,000.00 this year by having the responsible fathers pay directly to the mothers or the Public Welfare Department." Annual Report to Mayor submitted by Thomas C. Lynch, District Attorney, San Francisco, July 1, 1963–June 30, 1964, p. 32.

Under the supervision of the State Department of Social Welfare, the direct administering agency of public welfare programs in California is the county with authority vested in the board of supervisors and executed by a county welfare department. Initially and primarily, therefore, the responsibility rests upon the county welfare department to enforce parental liability for the support of minor children receiving public aid.[1005] The county welfare department is to investigate applications for aid[1006] and to determine family income and resources among other factors of eligibility.[1007] The department is responsible for the carrying out of the requirement that an absent parent

> complete a statement of his current monthly income, his total income over the past 12 months, the number of dependents for whom he is providing support, the amount he is contributing regularly toward the support of all children for whom application for aid is made . . . , his current monthly living expenses and such other information as is pertinent to determining his ability to support his children.[1008]

The department is directed, as soon as possible after an application is signed, to interview the absent parent if he is in the county and his whereabouts is known, to determine his ability to support his children, to make arrangements—preferably by entering into a support agreement—requiring him to meet his obligation, to discuss his parental responsibilities, and to explore family reconciliation and resumption of parental relationships.[1009]

Although Welfare and Institutions Code section 1571 contains a general requirement of immediate notice by the county supervisors to the district attorney whenever aid is granted to a child not being supported by a parent, referral is not required if "it is definitely established that the parent is financially incapable of providing such support," and the district attorney need not act upon the notice "unless and until the case has been referred to him by the county department."[1010] It is only if the enforcement efforts of the county department have proven ineffective or have little prospect of success that the district attorney is summoned into action. In that event, referral of the case to him is called for, not just notice of its existence.[1011] If the whereabouts of the parent is unknown, referral is to be made. If the whereabouts is known, and the county de-

---

1005. Cal. Welfare & Inst'ns Code §§ 200–01.1.
1006. Cal. Welfare & Inst'ns Code §§ 449.2, 449.5.
1007. Social Security Act § 402(a)(7), as amended, 53 Stat. 1379 (1939), as amended, 42 U.S.C. 602(a)(7) (Supp., 1964); Cal. Welfare & Inst'ns Code §§ 1500, 1511; AFDC Manual, Reg. §§ C–012(4), C–212.25, Handbook § C–210.
1008. Cal. Welfare & Inst'ns Code § 1564. "A violation of this section constitutes a misdemeanor." *Ibid.*
1009. Cal. Welfare & Inst'ns Code § 1571.
1010. *Ibid.*
1011. *Ibid.*

partment has not been able to enter a satisfactory support agreement within forty-five days, referral is to be made unless the department "has definitely determined that the man is financially incapable of supporting the child." Regardless of these conditions, section 1571 prescribes a referral in any of these circumstances: The parent refuses to provide necessary information or to be interviewed, or past relations with him indicate that the department's efforts "would be fruitless"; the parent refuses to contribute according to his ability, or, without good cause, has failed to comply with a support agreement for sixty days; there is reason to believe that the parent may flee or hide; legal action is necessary to establish paternity.

Once the referral has been made, the county department and the present parent are required to cooperate with the district attorney. The department is to report all information in the case record bearing upon nonsupport and the suitability of prosecution as a method of obtaining support.[1012] The present parent is to give "reasonable assistance," which specifically includes: Consent to be interviewed by the district attorney; willingness to sign a complaint against the absent parent; not dismissing the complaint; and not concealing the identity or whereabouts of the absent parent.[1013] The duties and powers of the district attorney are explicitly set forth in the Welfare and Institutions Code. Upon referral, he is to investigate immediately and "take all steps necessary to obtain support for the needy child."[1014] The steps are not only those prescribed in the Welfare and Institutions Code, but also those authorized in Penal Code section 270;[1015] and the enforcement remedies under the Welfare and Institutions Code do not preclude "any other remedy which he has under the law."[1016] Special provision is made for his powers in the case of parents who are divorced or legally separated or are engaged in a pending action for divorce or separate maintenance.[1017] In such circumstances the district attorney may apply to the superior court for an order directing the parents or either of them to show cause why a support order should not be issued, or the amount of a previous order increased, or the parent held in contempt for failure to comply with a previous support order.[1018]

---

1012. *Ibid.*
1013. CAL. WELFARE & INST'NS CODE § 1572.
1014. CAL. WELFARE & INST'NS CODE § 1571.
1015. CAL. WELFARE & INST'NS CODE § 1570.
1016. CAL. WELFARE & INST'NS CODE § 1579.
1017. CAL. WELFARE & INST'NS CODE § 1578.
1018. *Ibid.* The legislature has recently made a small effort to mesh the separate actions of the courts and the welfare departments with respect to the support of the children in pending divorce or separate maintenance cases. In addition to the optional scale mentioned earlier, CAL. WELFARE & INST'NS CODE § 1552.45, it has provided that the court shall direct the clerk to notify the district attorney and the county department "if, to the knowledge of the court, aid has been

## Methods in general.

The methods used by district attorneys and courts to enforce support obligations are characterized by diversities, uniformities, and an intermixture of support enforcement techniques with those used for the detection and prosecution of welfare fraud, theft, and perjury. They are characterized, too, by the imagination displayed in the invention of legal devices in the enforcement and criminal prosecution functions, the frequency with which such devices approach and transgress norms of legality and constitutionality, and the extraordinary way in which some district attorneys have made political capital out of their welfare role.

Typically, the district attorney hails the parent before him by a variety of informal and formal devices; interrogates, admonishes, and threatens him with criminal prosecution; and obtains a so-called "voluntary agreement" in writing by which the parent undertakes to pay a specified amount monthly for the support of the children.[1019] Typically, the district attorneys do not utilize their authority under Welfare and Institutions Code section 1578 to secure superior court orders in divorce and separate maintenance actions. Similarly, prosecution under Penal Code section 270 is resorted to only after other less formal remedies have been exhausted. But the amount of time and energy devoted to enforcement by any of these techniques varies greatly among the counties. Only the larger counties have family support units in the office of the district attorney. Follow-up on the "voluntary agreements" and payments under them—whether to the district attorney, the probation officer, or directly to the family—is subject to a great deal of local choice. Equally diverse is the handling by the district attorney and the municipal court of suits for failure to provide. Irving Reichert, in his study for the Welfare Study Commission,[1020] illustrated the differences in practice. In one large county, the judge called all support cases simultaneously and told the line-up of fathers to plead guilty and receive probation. The judge did this without a presentence report, without knowledge of the backgrounds

applied for or granted . . . or if the court . . . believes that within the near future there is a likelihood that aid will be applied for . . . . " CAL. WELFARE & INST'NS CODE § 1578.1. Reciprocally, if the county department learns about the law suit, it shall "notify the court that aid is being paid or has been applied for, and . . . furnish . . . such information as is available . . . as to the financial resources of the parents which might be applied to child support." *Ibid.*

1019. Though such agreements are not explicitly mentioned in the Welfare and Institutions Code, other than in connection with the welfare departments, they probably lie within the authorization to the district attorney to "take all steps necessary to obtain support for the needy child." CAL. WELFARE & INST'NS CODE § 1571. CAL. PEN. CODE § 270 and CAL. WELFARE & INST'NS CODE § 580(d) provide additional but limited authority. The latter declares that the probation officer is authorized to receive money "payable to a child, wife, or indigent parent when it has been alleged or claimed that there has been a violation of either section 270, 270a, or 270c of the Penal Code and the matter has been referred to the probation officer by the district attorney."

1020. Reichert, *Relationships Between Welfare and Law Enforcement Agencies in California,* in CAL. WELFARE STUDY COMM'N, CONSULTANTS' REPORTS, pt. II, app. F, at 253, 265–69 (1963).

of the fathers in providing support, with any inquiry into their ability to pay or the willfulness of their failure to do so.

> Sometimes they had been in court before and had prior convictions for the same offense; sometimes investigators and welfare workers had spent many hours in locating them and in making support agreements that had been broken. Sometimes a man was not guilty of the offense. . . . One such case involved a man who earned $56 a week, was physically handicapped, and was already supporting eight children. The man was found guilty despite the fact that he qualified for public assistance himself.[1021]

In another county the district attorney's investigator handles the case when it is first called in court. If the man pleads guilty, the judge may obtain a presentence report from the probation office, may ask the investigator about the case, and may immediately place the man on probation with an order to pay a specified amount. In one county, probation was denied in 97 out of 158 cases, in another, in only 5 out of 384.[1022]

One county, copying a measure long in existence for other purposes in other counties, passed a so-called resort ordinance and rigorously applied it to catch AFDC mothers in a penal net.[1023] The ordinance forbade "resorting" to any of a long list of places in town, country, or park for the purpose of extra-marital relations. Equally engulfing were the elements of the crime. The county fathers were not content with prohibiting the commission of the act itself. Resorting for the purpose of committing the act was sufficient and this was true whether the purpose was shared by both parties or held by only one. The application of the

---

1021. *Id*. at 269.

1022. *Ibid.* The judges in several counties worked out a sentencing practice designed to benefit the counties financially. After conviction under CAL. PEN. CODE § 270 a fine would be imposed and past welfare benefits ordered repaid. No order would be given for current child support. The fine enabled the county to collect money that did not have to be shared with the state and federal governments. Welfare grants could be cut by the monthly amount of the ordered restitution. This action could result in keeping families on aid unnecessarily and depriving them of any opportunity to get off. The second county in inter-county transfer cases was also adversely affected, the fine and restitution payments to the first county withdrawing what would otherwise be resources of the family to be taken into account in granting aid in the second county.

One counteractive of the practice considered by the State Department of Social Welfare was a simple adjustment-by-audit procedure treating fines and restitutions as refunds with the state and federal share recouped from the welfare subsidy to the county. Cal. Social Welfare Bd., Minutes, Oct. 9, 1962. This plan was not used because of the prospect of legislative solution. That came in 1963 by way of an amendment to the Penal Code providing: "In any case where there is a conviction and sentence under the provisions of either Section 270 or Section 270a, of this code, should a fine be imposed, such fine shall be directed by the court to be paid in whole or in part to the wife of the defendant or guardian or custodian of the child or children of such defendant, except as follows:

"If the children are receiving public assistance, all fines, penalties or forfeitures imposed and all funds collected from the defendant shall be paid to the county department. Money so paid shall be applied first to support for the calendar month following its receipt by the county department and any balance remaining shall be applied to future needs, or be treated as reimbursement for past support furnished from public assistance funds." Cal. Stat. 1963, ch. 834, § 2, at 2033, amending CAL. PEN. CODE § 270(d).

1023. Tulare County, Cal., Ordinance 719, March 10, 1960, reprinted in Cal. Dep't Social Welfare, Report on Tulare County at 11, Sept. 16, 1960.

ordinance was not so sweeping as its geography and psychology. It was selective and discriminatory; only AFDC mothers and those found with them became familiar with its penal sanctions. The methods of enforcement were those associated with the law of crimes: Investigation on suspicion or gossip, detectives operating in teams, night raids, simultaneous approaches to the back and front of the house, guns conspicuously displayed on hips, unceremonious entry, inmates interrogated at length and notes taken, the entire house searched without any particular care to secure permission, men and sometimes AFDC mothers arrested and hauled off to jail in the middle of the night.[1024] As thus administered the ordinance clearly violated the constitutional command of the equal protection of the laws and the constitutional guarantees to the right of privacy and security in persons, houses, papers, and effects. This and similar local measures were invalidated by the California Supreme Court not for these reasons but on the ground that the state preempted the field of regulating the criminal aspects of sexual activity and prostitution.[1025] The court reasoned that since the legislature had not defined cohabitation and fornication as crimes, it had "determined by implication that such conduct shall not be criminal . . . ."[1026]

Prosecution, trial, and probation techniques in some counties are illustrated by the much publicized case of the two Lucies.[1027] The district attorney lodged fraud and theft charges against two AFDC mothers, one for having a man in her home while receiving aid and the other for not reporting accurately the address in Mexico of her common-law husband. The man in the first case was also prosecuted for nonsupport of two of the children. After conviction or pleas of guilty, all three were placed on probation, conditioned on their not indulging in extra-marital relationships. All three were later jailed for violating this condition. These defendants, whose private lives and intimate relationships received the searching scrutiny of law enforcement officers and the obsessed attention of the press and public, were not only poor and uneducated but members of a minority group: Mexican-Americans. In Mexico free union is a legal form of marriage. The form of marriage of the poor, the rural, and the young, it accounts for one-fifth of Mexican marriages. When the crops improve, religious and civil ceremonies are often added.[1028]

1024. Cal. Dep't Social Welfare, Report on Tulare County, Sept. 16, 1960; Cal. Social Welfare Bd., Minutes, Sept. 23, 1960; Cal. Dep't Social Welfare, Office Memo, Tulare County, Oct. 13, 1960.

1025. *In re* Lane, 58 Cal. 2d 99, 102, 22 Cal. Rep. 857, 858, 372 P.2d 897, 898 (1962).

1026. *Id.* at 104, 22 Cal. Rep. at 860, 372 P.2d at 900. Apparently the defendant in the *Lane* case was not an AFDC mother and the modus operandi described by the court—in each case, the defendant went from the living room to the bedroom in her own home for the purpose of nonmarital relations—suggests commercial prostitution rather than spouse-like cohabitation.

1027. *In re* Turrieta, 54 Cal. 2d 816, 8 Cal. Rep. 737, 356 P.2d 681 (1960) (facts reported in *Ex parte* Turrieta, 2 Cal. Rep. 883 (1st Dist. 1960)).

1028. Hayner, *The Family in Mexico*, 16 MARRIAGE AND FAMILY LIVING 369–73 (1954).

The district court of appeal stated that one of the AFDC mothers had been denied constitutional right of counsel.[1029] The court emphatically rejected a plea that it should "tolerate . . . an undefined degree of laxity" in applying constitutional standards to these cases.

> When essential constitutional rights are in issue, the petty offender . . . is the equal of any other citizen, and entitled to the full protection of the Constitution, not just to a part of that protection, grudgingly given and imperfectly applied. . . . The accused who stands before a justice court for sentencing does not thereby become a second class citizen, entitled only to second class justice.[1030]

In another county, prosecution, trial, and probation practices took a different turn. The district attorney would charge AFDC mothers, as well as fathers, with nonsupport of their children. If the mother pleaded not guilty, she would be convicted and jailed. If she pleaded guilty, as the judge advised, she would be placed on probation, on condition either that she receive no further public aid or that she receive it on the terms laid down by the judge. In one case an AFDC mother came into court as a witness in her husband's nonsupport trial.[1031] At the trial she was charged with nonsupport and she immediately entered a plea of guilty. She was promptly sentenced, according to the transcript, "to serve sixty days in the custody of the sheriff of the county, which sentence was suspended on condition that defendant remove her two children from the relief rolls within thirty days." The husband, meanwhile, was released unconditionally.[1032] In these and numerous other cases, the district attorney and a municipal court judge forced AFDC mothers, under pain of punishment, to withdraw from the relief rolls and ordered them to go to work—without regard to health or ability to work, the children's need for the mother in the home, provision for the children's care, availability of employment, or eligibility of the family for public aid.[1033] Thus did they seek to solve at a penal stroke the human and social problems of welfare.[1034]

---

1029. "There can be no doubt that, when a party is convicted, but not sentenced, and is placed on probation, and thereafter probation is revoked and sentence is imposed, the constitutional right to counsel applies to the sentencing proceeding." *Ex parte* Turrieta, 2 Cal. Rep. 883, 884 (1st Dist.) (dictum), *vacated*, 54 Cal. 2d 816, 8 Cal. Rep. 737, 356 P.2d 681 (1960).

1030. 2 Cal. Rep. at 885.

1031. Cal. Social Welfare Bd., Minutes, Feb. 28, 1961 (Appeal of Ryan).

1032. Cal. Social Welfare Bd., Verbatim Transcript, Minutes, June 20, 1960, at 24, 42.

1033. Cal. Dep't Social Welfare, Report on Action of San Diego County and Municipal Court Relating to Failure To Provide Actions; see Cal. Social Welfare Bd., Minutes, June 21, 1960; Cal. Social Welfare Bd., Verbatim Transcript, Minutes, June 24, 1960, at 20; Cal. Social Welfare Bd., Minutes, Feb. 28, 1961 (Appeal of Turner, San Diego County); Cal. Social Welfare Bd., Minutes, Feb. 28, 1961 (Appeal of Ryan).

1034. In the same county a plan for the administration of aid had been devised to accommodate the greatly enlarged role of the district attorney. A special seventeen-man AFDC review unit was installed in the office of the district attorney to be housed adjacent to the welfare AFDC intake section, which in turn would be removed from the welfare buildings. The welfare department was required to refer all applicants for AFDC to the new unit along with all information and the tentative decisions of the department. Furthermore, the director of public welfare was required to

To correct these specific practices, the legislature added two provisions to the Welfare and Institutions Code designed to restrict the application of Penal Code section 270 and to confine the role of the district attorney.[1035] One declares that "the filing of an application for aid under this chapter shall not constitute and shall not be construed as a failure or refusal of any parent signing said application to carry out his parental responsibilities as provided in section 270 of the Penal Code." The other provides that support proceedings against the caretaker parent are not to be initiated by the district attorney "except on the request of the county welfare department."

Law enforcement officers in many counties use lie detectors on AFDC mothers and fathers.[1036] For example, in the case of Eula Henderson,[1037] the district attorney demanded that the mother submit to a lie detector test regarding her relations with men in order to determine the paternity of the child for whom aid was being asked. The mother had previously described her intimate relations in lurid detail.[1038] The district attorney defined submission to the test as part of the cooperation with law enforcement officers prescribed by Welfare and Institutions Code section 1572. The state social welfare board found that the mother had cooperated to the best of her ability in identifying the father and held that the district attorney could not make the polygraph test a condition of eligibility for AFDC.[1039] On appeal to the courts by the district attorney, the district court of appeal held that refusal of the mother to submit to the polygraph test does not as a matter of law constitute refusal to give "reasonable assistance" in determining the identity of the father and that the evidence supported the board's finding that the mother had cooperated.[1040]

---

deny or terminate aid to all applicants whom the district attorney considered uncooperative. The plan thus denied finality to the decisions of the welfare department on questions of eligibility for assistance, made other welfare department decisions tentative and reviewable, and in effect converted the welfare director into a subordinate arm of the office of the district attorney. The state social welfare board declared the plan illegal under state law and state and federal regulations, and violative of basic welfare concepts. See generally Cal. Dep't Social Welfare, Report on San Diego County Aid to Needy Children, Feb. 21, 1961.

1035. Cal. Stat. 1961, ch. 1784, § 1, at 3795, adding CAL. WELFARE & INST'NS CODE § 1570.

1036. For discussion of the use of lie detectors see Cal. Social Welfare Bd., Verbatim Minutes, May 3, 1960, at 59–67.

1037. County of Contra Costa v. Social Welfare Bd., 229 Adv. Cal. App. 879, 40 Cal. Rep. 605 (1st Dist. 1964). For prior history of the case see Cal. Social Welfare Bd., Minutes, Feb. 26, 1960 (Appeal of Henderson); Minutes, May 3, 1960 (denial of county request for rehearing); Minutes, July 22, 1960.

1038. See Cal. Social Welfare Bd., Minutes, Feb. 26, 1960 (Appeal of Henderson).

1039. *Ibid.* See Op. Cal. Legislative Counsel No. 4247, July 15, 1960, stating: "Use by a county of a lie detector as a means for verifying statements made by an applicant seems clearly inconsistent with the method of investigation prescribed in the regulations, especially where submission to a lie detector test is made a condition of eligibility. The use of such a device . . . . suggests a refusal on the part of the county to accept an applicant's statements as truthful and certainly does not demonstrate respect for the integrity and self esteem of the applicant as contemplated in the regulations."

1040. County of Contra Costa v. Social Welfare Bd., 229 Adv. Cal. App. 879, 40 Cal. Rep. 605 (1st Dist. 1964).

### Mass arrests and night calls.

The most spectacular of all of the techniques of fraud prevention[1041] and support enforcement used by the district attorneys, frequently in collaboration with investigators from fraud units of the welfare departments, are mass arrests and night calls. Often the two techniques are combined. In the mass arrests, cases of welfare recipients who are suspected of fraud are allowed to accumulate, and then, on a given day or night, all arrests are made. The district attorney may be motivated to employ this device with an eye to the deterrent effect of the publicity on other violators or potential violators or by the political advantage. Whatever the motive, the consequences are disastrous for welfare and of no special help to law enforcement.[1042]

Much more generally used than mass arrests are night calls, popularly known as "night raids," "bed checks," and "operations week-end." They may be made at the home of only one recipient but often they are a mass operation. The purpose is usually to determine whether there is an unreported man in the home of the recipient—whether he be husband, father, stepfather, or man assuming the role of spouse—whose presence

---

1041. In 1961, the Department of Health, Education and Welfare issued new regulatory materials dealing with deserting fathers and fraud. Bureau of Public Assistance, State Letters 537, 540 (1961). These are based on a hitherto little used provision of the Social Security Act that the states must "provide such methods of administration . . . as are found by the Secretary to be necessary for the proper and efficient operation of the plan. . . ." *E.g.*, Social Security Act § 402, 49 Stat. 627 (1935), as amended, 42 U.S.C. § 602(a)(5) (1958). See U.S. BUREAU OF PUBLIC ASSISTANCE, HANDBOOK OF PUBLIC ASSISTANCE ADMINISTRATION, pt. IV, § 2110. They require a more carefully defined working relationship between welfare and law enforcement departments, a more rigorous performance of the specific functions assigned to each, much more reporting to the state department, more particular administrative reviews and evaluations by the state department and the maintenance of registries and readily available central information. Prior to the issuance of the new federal regulations none of the requirements was in effect in this state. Recipient fraud had been left almost entirely to local county action and discretion, and county methods and procedures varied greatly. In some counties investigation of fraud was turned over almost entirely to the district attorney; in others the welfare departments played a large role. State regulations designed to carry out the federal requirements have since been prepared and issued. Cal. Dep't Social Welfare, Bulletin No. 624, May 1, 1962, revised Aug. 5, 1963.

1042. The consequences are itemized by Irving Reichert, *supra* note 1020, at 254.

"The press runs editorials or feature stories asking for a cleanup of 'the welfare mess;' boards of supervisors meet to discuss the problem; grand jury committees are spurred into action; welfare recipients are subjected to humiliation and embarrassment because their neighbors look upon them as chiselers who are not really in need; welfare workers ask to be transferred from ANC to some other aid program that will not subject them to ridicule as dupes or spendthrifts with the taxpayers' dollars; some recipients drop off the ANC rolls because they have been guilty of fraud and are afraid of being caught; some drop off because they do not want to be subjected to the humiliation of being looked upon as 'freeloaders;' some recipients are deterred from committing further fraud; some unstable people, similar to those who are inspired to rob a bank, when they read headlines of a wave of bank robberies, may decide they will try to get ANC money fraudulently; and some young people, who are deciding their future vocations, may be deterred from entering the field of social work.

"In the area of relationships, social workers tend to become hostile to law enforcement because of the damage that has been done by mass arrests. Some are reluctant to make future fraud referrals because of the fear of mass arrests. Welfare departments also resent being made to 'look bad' by this type of arrest and its attendant publicity. They are particularly indignant when they know the arrests involve fraud cases that were referred months ago for prosecution. Sometimes they believe that the district attorney planned the mass arrests for personal publicity to make law enforcement look efficient; sometimes they suspect that he has done this deliberately because of anti-welfare attitudes." *Id.* at 298–99.

may, on the one hand, determine eligibility or the amount of the grant and on the other hand constitute an element in the crime of welfare fraud or theft. Such calls are frequently made between 10 p.m. and 4 a.m. The normal procedure is this: Investigators working in two-man teams approach the front and back of the house simultaneously and ring the doorbell; the investigator identifies himself, asks to be admitted, either specifically to look for a man or to make a routine check of the conditions of the home and the children; once inside, the investigator admits his partner and the two then conduct a minute search of the house, looking into the children's and mother's bedrooms, in and under the beds, in the attic, cellar, shower, closets, drawers, and medicine chests, seeking a man or evidence of his presence. Adults and children in the home are interviewed, notes taken, and sometimes signed statements are secured without explanation of their intended use.

On January 4, 1962, the district attorney of Santa Clara County conducted one such raid on twenty-three AFDC homes. Thirteen of the cases had been referred to the district attorney's office by the welfare department for investigation of possible fraud. In some of the cases there were well-grounded suspicions; in others only unverified reports.[1043] The additional ten cases had been referred by the welfare department on the basis of failure to provide, nonsupport, or whereabouts of absent parent unknown. Following the night calls, a total of eleven complaints were filed involving a total possible overpayment of 3,495.21 dollars.[1044]

One of the most publicized of the mass night calls was that planned and partially executed in Alameda County in January 1963. The plan was to cover every AFDC family on successive weekends. The calls began at 6:30 Sunday morning on the first weekend. A cross section of the caseload was covered, suspected and unsuspected alike.[1045]

1043. One referral had been made as early as January 1961, others were made in March and April, two in July, another in August, one in September, two in October, two in November, and three in December.

1044. Santa Clara County Welfare Dep't, Report to Advisory Committee on Family and Children's Services, April 13, 1962.

"[R]eview of 22 of the 23 cases involved, reveals families with difficult problems affecting both the adults and the children. They are characterized by severe health and social problems; limited education; limited work experiences; minority group status; and difficult physical and emotional problems. Of the mothers, only four had completed high school. Two had no formal education. Seven have had no work experience and 11 others only irregular work histories. Many of these mothers have had a series of marital problems. Four have never been legally married. In ten cases the mother is not now legally free to marry, two who were legally free to marry recently married men who themselves were not legally free to marry." Santa Clara County Welfare Dep't, Report to Advisory Committee on Family and Children's Services, Jan. 31, 1962.

1045. One of the caseworkers, Benny Parrish, refused to serve on the night call on the ground that it was illegal and unconstitutional. He was fired for insubordination. His demand for reinstatement was rejected by the Alameda County Civil Service Commission (June 17, 1963) and by the Alameda County Superior Court. Parrish v. Civil Serv. Comm'n, No. 334175, Alameda County Super. Ct., June 19, 1964, *appeal filed*, File No. 1, Civ. 22556, 1st Dist. Cal., Jan. 7, 1965.

At the state social welfare board hearings, called to look into the practice of night calls, there was much criticism both on welfare and constitutional grounds.[1046] The practice, it was argued with obvious merit, impairs the necessary relationship of confidence between worker and recipient, weakens the foundations of self-esteem and social standing required for rehabilitation, and terrorizes the children.[1047] Viewed not as a fraud prevention or law enforcement device but as a method of determining eligibility for aid or the amount of the grant, the mass night-call technique was condemned by the state social welfare board as unnecessary and not in the public interest.[1048]

With equal merit, lawyers have pressed a charge of invasion of constitutional rights—rights of privacy[1049] and immunity from unreasonable searches under the fourth and fourteenth amendments of the United States Constitution[1050] and similar provisions of the state constitution.[1051] Since the night calls most emphatically are searches and are conducted without a search warrant, they can be sustained constitutionally only if the recipient waives her rights by freely and voluntarily giving her consent to the search.[1052] In the circumstances, it is hard to imagine that the consent can be voluntary even though given.[1053] Investigators ringing the doorbell in the middle of the night and identifying themselves as officials—whether they are from the district attorney's office, or the welfare department, or, perhaps especially, if they are caseworkers known to the recipient from past contacts in connection with welfare—do represent authority to the recipient, authority whose mere presence constitutes coercion to some degree and whose request to enter, however politely phrased, is in the nature of an order.[1054] Even more important, the

---

1046. *Hearings Before Cal. Social Welfare Bd.*, Los Angeles, Mar. 29, 1963; *Hearings Before Cal. Social Welfare Bd.*, San Francisco, Feb. 21, 1963.

1047. The points made by the welfare workers might be further summarized as follows: Illegal behavior by the department minimizes respect for law and order; infusion of the criminal investigator into welfare programs confuses the role of social worker; publicity from these sensational activities has detrimental effects on civil rights as well as minority opportunities in other areas; publicity also arouses community indignation and demands for curtailment of welfare benefits; night raids are costly and have proved ineffective to meet their avowed purpose. *Ibid.*

1048. Cal. Social Welfare Bd., Resolution, Jan. 24, 1963.

1049. "[O]ne's privacy against arbitrary intrusion by the police—which is at the core of the Fourth Amendment—is basic to a free society . . . . [and] therefore implicit in 'the concept of ordered liberty' . . . and as such enforceable against the States through the Due Process Clause [of the fourteenth amendment.]" People v. Cahan, 44 Cal. 2d 434, 438, 282 P.2d 905, 907 (1955) (quoting Wolf v. Colorado, 338 U.S. 25, 27 (1949)).

1050. See Ker v. California, 374 U.S. 23 (1963); Mapp v. Ohio, 367 U.S. 643 (1961); Irvine v. California, 347 U.S. 128, 132 (1954).

1051. Cal. Const. art. 1, § 19. See Cal. Pen. Code § 1525; People v. Cahan, 44 Cal. 2d 434, 438, 282 P.2d 905, 907 (1955).

1052. Stoner v. California, 376 U.S. 483, 488 (1964); People v. Gorg, 45 Cal. 2d 776, 782, 291 P.2d 469, 472 (1955); People v. Sanchez, 191 Cal. App. 2d 783, 788, 12 Cal. Rep. 906, 909 (2d Dist. 1961).

1053. *Cf.* People v. Gorg, 45 Cal. 2d 776, 291 P.2d 469 (1955).

1054. See Johnson v. United States, 333 U.S. 10, 16 (1948); Amos v. United States, 255 U.S. 313 (1921); Judd v. United States, 190 F.2d 649 (D.C. Cir. 1951).

readily available means by which authority may be exerted is sharp in her mind. She is almost certain to feel that refusal to consent will bear adversely on her aid grant and thus deprive her and her children of their only source of support. She has been told repeatedly in writing and by her caseworker that she must cooperate in establishing the facts on which her eligibility depends. She knows that among other things she must submit to home visits by her worker,[1055] one at the time of the initial application and regularly thereafter in connection with the six-month reinvestigation. She thus has ample ground in fact to know, what she might well infer from the circumstances anyway, that failure to admit could easily be equated with failure to cooperate. In these circumstances of fear of loss of support and intimidation at the sight of authority, if the consent can be considered to have been given at all, it should be found only upon a clear showing sufficient to overcome a strong presumption to the contrary.[1056] These night call cases may present a precise illustration of the judicial conclusion that "the circumstances of the defendant's plight may be such as to make any claim of actual consent 'not in accordance with human experience,' and explainable only on the basis of 'physical or moral compulsion.' "[1057] Such particularly is the plight of these female defendants when they stand before authority in their nightclothes. Only slightly educated—a third of them have not passed beyond grammar school and they average a ninth-grade education—they are almost invariably involved in abnormal family situations. The home either has been broken or was never established. Many have never been employed; those who have were mainly domestics or waitresses. Their poverty is intense and their dependence on public assistance absolute. They have no financial reserves. If removed from the public assistance rolls they have no means of support, no financially able relatives on whom to rely, no training that will enable them to secure employment. AFDC recipients are typically members of minority groups; in some counties the percentage runs as high as eighty per cent and the overall state average

---

1055. See AFDC Manual, Reg. §§ C–012.50, C–015.30. Section C–012.50 of the handbook explains what the worker should do at the required home visit: "1. Review with the applicant the family situation as told at the application interview. Discuss any inconsistencies or conflicts in the information obtained and give the applicant an opportunity to clarify the questions or suggest means of obtaining additional supporting evidence. . . . 3. Review the family's circumstances for clues to income or potential resources which may have been previously overlooked. . . . 6. Explain again the family's reporting responsibilities."
1056. Tompkins v. Superior Court, 59 Cal. 2d 65, 67, 27 Cal. Rep. 889, 891, 378 P.2d 113, 115 (1963): "Petitioner [defendant] made a prima facie case that his arrest and the search and seizure were illegal when he established that they were made without a warrant. The burden then rested on the prosecution to show proper justification." *Accord*, Judd v. United States, 190 F.2d 649, 651 (D.C. Cir. 1951); People v. Roberts, 47 Cal. 2d 374, 303 P.2d 721 (1956); People v. Contreras, 211 Cal. App. 2d 641, 645, 27 Cal. Rep. 619, 622 (2nd Dist. 1963).
1057. Judd v. United States, 190 F.2d 649, 651 (D.C. Cir. 1951) (quoting Ray v. United States, 84 F.2d 654, 656 (5th Cir. 1936)).

is over sixty.[1058] On the issue of consent to search, "disparity of position" between a government official and a "humble" citizen is an important factor. The disparity here is unusually great.[1059]

It is no answer to these constitutional arguments to say that the night inspections are not searches for evidence of crime but rather are simple home visits to determine eligibility and thus are not within the protection of the fourth and the fourteenth amendments. In the light of the purposes of those amendments and current judicial interpretation, any distinction as to the object of the search is irrelevant. "The basic premise of the prohibition against searches," writes Judge Prettyman,

> was not protection against self-incrimination; it was the common-law right of a man to privacy in his home, a right which is one of the indispensable ultimate essentials of our concept of civilization. . . . To say that a man suspected of crime has a right to protection against search of his home without a warrant, but that a man not suspected of crime has no such protection, is a fantastic absurdity.[1060]

Although health inspection was upheld in *Frank v. Maryland,*[1061] it was on the ground that the inspection was reasonable, not because the amendments did not apply. The searches of the homes of AFDC mothers are not hedged about with safeguards existing in the *Frank* case. They are the very "knock at the door" in the night which the Court has said cannot be tolerated.[1062] In any event, the distinction is immaterial because evidence of crime is usually the main motive and is always one of the motives.[1063]

### Vagrancy and the Family Law of the Poor

From Sir James Fitzjames Stephen's account of the history of vagrancy in England, it appears that during the period from 1349 to 1547 vagrancy was viewed as forming the criminal aspect of the poor laws; during the period from 1547 to 1824, as a crime of status; and from 1824 to the time of his writing, as a crime of conduct.[1064] In America these

---

1058. Cal. Dep't Social Welfare, Characteristics of Recipients of Aid to Needy Children 3 (Research Series Report No. 20, July 1963).

1059. See Canida v. United States, 250 F.2d 822, 825 (5th Cir. 1958).

1060. District of Columbia v. Little, 178 F.2d 13, 16–17 (1949), *aff'd*, 339 U.S. 1 (1950).

1061. 359 U.S. 360, 373 (1959).

1062. Wolf v. Colorado, 338 U.S. 25, 28 (1949).

1063. In addition, such dragnet police methods, for such they would seem to be whether employed by welfare workers or law enforcement officers, have in other circumstances, such as the automobile check at a blockade, been held unconstitutional in California because they do not distinguish between the guilty and the innocent, but treat all persons as suspect. For discussions of the welfare night searches and conclusions as to their constitutionality see Reich, *Midnight Welfare Searches and the Social Security Act*, 72 YALE L.J. 1346 (1963); McKinlay, Assistant Corp. Counsel, City of Detroit, Report to Department of Public Welfare, April 3, 1964.

1064. See 3 STEPHEN, HISTORY OF THE CRIMINAL LAW OF ENGLAND 266–75 (1883).

three stages have not been successive but simultaneous.[1065] And so they are today in California.

From the adoption of the Penal Code in 1872 and before, vagrancy as idleness and economic irresponsibility has been associated with persons of other status and activity, such as the dissolute and suspicious.[1066] To these the legislature eventually added pickpockets, thieves, burglars, confidence operators,[1067] drug addicts, and others,[1068] thus enlarging the net and rendering the intended catch even more miscellaneous and ill-assorted. Crimes based on the elements of idleness, poverty, and wandering, singly or in various combinations, hitherto the heart of the vagrancy statute, sank more and more into the background. In 1955, the legislature removed the word "idle" from the phrase "every idle, lewd, or dissolute person."[1069]

Though occasionally the subject of judicial animadversion and in recent years a shifting judicial attitude, these provisions have generally been upheld by the California courts against constitutional attacks on the grounds that they were unduly vague,[1070] discriminatory in classification or application,[1071] lacked police power justification,[1072] and invaded personal liberty.[1073] The dictum in the 1908 *McCue* case that the legislature cannot denounce mere inaction, without some qualification, as a crime[1074] has never been transformed into holding. The courts have always been able to find the qualification. Mr. Justice Peters, in 1956, thought the provision regarding those who are idle, able-bodied, and

---

1065. See generally Douglas, *Vagrancy and Arrest on Suspicion*, 70 YALE L.J. 1 (1960); Foote, *Vagrancy-Type Law and Its Administration*, 104 U. PA. L. REV. 603 (1956); Perkins, *The Vagrancy Concept*, 9 HASTINGS L.J. 237 (1958); Sherry, *Vagrants, Rogues and Vagabonds—Old Concepts in Need of Revision*, 48 CALIF. L. REV. 557 (1960); Note, 37 N.Y.U.L. REV. 102 (1962).
1066. See Cal. Stat. 1855, ch. CLXXV, § 1, at 217, as amended, Cal. Stat. 1863, ch. DXXV, § 1 at 770.
1067. Cal. Stat. 1891, ch. CXVII, § 1, at 130.
1068. Cal. Stat. 1929, ch. 35, § 1, at 78.
1069. Cal. Stat. 1955, ch. 169, § 2 at 638, amending Cal. Pen. Code § 647 (1961).
1070. *In re* Cregler, 56 Cal. 2d 308, 14 Cal. Rep. 289, 363 P.2d 305 (1961); Phillips v. Municipal Court, 24 Cal. App. 2d 453, 75 P.2d 548 (2d Dist. 1938); *In re* Cutler, 1 Cal. App. 2d 273, 36 P.2d 441 (4th Dist. 1934); *In re* McCue, 7 Cal. App. 765, 96 Pac. 110 (2d Dist. 1908). The leading void-for-vagueness case is Lanzetta v. New Jersey, 306 U.S. 451 (1939).
1071. *In re* Cregler, 56 Cal. 2d 308, 14 Cal. Rep. 289, 363 P.2d 305 (1961) (by implication); *Ex parte* Hayden, 12 Cal. App. 145, 106 Pac. 893 (2d Dist. 1909).
1072. People v. Babb, 103 Cal. App. 2d 326, 229 P.2d 843 (2d Dist. 1951); Phillips v. Municipal Court, 24 Cal. App. 2d 453, 75 P.2d 548 (2d Dist. 1938); *Ex parte* Hayden, 12 Cal. App. 145, 106 Pac. 893 (2d Dist. 1909); *In re* McCue, 7 Cal. App. 765, 96 Pac. 110 (2d Dist. 1908).
1073. Phillips v. Muncipal Court, 24 Cal. App. 2d 453, 75 P.2d 548 (2d Dist. 1938); *In re* Cutler, 1 Cal. App. 2d 273, 36 P.2d 441 (4th Dist. 1934). Vagrancy statutes have been invalidated as unconstitutional invasions of personal liberty, People v. Belcastro, 356 Ill. 144, 190 N.E. 301 (1934); *Ex parte* Smith, 135 Mo. 223, 36 S.W. 628 (1896), or as involving compulsory labor in violation of state and federal constitutional prohibitions against involuntary servitude, *Ex parte* Hudgins, 86 W. Va. 526, 529, 103 S.E. 327, 330 (1920) (statute required all able-bodied men to work at least 36 hours a week, regardless of financial condition or physical capacity). A statute similar to that in *Hudgins* was upheld in Delaware as an emergency wartime measure. State v. McClure, 30 Del. (7 Boyce) 265, 270, 105 Atl. 712, 714 (Ct. Gen. Sess. 1919).
1074. *In re* McCue, 7 Cal. App. 765, 766, 96 Pac. 110, 111 (2d Dist. 1908).

without visible means of support, and who do not seek or accept employment, was "apparently based on the outdated concept that it is a criminal offense not to work."[1075] Prohibiting solicitation of alms as a business has never been challenged in the appellate courts on constitutional grounds. It was held in 1895 that one act of begging is not enough to show that a person is engaged in the business.[1076] In 1934, the prohibition against the poor wandering was declared not to infringe whatever constitutional right one may have to go and come as he pleases. The legislature may make punishable "pointless, useless wandering from place to place within the state without any excuse for such roaming other than the impulse generated by what is sometimes denominated wanderlust . . . ."[1077] In 1951, an appellate court rejected attacks on the vagrancy act based on its creation of crimes of personal condition. "A general course of conduct," said the court, "practices, habits, mode of life, or status which is prejudicial to the public welfare may be prohibited by law . . . ."[1078] In 1960, however, the California Supreme Court held the "common drunkard" clause unconstitutional on the ground that it was ambiguous and vague, a criticism certainly relevant in various degrees to other clauses of the act.[1079]

In 1961, the entire act was repealed, recast, and reenacted.[1080] The language was made somewhat more definite. The name of the offense was changed from vagrancy to disorderly conduct. Wherever possible, acts were emphasized as against status alone. Being lewd, dissolute, or a common prostitute is no longer enough: one must engage in the conduct or solicit others to do so.[1081] Begging as a business has now been changed to accosting others in a public place for the purpose of soliciting alms, whether as a business or not.[1082] Mere roaming about from place to place by persons without visible means of support is no longer forbidden; one must also refuse to identify himself and to account for his presence when requested by a peace officer to do so, "if the surrounding circumstances are such as to indicate to a reasonable man that the public safety demands such identification."[1083] Eliminated from the act altogether is the provision requiring the idle poor to seek and accept labor.

Exit, thus, as a straightforward, unalloyed, uncomplicated criminal

---

1075. People v. Wilson, 145 Cal. App. 2d 1, 6, 301 P.2d 974, 977 (1st Dist. 1956) (dictum).
1076. People v. Denby, 108 Cal. 54, 40 Pac. 1051 (1895).
1077. *In re* Cutler, 1 Cal. App. 2d 273, 280, 36 P.2d 441, 445 (4th Dist..1934).
1078. People v. Babb, 103 Cal. App. 2d 326, 328, 229 P.2d 843, 845 (2d Dist. 1951). *Accord*, People v. Allington, 103 Cal. App. 2d 911, 919, 229 P.2d 495, 500 (Super. Ct., App. Dep't 1951).
1079. *In re* Newbern, 53 Cal. 2d 786, 3 Cal. Rep. 364, 350 P.2d 116 (1960).
1080. Cal. Stat. 1961, ch. 560, §§ 1–2, at 1672.
1081. CAL. PEN. CODE § 647(a), (b).
1082. CAL. PEN. CODE § 647(c).
1083. CAL. PEN. CODE § 647(e). See People v. Bruno, 211 Cal. App. 2d 855, 862, 27 Cal. Rep. 458, 463 (Super. Ct., App. Dep't 1962).

character the sturdy rogue, the idle vagabond, the true vagrant. Through the ages he had known the heavy hand of parliaments and kings, the covetous grasp of feudal lords and agricultural employers, the outrage of the righteous and ambitious, the undisguised hatred of overseers of the poor and the taxpayer, the moral opprobrium of the United States Supreme Court and the puritan, the oppression of discriminatory treatment in statute and constitution, the fear of the owner of property and the accumulator of worldly goods, the steady, sometimes brutal pressure of the forces of stability, tranquility, and social order. Whether haughty, servile, or indifferent, he has been the victim of every sort of epithet, reviled by judges as a social parasite,[1084] and by Harvard historians as "no more than a festering part" of society.[1085] He leaves more quietly than he lived, shuffled offstage in a mere recasting of small sections of a minor statute, unnoticed by press and public—his wandering offstage as pointless, idle, and without purpose, in the broader social sense, as his services on it. He still remains in the vicinage, however, to play bit parts, and to lurk, prowl, and roam about in other statutory crimes.

We see him still in the absent father provisions of the AFDC program —so panoplied with penal power—surrounded by district attorneys, court orders for support, probation, contempt, and prosecution under Penal Code section 270.[1086] We see him in the "man in the home" provision of the Welfare and Institutions Code with special obligations of child support though he is not the father nor married to the mother,[1087] and made a misdemeanant for eating the food and drinking up the aid money of the needy family.[1088] We see the female vagrant still in those resort ordinances that single out AFDC mothers for special punitive treatment in matters of sex relations.[1089] We see them all again in the modern version of the house of correction, the work requirement of the welfare programs.[1090] They are caught in the sweep of the dragnet and the night raid.[1091]

The economic offense has been largely removed from Penal Code section 647, California's present form of its old vagrancy statute. This, however, is not because poets have elevated wanderlust to a virtue; nor because mobility has become the habit of the nation and a necessity of the working force; nor because the concept that it is criminal not to work has

---

1084. See, *e.g.*, People v. Babb, 103 Cal. App. 2d 326, 329, 229 P.2d 843, 845–46 (2d Dist. 1951) (quoting State v. Harlowe, 174 Wash. 227, 233, 24 P.2d 601, 603 (1933)).
1085. See JORDAN, PHILANTHROPY IN ENGLAND 1480–1660, at 79 (1959).
1086. CAL. WELFARE & INST'NS CODE §§ 1500, 1564, 1570, 1571, 1579.
1087. CAL. WELFARE & INST'NS CODE § 1508.
1088. CAL. WELFARE & INST'NS CODE § 1575.
1089. See text accompanying notes 1023–26 *supra*.
1090. CAL. WELFARE & INST'NS CODE §§ 1503.1, 1523.5–.9.
1091. See text accompanying notes 1041–63 *supra*.

become outdated—idleness in the rich has always been envied rather than punished and in the poor it is as socially reprehensible as ever—nor because in the modern industrialized, mechanized, automated economy there is unavoidable unemployment for the economically and socially marginal; nor because the equal protection of the laws, now given such renewed vitality by the United States Supreme Court, has invaded this field or reached the poor; nor even because the police have found these dragnet statutes futile or have realized that many of them must fall for vagueness. These are not the reasons for the abolition of vagrancy outright in Illinois,[1092] the growing attack on such statutes, and the changes made in California, though to some extent all of these will have been elements, to one degree or another, in some minds. Basically, this class of offenders, for such they are still regarded, has simply been moved along with penal sanctions to the welfare program. The relationship of the poor law and other public aid provisions to the vagrancy statutes is as intimate today as it was in the time of the Tudors.[1093]

*Conclusion*

In content, purpose, legislation, administration, and enforcement, California today has a family law of the poor distinct from the family law of the rest of the community.

In content, the rules differ with respect to property and support relations of husband and wife, and, less formally and completely, with respect to creation and termination of the marital relation. By contrast with civil family law, in the family law of the poor: Mutual support obligations and interests in property are dissevered from contract and community and separate property precepts; the family is viewed as an integrated unit with a common pool of resources from which the needs of all members equally must be met; divorce is often by simple desertion, made necessary by poverty; marriage, by simply assuming the role of spouse, often made necessary by undissolved formal marital obligations and fostered by family habits and cultural mores of ethnic minorities, whose status in the community and economic marginality insure their poverty and their presence in the relief system. Some relatives responsibility provisions in the family law of the poor have been retained and strengthened; others are in a state of flux and abandonment on policy and constitutional grounds. They are separated by a legislatively and judicially maintained wall from liability provisions in civil family law which are

---

1092. ILL. ANN. STAT. ch. 38, § 35–1 (Smith-Hurd 1964), repealing Ill. Laws 1877, at 87.
1093. For an account of this relationship and its migration to California see tenBroek, *California's Dual System of Family Law: Its Origin, Development, and Present Status* (pts. 1–2), 16 STAN. L. REV. 257, 259, 268, 277–78, 291–92, 294, 296, 310, 900, 902–03 (1964).

substantively different and virtually static. Actual support and the right to custody of minor children being separated and in different hands in the family law of the poor, the whole structure of parental rights and duties otherwise integrated in custody is weakened and the various rights and duties are individually and independently considered in the light of the interests of the child. Parental right is not necessarily paramount, parental fitness is examined rather than presumed, and the management, morality, and other conditions of the home are subject to the active interest of public officials. In the family law of the poor, the parents' liability for support of minor children is stated in terms of: Conditions of eligibility of the children for AFDC; rules about the utilization of family resources, whether income or property, to meet current and some future needs; and the duty assigned the workers to investigate and determine parental ability to pay. The norms of the Civil Code as to the relative wealth and situations of parents and children and their standards of living do not apply; no distinction is made between father and mother or primary and secondary duty of support. Strikingly, the liability for child support has been extended to include stepfathers and unrelated adult males living in the relation of spouse, whatever their relations to the children.

Today in California, no less than in Elizabethan England, the family law of the poor derives its particular content and special nature from the central concept of the poor law system: public provision for the care and support of the poor. He who pays the bill can attach conditions, related or unrelated to the purpose of the grant, and almost always does. He will wish to make certain that his payments are needed, and he will insist that the family first use all of its own resources. The whole intricate system of the family law of the poor, the source of its difference from the civil family law, and the basis of its perpetuity proceed from this wish and this insistence. The concept of the family itself, its nature and members, the relation between husband and wife especially as to support obligation and property interests, the imposition of legal liability upon relatives to support their destitute kinsmen, the special pattern of parental rights and duties with respect to minor children, and the extension of support liability to stepfathers and unrelated adult males assuming the role of spouse to the mother—all of these basic and determinative elements of the family law of the poor emanate from the public assumption of responsibility and the need to keep the bill down. The basic motive, thus, once the original step is taken, is fiscal and economic: to conserve public funds to the fullest extent possible consistent with the original undertaking. Although this fundamental motive from time to time has been

[676]

augmented by the punitive, the moralistic, the political, and restrained by the humane and the rehabilitative, it has been determinative in molding the character and fixing the features of the law of the poor in general and the family law of the poor in particular.

For the same reason, the family law of the poor has always been and is today the creature of the legislature. Involving as it does great issues and elements of public policy—large-scale governmental outlays, social problems among great numbers of people, conditions of the economy which together with personal factors account for privation, a ready field for political activity both in the broad and in the narrow sense—the law of the poor inevitably comes within the legislative province and is the subject of continuing legislative activity. For these same reasons, too, that law is carried out by welfare workers rather than judges, administrative agencies rather than courts. Many of the rules which determine family relationships are not addressed to the members of the family but to the welfare workers and are expressed in the form of their duties in administering the programs. Sanctions are to be found in the ordinary administrative machinery and in the withdrawal of support. To this are added the machinery and sanctions of the criminal law. All of this contrasts sharply with the private, civil, judicial family law applied to the rest of the community—a system of law built upon a concept of the family relatively more independent of the state's fiscal and administrative role. In the civil family law, judges determine family relationships and distribute family, not public, resources among family members, on a comparative rather than a uniform basis.

In the creation and administration of civil and political family law, the legislative, executive, and judicial branches of the government do not function in accordance with the traditional tripartite separation of powers. The courts and the legislative-administrative organs do not here perform different functions and exercise different types of power. The one does not make and the other interpret the law. They perform identical functions and exercise identical powers. Both make and both interpret the laws. Separated here are the products of the process and the groups to whom they apply. The courts do exactly what the legislature and its annexed administrative machinery do; they create and administer a body of rules about family relations; they amend, repeal, and change the rules from time to time and enact new ones; they interpret, implement, and apply. Their jurisdiction is limited not by the type of power, the nature of the function, or the character or phase of the process, but by the group or class of people subject to the rules. The legislature and welfare administration make and apply the family rules for the poor;

the courts make and apply them for those in more comfortable circumstances. That the rules are different is only to be expected since they are made by different legislative bodies, for different purposes, and to be applied to different segments of populations.

In this historic, dual system of family laws, reembodied in California's present-day welfare programs, two new elements are beginning to emerge: Welfare purposes beyond relieving the distress of poverty are influencing the character of the law of the poor; the poor are beginning to receive the safeguards and protections of the Constitution. In both areas, much lip service is preceding the actual happening of the event. The emergence of these new elements has not yet threatened the destruction of the wall of separation between the two systems. To the extent that the event is occurring, and to the much greater extent that it is discussed, it has operated on the poor law side of the wall to introduce a whole new spectrum of considerations.

The new welfare element can be simply stated: Public assistance must be directed as much toward opportunity as toward security; it must be geared to rehabilitation, employment, and self-support, as well as to relief; it must help people out of their distress, not merely in it; it must represent not a handout to the helpless but an active encouragement of their capacities for self-reliance and self-help. The purpose clause of California's Welfare and Institutions Code has long contained a declaration along these lines.[1094] In 1956, the Federal Social Security Act was amended to include the purpose "to promote the well-being of the Nation by . . . helping to strengthen family life and helping needy families and individuals attain the maximum economic and personal independence of which they are capable."[1095] The purpose clauses of the several public assistance titles repeat and reaffirm these goals with minor variations.[1096] Little direct action, however, has been taken to implement either the state or national declarations. But they do formulate a goal and thus constitute a start. Operative rehabilitative provisions crop up in state and federal laws allowing the recipients to retain specified amounts of earnings and other resources useful in a plan for self-support. To the extent that these provisions are successful, they help persons escape the relief rolls, thus combining fiscal gain with the broader welfare objectives. Similarly, length of residence requirements for eligibility are being eliminated. Justified in the past by their effectiveness in con-

---

1094. CAL. WELFARE & INST'NS CODE § 19: "Due regard for the preservation of family life . . . and . . . to encourage self-respect, self-reliance, and the desire to be a good citizen, useful to society."
1095. Social Security Amendments of 1956, § 300(b), 70 Stat. 846, 42 U.S.C. § 301n (1958).
1096. Public Welfare Amendments of 1962, §§ 104(c)(2), (3), (4), 76 Stat. 186, 42 U.S.C. §§ 601, 1201, 1351 (Supp. V, 1964).

fining the poor to their home counties, thereby localizing the burden of support, identifying the government unit responsible, and insuring an accurate determination of need, such requirements are inconsistent with the aspirations of a free society, the demands of an industrial economy, and the economic opportunity of the individual.

Responsibility of relatives provisions, invented and always sustained to cut the costs of public welfare, were abolished in California's blind and disabled programs because of increasing popular and professional opinion that they are not fiscally productive, are disruptive of family relations and rehabilitation plans, and have other socially undesirable consequences. Conversely, liability of stepfathers and unrelated males has been brought about by financial considerations, augmented by a community sense that the obligation of a parent, natural, legal, or quasi-legal, toward a minor child is different from other relatives' liabilities and by community attitudes toward immorality, illegitimacy, and the fact that a major fraction of families on relief belongs to minority races with deviant mores.

A striking but rare example of a program in which welfare considerations have now prevailed over the purely fiscal is that dealing with adoptions. In the past this program has been used primarily to shunt the support burden from the public to an adoptive couple. In the last generation, however, a complete shift has occurred. The interests of the child are to be viewed as paramount. The needs of the natural parents, the adoptive couple, and the public treasury are secondary, though not to be ignored. The adoptive home is to be investigated and evaluated in terms of its suitability for the child and the adoptive couple in terms of matching his requirements. He is not to be separated from his parents or parent unnecessarily. He is not to be placed for adoption unless he is capable of benefiting from family life and does not require special care or treatment only available elsewhere. The adoptive couple is to receive a child available for adoption with known background and conditions of health. The natural parents are to be given full opportunity to make a deliberate decision in the light of knowledge about available alternatives. Above all, children are not to be separated from their mothers for financial reasons alone. Public aid makes it possible for them to remain together instead of constituting the reason for their separation.

Historically in this country as well as in England the poor, generally stigmatized as indigents, paupers, or vagabonds, have not been the beneficiaries of constitutional guarantees to citizens and persons. They have, however, been recognized in the Constitution as proper objects for exercise of the police powers of the states, to be controlled, regulated, and suppressed. In this respect, the poor and racial minorities, often two names for but a single class, have stood upon the same constitutional footing. Discrimination against them in public welfare programs—and even worse, the perversion of welfare, constitutional, and statutory concepts and provisions to control and exclude them—has had great impact on welfare ideas and institutions. Among the factors which have further compounded confusion with respect to the historical purposes of welfare and the protections of the Constitution have been: Enslavement and control of the Indian through the use of the traditional indenture system and vagrancy provisions; exclusion and control of the Chinese through public health, welfare, safety, and morals notions and provisions; attacks upon the present-day AFDC program caring for a high proportion of children who are of Mexican-American and Negro parentage. All these have accustomed Californians to associate welfare with punitive, repressive, discriminatory, exclusionary goals as well as with relief and rehabilitation.

Traditionally the constitutional grant of power which has been invoked to deal with racial minorities and the poor of all races has been the police power, not the general welfare power. When problems of poverty are handled under the police powers of the Constitution, poverty comes to be equated with disease, immorality, and disorder. Indeed, historically these were inseparable conditions. The police power has generally been utilized to protect one part of the community from another—the comfortable against the needy.

A classic illustration is to be found in the famous case of *City of New York v. Miln*,[1097] decided by the United States Supreme Court in 1837. It is "as competent and as necessary for a State," said the Justices in that case,

> to provide precautionary measures against the moral pestilence of paupers, vagabonds and possibly convicts as it is to guard against the physical pestilence which may arise from unsound and infectious articles imported, or from a ship, the crew of which may be laboring under an infectious disease.

Accordingly, the Court held valid a New York statute designed to exclude the poor brought to New York from other states or from foreign countries. The statute was found to be a regulation of police, not of commerce, and therefore within the power of the state.

By this doctrine the constitutional power of the states to deal with the poor is the police power—the power to preserve public order, quarantine contagion, protect morals, and maintain safety. Poverty entails constitutional no less than social degradation. Financial, physical, and mental well-being are thus prerequisites to constitutional rights. Welfare programs founded in these conceptions and sustained by the police power

---

1097. 36 U.S. (11 Pet.) 357, 369 (1837).

focus on problems of behavior, utilize instruments of coercion and restraint, and are oriented toward keeping the peace and maintaining public order. They are designed to safeguard health, safety, morals, and well-being of the fortunate rather than directly to improve the lot of the unfortunate.

Though they do not have quite the unquestioned dominance of a century ago, these ideas survive today to plague welfare administration and trouble constitutional interpretation. They emerge undisguised in county resort ordinances, discriminatorily applied to welfare mothers; in night raids, polygraph tests, and searches without warrants; in probation conditions forbidding mothers to secure public aid for their children, regardless of need or eligibility; in commands to support their children under threat of imprisonment, whatever their ability, the need of the children for their care, or the unavailability of jobs; in judicial attempts to dictate morality by ordering recipients to be "good," whatever their family culture and group mores, whatever their individual retardations and instabilities.

Although the recipients of public aid programs are still effectively outside the jurisdiction of the United States Constitution, a new spirit in constitutional law has given positive signs of its future potential. In two lines of decisions the Supreme Court has furthered the right to equal justice. In the first, it upheld the right of the poor to appeal decisions whenever others can do so, and to have writs and records supplied free.[1098] In the second, it held that all criminal defendants must have the aid of counsel, to be supplied free if they cannot afford to bear the costs.[1099] There can be no equal justice, the Court now holds, where the kind of trial a man gets depends on the amount of money he has. Welfare may take some departure and inspiration, too, from *Brown v. Board of Educ.*,[1100] a decision in another contested arena of public services—that of education. The issue in that case was over the arbitrary criterion of race used as a basis of segregation of the public schools. Is poverty a less arbitrary criterion when used as a basis of segregation in family law? The unexcelled rhetoric of Mr. Justice Jackson in *Edwards v. California*,[1101] the modern counterpart of the *Miln* case, is directly in point:

> Does "indigence" as defined by the application of the California statute constitute a basis for restricting the freedom of a citizen, as crime or contagion warrants its restriction? We should say now, and in no uncertain terms, that a man's mere property status, without more, cannot be used by a state to test, qualify, or limit his rights as a citizen of the United States. "Indigence" in itself

---

1098. Hardy v. United States, 375 U.S. 277 (1964); Griffin v. Illinois, 351 U.S. 12 (1956).
1099. Gideon v. Wainwright, 372 U.S. 335 (1963).
1100. 347 U.S. 483 (1954).
1101. 314 U.S. 160, 184–85 (1941) (concurring opinion).

is neither a source of rights nor a basis for denying them. The mere state of being without funds is a neutral fact—constitutionally an irrelevance, like race, creed, or color.

Pessimistically, it can be observed that this was a dissenting view in 1941. Optimistically, however, it was at least a minority view—marked judicial progress in the century since *Miln*.

When "the mere state of being without funds is a neutral fact—constitutionally an irrelevance"; when classifications based on poverty and handicap are measured by equal protection standards of constitutional purpose and proper classification; when constitutional rights cannot be sacrificed as a condition of granting public assistance; when law enforcement and penal intrusions into the law of welfare are fully restrained by the fourth, fifth, and fourteenth amendments; when free movement is recognized as a constitutional right forbidding residence restrictions in welfare; when the highest court in the land as well as the highest court in California see responsibility of relatives provisions as arbitrary and discriminatory taxation; when welfare categories and constitutional classifications coincide; when the granting and withholding of assistance and the variation of requirements among and between programs are subjected to due process and equal protection norms; when a presumption of competence and responsibility of clients becomes a welfare counterpart of the criminal law presumption of innocence—when these things happen, then indeed will the law of the poor feel the full impact of the pronouncement that "separate" is "inherently unequal," generating among aid recipients "a feeling of inferiority as to their status in the community that may affect their hearts and minds in a way unlikely ever to be undone."[1102] Until that time, however, California's separate, different, and unequal system of family law of the poor will continue in force basically in the form in which Henry VIII and Elizabeth I gave it to England and the English-speaking world.

---

1102. Brown v. Board of Educ., 347 U.S. 483, 494 (1954).

# Index